Florence Nightingale:
Measuring Hospital Care Outcomes

Excerpts from the books
*Notes on Matters Affecting the Health, Efficiency, and
Hospital Administration of the British Army Founded
Chiefly on the Experience of the Late War*
and
Notes on Hospitals
by Florence Nightingale

With Contributions by
*Mary O. Mundinger, RN, DrPH
Duncan Neuhauser, PhD
Paul B. Batalden, MD
Julie J. Mohr, MSPH
Lisa I. Iezzoni, MD, MSc*

Joint Commission
on Accreditation of Healthcare Organizations

Joint Commission Mission

The mission of the Joint Commission on Accreditation of Healthcare Organizations is to improve the quality of care provided to the public through the provision of health care accreditation and related services that support performance improvement in health care organizations.

Joint Commission publications support, but are separate from the accreditation activities of the Joint Commission. Purchasers of our publications receive no special treatment in, or confidential information about, the accreditation process.

The inclusion of an organization name, product, or service in a Joint Commission publication should not be construed as an endorsement of such organization, product, or service; nor is failure to include an organization name, product, or service to be construed as disapproval.

Parts of this book are reprinted from original books by Florence Nightingale: *Notes on Matters Affecting Health Efficiency and Hospital Administration of the British Army Founded Chiefly on the Experience of the Late War,* originally published in 1858; and *Notes on Hospitals,* originally published in 1859.

Printed in the United States of America   5   4   3   2   1

Requests for permission to make copies of any part of this work should be mailed to:

Permissions Editor
Joint Commission on Accreditation of Healthcare Organizations
One Renaissance Boulevard
Oakbrook Terrace, Illinois 60181

ISBN: 0-86688-559-5
Library of Congress Catalog Number: 99-62729

For more information about the Joint Commission, visit our Web site at www.jcaho.org.

The Joint Commission
on Accreditation of Healthcare Organizations
wishes to thank the following organizations
for helping to support the publication of this book.

Case Western Reserve University
Health System Leadership Fund

Columbia University School of Nursing

Henry Ford Health System

iv

Coordinating Editor

Duncan Neuhauser, PhD
Charles Elton Blanchard, MD
   Professor of Health Management
School of Medicine
Case Western Reserve University
Cleveland, Ohio

Contributors

Paul B. Batalden, MD
Professor
Center for Evaluative Clinical Sciences
Dartmouth Medical School
Hanover, New Hampshire

Lisa I. Iezzoni, MD, MSc
Division of General Medicine and Primary Care
Department of Medicine
Beth Israel Deaconess Medical Center
Boston, Massachusetts

Julie J. Mohr, MSPH
Center for Evaluative Clinical Sciences
Dartmouth Medical School
Hanover, New Hampshire

Mary O. Mundinger, RN, DrPH
Dean and Centennial Professor in Health Policy
Columbia University School of Nursing
New York, New York

Contents

vi

Foreword
By Mary O. Mundinger, RN, DrPH

In a clinical nursing career that was less than three years long, Florence Nightingale changed the very nature of the profession and introduced scientific measurement of nursing practice and outcomes. This occurred in the third quarter of the 19th century, at a time when medicine had not yet begun to measure its efficacy. How did she do it? With a steely resolve, a spiritual commitment to caring for people, a commitment religious in its fervor, with private funds and family connections when all else failed, and by using her (then rare) training in mathematics and philosophy.

Nightingale grew up in a privileged family in Victorian England. Her father had no qualms about educating his daughter, and he tutored her in philosophy, mathematics, Latin, Greek, and Italian. Having learned how to think, analyze, and apply mathematics to the study of social phenomena, Nightingale, against her family's wishes, left home at the age of 31 to take up the study of nursing—first in a Protestant hospital in Dusseldorf, then in a Catholic hospital outside Paris. She then returned to London where she served for a year as a nursing administrator.

Nightingale maintained the governmental and social ties of her wealthy and influential family, and at age 34 was sought by the British government, with support from *The London Times,* to become chief nurse for those wounded in the Crimean War. She arrived with 38 nurses at Scutari, Turkey, to find abysmal conditions. British soldiers had a horrifying mortality rate, with nearly 43% of the hospitalized wounded dying. The sanitary conditions were medieval but the army was dead set against a reformer who was a woman, nurse, and civilian, telling them how to improve.

First, Nightingale forbade the poorly trained domestic nurses from drinking and consorting with the patients. She did not allow the other nurses to visit the wards at night, but she made rounds herself, finding her way among the cots with her little lamp, an emblem to this day of professional nursing care. She used the resources at hand to improve sanitary conditions, and when the army refused to purchase boilers to heat water for cleansing, she paid for them herself out of private funds.

As important as the reforms Florence Nightingale put in place were, the measurements she made of these reforms were equally important. Inventing polar charts that showed the month-by-month improvements in mortality associated with the sanitary reforms, she built an incontrovertible case for cause and effect. Not only did she establish the local improvements in field hospitals, but she compared the health of British soldiers in these hospitals with the health of British soldiers quartered in England, demonstrating by the end of the war that battlefield mortality was only two thirds of that of soldiers at home. Six months after Nightingale and her nurses arrived at Scutari, the 43% mortality rate had dropped to just over 2%. These breathtaking changes were not lost on the British government. She sent her statistics to Parliament and *The London Times,* which had initially published reports of the devastating conditions and had continued to follow her success.

Returning to London after creating a revolution in military health care (in a mere 20 months!), Nightingale retired to her bedroom to continue the assault on outmoded ways of treating the sick. She lived 54 more years to the age of 90, essentially a recluse and invalid, but her voice never wavered, and she continued to transform health for the army and for civilians. In 1860, she established the Nightingale School for Nurses at St. Thomas Hospital in London, the place where nursing as a learned profession had its true beginning.

Today, 179 years after Nightingale's birth, and 145 years after Scutari, the health care community is identifying outcomes measurement as the key to quality achievements and the answer to cost effectiveness decisions. Florence Nightingale knew this long ago.

Nightingale clearly identified the link between outcomes measurement and improved health care. Today nursing has an even more powerful claim than the historical one, as a leader in health care outcomes measurement. Medical interventions are inherently episodic, oriented toward illness and cure. Nursing care incorporates the management of medical conditions and the education, empowerment, and disease prevention activities that make for a lasting, positive outcome. The scope of nursing is broad, extends over time, and works within the context of a patient's resources and will.

This historical connection is certainly one to celebrate. But it is also a call to action and accountability for the nations' nurses, who must take up the challenge to use outcomes as a powerful guide to practice.

x

Preface
By Duncan Neuhauser, PhD

On November 18, 1996, Mary Mundinger, Dean of the Columbia School of Nursing, and I walked from her office to the Columbia University Health Sciences Libraries' Rare Book Room. We were met there by Susan Box, then Head of Archives and Special Collections. Before the meeting, Dean Mundinger had asked if she could locate a copy of Florence Nightingale's *Notes on Matters Affecting the Health Efficiency and Hospital Administration of the British Army,* originally printed in 1858.

While looking for the book, Ms. Box had found an entire shelf of uncatalogued Nightingale books and original letters. This collection was apparently organized by two nursing students over half a century ago and then forgotten. And here on the table was this very rare book, an original copy of the *Notes on Matters Affecting the Health Efficiency* that Dean Mundinger had requested.* When Ms. Box showed us the book, we found the pages were uncut. No one had ever read this copy before!

This book carefully reports the most extraordinary improvement in hospital care ever documented and demonstrated. Florence Nightingale (1820–1910) is rightfully well known for her role in the development of modern nursing. She is less well known for her quantitative analyzes of hospital mortality, particularly her analysis of the improvement in mortality during her stay at the Scutari hospital in Turkey during the Crimean War from 1854 to 1856.

We are pleased to reprint in this book two extensive reports by Nightingale describing her work, both excerpts from books published in London during that era. A foreword by Mary Mundinger, an introduction by myself, and commentary by Paul Batalden and Julie

*There are fewer than a dozen known originals in the United States.

Mohr are included. An article by Lisa Iezzoni discusses the consequences of misinterpreting Nightingale's data, and discusses why hospitals in Nightingale's era were considered "places where you go to die."

Florence Nightingale: A Passionate Statistician
By Duncan Neuhauser, PhD

During the first seven months of the Crimean War, a British soldier wounded in battle likely had a better chance of survival if left on the battlefield than if transported to an army hospital where infectious diseases took more soldiers' lives than did battle wounds. During the last six months of the Crimean War, a wounded British soldier's chance of survival was about the same as a guard stationed in England, away from the war.[1]

What happened in the year of war between these periods to affect such a change? The arrival and work of Florence Nightingale. While the Crimean War raged on, Nightingale waged a battle of her own against the deplorable conditions at British army hospitals. The results of her efforts can still be seen in the standards set at hospitals today, over a century later.

The Crimean War
In the summer of 1853, the Russian Black Sea fleet destroyed the Turkish fleet. In the eyes of the English and French, this positioned the Russian fleet to capture Istanbul and the Bosphorus passage into the Mediterranean, threatening the British link to India and French interests in the Eastern Mediterranean. In a ground swell of popular enthusiasm, the British declared war on Russia in March 1854,[2] sending troops, along with the French and Turks, to the Crimean peninsula on the north shore of the Black Sea. Between 1854 and 1855, a series of battles was fought: Alma, Balaclava, Inkerman, and Sebastopol. Soldiers wounded there were transported by ship primarily to the large base hospital at Scutari in Turkey. At the end of 1855, the town of Sebastopol fell and on April 29, 1856, peace was declared.

The Crimean War was the first European war fought by the English since the Napoleonic wars, when the

Duke of Wellington fought on the Spanish Peninsula and at Waterloo. In the words of Lytton Strackey, "The whole organization of the war machine was incompetent and out of date. The old Duke had sat for a generation at the Horse Guards repressing innovation with an iron hand."[3] Another writer, a young Leo Tolstoy, then an artillery officer in the Crimean War, offered a Russian perspective in his diary[4] and stories.[5] Tolstoy's *Sebastopol* discussed three doomed Russian soldiers, but did not relay the fact that two out of the three soldiers in the story died of starvation or sickness and only one in three from enemy fire.[2] Likewise in the British army, more soldiers died from cholera; infection; or lack of food, water, sanitation, and shelter than died from bullets.

The winter of 1855 was a disaster for the British troops. "This army has melted away almost to a drop of miserable, washed out, worn out spiritless wretches who muster out of 55,000 just 11,000 now fit to shoulder a musket,"[6] wrote one observer.

For all these reasons, the Crimean War is usually regarded as the worst managed campaign in English history.[8] However, the war also saw innovations—the telegraph, the camera, and, most important for Nightingale's cause, newspaper reporting. Reporters had plenty to tell the British public about military incompetence, particularly regarding the lack of care for sick soldiers at Scutari Hospital near Istanbul. The resulting public outrage led the British Secretary of War to invite Florence Nightingale to create a private nurse corps.[6]

The Role of Florence Nightingale
While the invitation was extended, the perceived intrusion of Nightingale's mission was anything but welcomed by British army commanders. The British command was not about to learn anything new or change its actions.[7] Nightingale's ultimate success rested on several factors: (1) her ability, availability, and determination; (2) her aristocratic connections; (3) the role of public

opinion and the threat of exposure; (4) Queen Victoria's close attention to the issue; (5) Nightingale's access to money independent of the military; and (6) her careful collection and analysis of data and reasoned conclusions. She needed all this to face the obstacles ahead of her.

Nightingale and her party left England on October 21, 1854[8] and arrived at Scutari Hospital on November 3. The chaos at Scutari was total. Nightingale documented that most of the deaths there were caused by "zymotic" or "scorbutic" diseases. Zymotic diseases are what would be called infectious today, but then would have been considered the result of miasma or "poisonous" air. Scorbutic diseases included poor nutrition and frost bite. At Scutari, Nightingale focused on improving cleanliness, sanitation, nutrition, administrative order, and patient care.

Nightingale also visited the hospitals in the Crimea, where Chief Medical Officer Hall tried to thwart her efforts through such petty devices as not providing food for her party (she brought her own). By May 1855, Nightingale was determined to reform the practices of British army hospitals. She stayed on after peace was declared on April 29, 1856, not leaving for England until after the last patient was discharged from Scutari.[8]

Report to the Secretary of War
As soon as she returned to England, Nightingale put her energy into the creation of a Royal Commission to report on the health of the army.[8] She faced months of resistance over creating the committee, selecting its members, and defining its charge, eventually overcoming these obstacles by threatening to go public and publish her experiences. Even in poor health, she worked industriously for six months to finally produce her report, *Notes on Matters Affecting the Health, Efficiency and Hospital Administration of the British Army.*[1]

This monumental, rare, and virtually unobtainable piece[15] was privately printed as a report to the Secretary of State for War of the United Kingdom.[8] In it, the health services provided by the British army during the Crimean War (1854–1856) were reviewed. It also addresses the health of British solders in peace time and, among other topics, tells how to provide nourishing food for 1,000 soldiers with only 26 cooking pots. This report differs from Nightingale's falsely sentimental image as "The Lady With the Lamp" of Scutari Hospital.

In the words of Lytton Strackey, "This extraordinary composition. . .laying down vast principles of far-reaching reform, discussing the minutest details of a multitude of controversial subjects containing an enormous mass of information of the most varied kinds—military, statistical, sanitary, architectural—was never given to the public for the need never came, but it formed the basis of the Report of the Royal Commission; and it remains to this day (1918), the leading authority on the medical administration of the armies."[3] Ultimately, the Royal Commission report "embodied almost word-for-word the suggestions of Miss Nightingale."[3] Changes in the government, resultant from these suggestions, were implemented from 1859–1861.[3]

This report is still fascinating because of Nightingale's vivid prose, her presentation of the dramatic differences in mortality rates, and her sophisticated and sometimes quite subtle analysis of statistical data.

A Passionate Statistician

In her quest to bring reform to the British army's hospitals, Nightingale expertly employed the statistical information she presented to forward her cause.

Statistical information became one of the ruling forces of her life:

> "She was ... a Passionate Statistician. Statistics were to her almost a religious exercise. It was by the aid of statistics that law in the social sphere might be ascertained and aspired.

". . . there were enormous masses of statistical data already pigeon-holed in government offices or easily procurable by government action of which little or no use was made.

"What we want is not so much . . . an accumulation of facts as to teach the men who are to govern the country the use of statistical facts."[9]

And teach she did, through her statistical study of army hospital care.

A Study of Quality of Care in Army Hospitals

The rise of mortality at Scutari and its decline after the introduction of sanitary reforms provides a unique natural experiment in the study of quality of care. Even with the passage of a century, "history does not afford its equal;" it is "a complete example of an army falling to the lowest ebb of disease and disaster from neglect committed and raising again, to the highest state of health and efficiency from remedies applied. It is the whole experiment on a colossal scale," in Miss Nightingale's prose.

She preached and scolded further; "We had, in the first seven months of the Crimean campaign, a mortality among the troops at a rate of 60% per annum from disease alone (excluding combat injury)—a rate of mortality which exceeds that of the Great Plague of 1665 (in London). We had during the last six months of the war a mortality among our sick little more than among our healthy guards at home and a mortality among [all] the troops at home."[1]

The mortality rates for patients over time at Scutari and the smaller Kulali hospitals are shown in Table 1. The second hospital is spelled in several ways: Kulali, Kululi, Koulali.

Nightingale noted that most of the deaths were due to zymotic diseases such as scurvy, fever, cholera, diarrhea, and dysentery and not directly to wounds. She saw and understood the association between the overcrowding of patients in the hospital and the mortality rate.

6

TABLE 1
Mortality in the Hospitals at Scutari and Kulali
From October 1, 1854 to September 30, 1855

	Dates	Deaths per 1,000 Sick Patients*	Comments
1854	October 1–14 October 15–November 11 November 12–December 9 December 10–January 6	192 85 155 179	
1855	January 7–January 31	321	
	February 1–February 28	427	Kulali: 520
	February 25–March 17	315	
	March 18–April 7	144	March 17, 1855: Commencement of sanitary improvements
	April 8–April 28	107	
	April 29–May 19	52	
	May 20–June 9	48	Improvements nearly complete
	June 10–June 30	22	
	July 1–September 30	22	
1851	Military Hospitals in London	20.99	
1837–1846	All Guard Troops in England	20.4	
1855	All Crimea Troops (Last five months of war)	11.5	

* Number of patients based on the mean of admissions and discharges and deaths.

The sanitary improvements Nightingale made included removing 5,114 "hand-carts or large basketfuls of filth;" flushing out stopped up sewers and latrines 466 times; burying 35 carcases of animals found in and about the hospitals; washing of bed sheets and shirts; and replacing dirty clothes that soldiers had been wearing since they left the battlefield. Nightingale explains the increase in mortality to be due to "frightful overcrowding" and want of ventilation, drainage, cleanliness, and hospital comforts.[1]

She was well aware that opponents to her proposed reforms might argue that these differences in mortality rates were not due to conditions at the hospital, but to varying severity of patients' wounds and illnesses when they arrived at the hospital from the transport ships. To answer this potential criticism, she showed (1) the association between the sanitary improvements and mortality; (2) that the mortality was not due primarily to wounds, but to secondary infections; (3) that mortality rates in the transport ships were not associated with mortality in the hospitals (mortality in the transports was falling while it was rising in the hospitals); and finally, (4) with heavy irony Nightingale wrote, "The Principle Medical Officer himself (no political ally of hers) has shown that cases which were fortunately so bad as to be unfit for removal (from the battlefield to the hospitals via ship) in February 1855 suffered only a fifteenth part of the mortality which, had they been sent to Scutari, would have been their fate."[1]

In order to press her case for reform in the British army, Nightingale went on to demonstrate the high mortality among the peace time British soldiers stationed in England. This involved comparisons of yearly mortality per 1,000 persons, controlling for age in large English towns with soldiers in the Line and Guards regiments. See Table 2.

Her case was strengthened by showing how conservative these comparisons were. British soldieries were, she observed, carefully screened for their health and physical

TABLE 2
Annual Ratio of Deaths per 1,000 Living Persons*

Age	Civilians in Large English Towns	Soldiers In The	
		Guards	Line
20–25	9.6	21.6	17.8
25–30	10.4	21.1	19.8
30–35	11.4	19.5	19.8
35–40	16.1	22.4	21.0
40–45	16.7	26.2	23.4
45–50	24.5	26.2	23.4

* Original data from Sir A. Tulloch, "Statistical Report on the Sickness, Mortality, and Invaliding Among the Troops in the United Kingdom" (1885)

fitness, especially the elite Guards. As a result, some of the healthiest men were drawn out of the civilian population. Secondly, the sick are "invalided out of the service" and there is a very high mortality among invalided soldiers, which is not included in the figures shown in Table 2.

In a barbed shaft of 19th century patriotism carefully aimed at the military leadership, Nightingale said, "The British army consists of only the finest specimens of the finest physical race in the world, with the exception, perhaps, of some part of our aristocracy."[1] Furthermore, they had access to good medical care by the standards of her day.

Nightingale was then in a position to decry the lack of sanitary conditions in the army barracks.

Given the poor quality of data available to her, this report is, indeed, a marvel of statistical analysis. Today's quality of care literature would be very different if researchers were working with such variation in mortality figures.

Notes on Hospitals

Notes on Hospitals, the only modern book on hospital management in the 19th century, was published in the year following the publication of *Notes on Matters Affecting the Health, Efficiency, and Hospital Administration of the British Army.* In the first edition, she included information about the Crimean War and the hospital at Scutari. Other related books then in publication focused on hospital architecture, the implication being that, once the building structure was correct, nothing of significance remained for discussion. Nightingale was interested in information systems, statistics, and outcomes[10]—all issues of importance to hospitals today. This book, along with her personal written advice, influenced hospitals of her time all over the world.

References

1. Nightingale F. *Notes on Matters Affecting Health, Efficiency and Hospital Administration of the British Army.* London: Harrison and Sons, 1858.
2. Crimean War. *Encyclopedia Britannica, 14th Edition.* 1939; 6:708.
3. Strackey L. *Eminent Victorians.* New York: Capricorn, 1963, pp 138, 171, 172, 175.
4. Tolstoy LN. *The Private Diary of Leo Tolstoy:* 1853-1857. New York: Doubleday, 1927.
5. Tolstoy LN. Sebastopol. *The Novels and Other Works of Leo N. Tolstoy, Vol. XI.* New York: Charles Scribner's Sons, 1923.
6. Knightly P. *The First Casualty.* New York: Harcourt Brace Jovanovich, 1975, pp 12, 14.
7. Woodharn-Smith C. *The Reason Why.* New York: McGraw-Hill, 1953, p 12.
8. Woodharn-Smith C. *Florence Nightingale.* London: Constable, 1950, pp 146, 255, 282.
9. Cook E. *The Life of Florence Nightingale.* London: Macmillan, 1914; 2:395–396.
10. Nightingale F. *Notes on Hospitals, 1st Edition.* London: Parket and Son, 1859.

An Invitation from Florence Nightingale: Come Learn About Improving Health Care

By Paul B. Batalden, MD, and Julie J. Mohr, MSPH

"Those who seek to honor the wisdom of old people would do well to seek what they were following and not simply try to follow them."

Chinese proverb
(paraphrased)

How can a history lesson help today's leaders who are trying to effect change in health care? Florence Nightingale, as a health care improvement pioneer, provides us with an example of a leader who learned and helped others learn. She knew about statistical thinking, the importance of scientific thinking about the work of health care, and the reality of systems and processes. She personally understood something about the magnitude of waste and knew something about the psychology of work, worker, workplace. Furthermore, Nightingale had a passionate personal commitment to improvement in her actions and her words.

User of Statistical Thinking

Nightingale was a pioneer in the use of statistics as an aid in the improvement of health care. This included using denominators, operational definitions, and the graphical display of information/data using polar plots. She understood the intended purpose of statistics and realized that if judgments of outcomes were to matter, it would require attention to accurate data collection and accurately defined measures, lest people draw erroneous conclusions. She illustrated her conclusions with practical examples. She proved her own humanity as she revealed her limits as a computational wizard.

12

Encouragement of Scientific Thinking

Nightingale was a leader of the improvement of health care who pressed for the use and encouragement of scientific thinking and continued learning as a means of guiding the actions leaders take. Her interest in creating a hygienic environment is illustrative of her understanding of cause and effect—particularly with respect to actions on preventable causes of disease, and she recognized the multiple causes of disease. She was a pioneer in the use of coding schemes that would allow for more systematic study of care and illness. She recognized the importance of encouraging study and learning at work—and she understood that to do so meant that the leader might have to free people from their regular duties. She encouraged the presentation of alternative treatments, with a view to understanding their association with the outcomes of care.

User of Information

Nightingale knew the importance of using timely information for operations and to create tension for change. She did not hesitate to use information to connect the phenomena she was trying to make vivid with other phenomenon her audience knew. She anticipated the benefits of recognizing "best practices"—what today we might call "benchmarking."

Knowledge of Processes, Systems, Structures, and Waste

Nightingale was a leader with insight into the structure, systems, processes, and waste of organizations. She set standards for staffing and matched people with the job. She understood that when things were missing, it could be a "system" problem—not any "person's fault." According to Nightingale, there was a role for inspection—to gather data for action—which allowed people to work to become as good as possible. She was a practitioner of many of the management principles that people seem to think they are "discovering":

- Centralize support services, decentralized operations;
- Make partners of your suppliers;
- Understand the "hand-offs" in a process for the common sources of failure that they are; and
- Identify the failures and inquire into them.

Knowledge of Psychology of Work, Worker

Nightingale had insight into the psychology of work and the worker, understanding the importance of recognition for work done well and taking pride in one's work. Her observations about the needs and care of the sick, her clever management of the problem of off-hours drinking and carousing, and her insistent pressure to be mindful of how caregiving practices themselves can contribute to the burden of illness were classic.

Center for the Evaluative Clinical Sciences

In the Center for the Evaluative Clinical Sciences at Dartmouth College, we teach a course, "The Continual Improvement of Health Care," that offers participants an opportunity to discover and preview the knowledge, methods and skills necessary to participate in and help lead the continual improvement and innovation of health care. Students pursuing a master's degree in evaluative clinical sciences are from diverse backgrounds ranging from recent college graduates to mid-career clinicians and administrators. As part of the course, we include a session on some of the historic leaders of quality improvement— those pioneers who helped create the substantial body of knowledge that is available to us today for the improvement of health care. The session introduces students to the thinking and contributions of Florence Nightingale as well as those of Ernest Codman, W. Edwards Deming, Walter Shewhart, Avedis Donabedian, and Joseph Juran.

To prepare for the session, students are assigned to groups and are asked to complete readings written by, and about, the selected leaders. For an in-class discussion, each group takes on the persona of a leader. For example, a group of students represents Florence Nightingale. Persona groups are asked to prepare a brief presentation about their leader, considering the basic biographical facts, the historical context in which they lived and worked, some of the basic ingredients of the leader's thinking, evidence of the evolution of the leader's thought, key accomplishments we should recognize, and a story, symbol, or signature event that might help us understand the person. Although the leaders may not have lived during the same time throughout history, we invite the persona groups to participate in a round table discussion during class to help us think about the challenges we are facing in health care today.

Some questions we have asked the leaders to help us with are:

- We have no illusions that we can move forward with any sense of security about the future if we don't have our staff with us. Do you have any advice for us?
- What advice do you have about measuring quality, when everyone seems to want to measure quality differently?
- How do we accelerate the improvement of health care given the distractions and pressures of the environment?
- Limiting social expenditures for health care is a pressing issue for many in our society today. How should this be done to minimize its impact on the quality of the care for patients?
- We're trying to become a more integrated system of care for patients and their communities. What advice do you have for us?
- As you look out on the challenges being faced by contemporary leaders in health care in the United States, how are they alike and different from those that you faced?
- Are there some threads that connect your thinking to the others we've invited here today?

Over the last four years of teaching this course and using this exercise, we have been reminded of Nightingale's contributions. The message to us and to our students is that historic persons—Florence Nightingale and many others—have a very contemporary contribution to make to our understanding of the improvement of health care.

NOTES ON MATTERS

AFFECTING THE

HEALTH, EFFICIENCY, AND HOSPITAL ADMINISTRATION

OF THE

BRITISH ARMY,

FOUNDED CHIEFLY ON THE EXPERIENCE OF THE LATE WAR

BY

FLORENCE NIGHTINGALE

———

Presented by request to the Secretary of State for War.

———

LONDON

PRINTED BY HARRISON AND SONS, ST. MARTIN'S LANE, W.C.

1858

18

PREFACE

TO

SECTION II

It is now well-known that a large element in the mortality during the winter of 1854-55 was the loss of life on board the Sick Transports between Balaclava and Scutari.

The sick, from the landing in the Crimea, September 15, 1854, to the end of January, 1855, were brought to Scutari in 56 Transports, some of which were sailing vessels and others steamers.

The sick were received on board, and sometimes detained for several days before the vessel sailed. The voyage for sailing ships was usually six days, and for steam ships under two days: but the average time the sick were detained on board was eight days and a-half from the time of their embarkation at Balaclava till they were disembarked at Scutari. The numbers of those who died on board are variously stated, but they are probably, in every instance, understated.

It appears, that about 13,093 sick were embarked during the four and a-half months, of whom about 976 died. This is a mortality of no less than seventy-four and a-half per 1,000 in the short space of eight and a-half days. When we reduce this proportion to the proportion of deaths per annum, we find that, had the embarkation of sick gone on for twelve months at the same rate of mortality, no less than 3,182 men would have died out of every 1,000 embarked; in other words, the whole population of the Sick Transports would have perished on the Black Sea upwards of three times.

74½ per 1,000 Mortality of Sick on board Transports for 4½ Months.

The following Table gives the monthly details of this catastrophe.

Upon a voyage no longer than from Tynemouth to London, there died 74 out of every 1,000 sick embarked, during a period of 4½ months.

The loss in individual Transports was much greater than this average. The "Caduceus" embarked 430 sick on Sept. 23, 1854, and disembarked them at Scutari on Sept. 29. During the six days the sick were on board, there died no fewer than 114 men,

20

MORTALITY ON BOARD SICK TRANSPORT SHIPS

ARRIVED AT SCUTARI

1854. Months.	Sick embarked arriving at Scutari during the month.	Died on Passage.	Deaths per 1,000 embarked.	Deaths per 1,000 on cases treated at Scutari.	Deaths per 1,000 per ann. on board Sick Transport Sept. 15, 1854, to Jan. 31, 1855.
Sept. 15—30	3987	311	78		
Oct.	567	15	26·4		
Nov.	2981	162	54·3		
Dec.	2656	226	85		
1855.					
Jan.	2902	262	90	321	
	13,093	976	74·5	198*	3182
Feb.	2178	41	19	427	
Feb. 25 to Mar. 17	1067	5	4·7	315	
Mar. 18 to April 7	860	4	4·6	144	

being 26½ per cent. of the total number embarked, or in the incredible ratio of 16,160 per 1,000 per annum.

1. Either Transports unfit for Sick or Sick unfit for Voyage.

1. In considering what possible causes could have led to such a calamity, we can but come to one of two conclusions.

Either these Sick Transports were in a condition utterly unfit for sick as regards their Sanitary state, or sick were shipped in a condition utterly unfit for such a voyage. From the imputation of one neglect or the other we cannot escape. We have positive evidence that the Transports were, many of them, unfit for the purpose. They were overcrowded, badly ventilated, not clean, and not fitted up for the reception of sick. The attendance on board was also deficient. The superficial space, allowed in these Transports, was fixed by a Board of Inspection formed at Balaclava, December 12, 1854, at 6 ft. by 2½ ft. for sick and 6 ft. by 3 ft. for wounded men. The height between decks varied from 6 ft. to 8 ft. In one instance alone was it 8½ feet, and in one other 9 feet in some parts. We know, on the other hand, that many cases of Choleraic Disease were put on board, and, as might have been expected, great was the mortality in consequence. Those who were brought ashore alive often arrived in a state of collapse, only to die.

It has been usual to refer the terrible episode of these Transport Ships to the condition of the sick in camp as the cause. The cases, it is said, were bad cases, *therefore* they died

* Viz., from October 1, 1854, to January 31, 1855.

in large numbers on board the Transports and in the Hospitals at Scutari when they arrived there: *therefore* the occurrence of the catastrophe at Scutari and on the voyage was unavoidable.

It is, however, too late, and men know too much for such an apology to be accepted now for this sacrifice of the soldier. If the cases were so severe, the worst that could be done with them was to ship them in unwholesome Transports for the "polluted" Hospitals at Scutari. To have begun by putting Ships and Hospitals into a Sanitary state fit to receive the sick—to have kept the cases which it was unsafe to move at Balaclava—this, it would seem, would have been the more practical conclusion to be drawn from the above as to what ought to have been done.

The sick could but have died at Balaclava. But the Principal Medical Officer himself has shown that cases which were fortunately so bad as to be unfit for removal, in February 1855, suffered only a fifteenth part of the mortality which, had they been sent to Scutari, would have been their fate.

We do not allude, of course, to those times of which the sailing of the Caduceus may have been one, when, an Army being on the march, it is imperative to remove the sick, however perilous to them such removal may be; but, at such times, how much more imperative is it–to have good Sanitary conditions on board the Transports!

2. During February it will be seen that the character of the cases from the Crimea improved. The per centage of mortality upon those embarked on board the Transports fell from 90 to 19 per 1,000; but the mortality at Scutari rose, viz. from 321 to 427. And even, during the three weeks ending March 17, when the mortality on board the Transports, which had been above 74 per 1000 from Sept. 15, 1854, to Jan. 31, 1855, fell to under five per 1,000, the mortality at Scutari still maintained its fatal pre-eminence, and continued at 315 per 1,000, a far higher rate, indeed, than it had been for the four months ending Jan. 31, 1855, which was 198 per 1000.

2. Mortality at Scutari did not fall with that on board Sick Transports.

3. If we take the Sick whom we received alive at Scutari, the dead being deducted, a still more fatal per centage presents itself, being of Deaths to 1,000 living disembarked, as follows:

3. Mortality on board Sick Transports per 1,000 of living landed.

Months.	Sick disembarked at Scutari.	Died on voyage of those embarked from the Crimea.	Deaths to 1,000 living landed.
1854.			
Sept. 15—30......	3676	311	84·6
Oct.	552	15	27
Nov.	2819	162	57·4
Dec.	2430	226	93
1855.			
Jan..............	2640	262	99·2
	12,117	976	80·5

In the month of January we actually lost ten to every 100 who arrived alive.

NOTES ON THE CAUSES OF DISASTER AT SCUTARI

With regard to Scutari, it appears that there is now no difference of opinion in acknowledging the colossal calamity which befell us there in the winter of 1854-55. At least, such is the assertion of the world *versus* that of three men.

Regarding the causes of this calamity, there is still some difference of opinion.

It is not, however, now the question how much may be assigned to the condition of destitution and exhaustion in which the patients were sent down from the Crimea, and how much to the five conditions which reigned at Scutari, viz.:—

1. Frightful overcrowding.
2. Want of ventilation.
3.   "   drainage.
4.   "   cleanliness.
5.   "   Hospital Comforts.

But, if the men were sent down to Scutari in such a state as the Medical Officers allege, and allege truly, from over-work in the trenches, salt rations, insufficient clothing and shelter,how much more would such conditions as those which reigned at Scutari act upon them, how much more ought they to have been placed under such circumstances as would make the least call upon their shattered vital powers! Instead of this, bad air, bad cooking, want of cleanliness did their best or their worst to complete what bad food, bad clothing, over-work had begun. The men had not a chance. As has been said of the Cavalry so may be said generally,—

"Whatever was accomplished in the wars in which we have been engaged must be set down to the daring and discipline of our men, and the heroic examples of their leaders. They offered their blood in atonement of professional ignorance, and England accepted the sacrifice without taking a single step thereafter to avert so cruel a waste of energy, intrepidity, and patriotism."

Such conditions as those of Scutari must work with tenfold power on the exhausted constitutions submitted to them, with far more deadly effect than they would have done on any part of the civil population of London. And again, the worst part of the civil population of London is never submitted to such conditions.

Three facts will corroborate this:—

1. The fact that patients from the Land Transport Corps were sent down in exactly the same condition in 1855-56, as all

Margin notes:

What Proportion of the Mortality should be assigned to the conditions under which the men were Treated at Scutari?

Three Facts in answer to this Question.

24

our patients in 1854-55, and did recover, under different conditions, in Scutari Hospitals.

2. The fact that, after each in-rush of patients in 1854-55, there used to be a frightful increase of mortality.

3. The fact that the mortality from Diseases of Stomach and Bowels was at Scutari as 23.6 to (in the Crimea) 18.3, or nearly 25 per cent. more.

But it is now impossible to assign each cause of mortality its relative value. It would have been necessary, in order to do this, to have ascertained how, when and where each case of Disease originated, which was not done.

The Five great causes of Mortality at Scutari.
1.
Overcrowding

It is only necessary, therefore, now to add authentic and official testimony of each of the five causes assigned to the calamity.

1. Frightful overcrowding. Our Hospital Regulations assign 2 feet as the space to be assigned between each bed. Dr. Christison, of Edinburgh, assigns as the minimum space for each patient, 9 feet from head to head, 10 feet from head to middle of ward, 14 feet in height. Guy's Hospital gives a space of from 4 to 10 feet between bed and bed; the London Hospital, 8 feet; the London Fever Hospital, 9 feet; King's College Hospital, 6 feet; St.Bartholomew's, 5 feet; the Naval Hospitals, 4 feet between the beds.

The following Hospitals give respectively:—

CUBIC FEET OF SPACE PER PATIENT

London Fever	2,000
King's College	1,800—2,000
London	1,700
Guy's	1,300—2,000
St. Bartholomew's	1,377
Lariboisière (at Paris)	1,686
Naval Hospitals	1,200—1,500
Military	500—700
N.B.—Barracks give only	300—500

Dr. Christison is of opinion that 1,300 cubic feet of space per patient is enough; it requires ample ventilation to make it so. It never can be sufficiently repeated that the amount of cubic space is not so important as the ensuring a constant change of the air in that space. Not less than 2,000 cubic feet of air should be supplied to each Patient every hour.

It is obvious that, if the piling the cubic space on the top of the patients would answer the purpose, this may be done by placing them as close as possible in the open air, in which case any number of cubic feet may be obtained, arranged perpendicularly over the patient. But this does not answer the purpose. On the contrary, the front ranks in a march are always the least distressed, those behind the most. And persons have died by suffocation in the open air, in a crowd.

Space between the patients, both between their heads and at the feet, is the essential; and, above 16 feet, the height does not much matter.

In the corridors of the Barrack Hospital, Scutari, scarcely three feet was allowed between foot and foot. Two persons could hardly pass abreast; and, transversely, between the bed-sides, although two feet is the meagre space allowed by regulation, this was not adhered to, and there was scarcely room for one person to pass.

By the Report of the Cumming Maxwell Commission, two of whom were Army Surgeons, it appears that, from Inkermann to December 19, nearly twice the legitimate number of patients was inserted, even in the narrow space allowed, viz., 2,000 instead of 1,220 patients.

On December 17, repairs were finished, just in time to open a whole wing to an in-rush of patients, which began that very day, and reached in seventeen days, altogether, the number of 4,000. Yet, notwithstanding this fortunate occurrence, the overcrowding from December 19 to January 27, was 2,200, in the space allotted to 1,600, in the Barrack Hospital.

"A similar comparison will lead to a more unfavourable conclusion in the case of the Barrack Hospital. From the battle of the Alma to that of Inkermann, it afforded room for only 951 patients; but the average number in the building during that time was 1,276. From the last-mentioned date until the 19th of December there was room for only 1,220, while the average number in Hospital during the same period exceeded 2,000. From the 19th of December to the 27th day of January, the accommodation was sufficient for 1,643 patients, but the actual average number, according to the weekly state, was 2,228. The addition of the eastern half of C. corridor made the total accommodation fit for only 1,704; but we regret to state that the Hospital has continued down to within the last few days over-crowded by about 400 patients." Cumming Maxwell Commission.

February 23, 1855.

"Upon comparing the maximum number which the General Hospital can in our opinion accommodate, viz., 968 patients, with the numbers appearing in the weekly states of that Hospital, and which will be

26

found below, we think that it was not over-crowded until the last week in December, and that, with the exception of one week in January, it has been over-crowded since that date."

NUMBER OF PATIENTS in the several HOSPITALS at SCUTARI at the end of the Weeks ending on the hereunder-mentioned Days.

DATE.	General Hospital.	Barrack Hospital.	Haidar Pasha.	Stables.	Kuleli	Total Number of Sick, not including Hospital Ships.
1854.						
October 7	724	1,198	..	..	..	1,922
14	694	1,174	..	..	..	1,868
21	658	1,267	..	..	..	1,925
28	620	1,242	..	..	..	1,862
November 4	800	1,500	..	..	..	2,300
11	734	2,062	..	..	..	2,796
18	907	1,958	..	..	..	2,865
25	856	2,183	..	..	..	3,039
December 2	829	2,202	..	..	110	3,141
9	746	2,176	..	..	179	3,101
16	710	1,900	..	..	240	3,750
23	957	2,434	..	..	240	3,721
30	1,034	2,401	..	..	234	3,669
1855.						
January 6	1,008	2,387	386	..	234	4,341
13	875	2,249	307	60	508	3,999
20	1,006	2,179	304	60	508	3,545
27	1,007	2,221	350	63	495	4,016

	Date.	General Hospital.	Barrack Hospital.	Haidar Pasha.	Hospital Ships.	Kuleli.	Total Number of Sick
Average Daily No.	February	969	2,043	488	707	908	5,115
"	Up to March 15 }	828	1,650	434	312	878	4,102

When we re-consider that the space allotted by the Regulations of the Service is only two feet between the beds, that the filling both wards and corridors with patients is, under the most favourable circumstances, like building* two

* "The wards and corridors being both occupied by the sick, they could, in fact, be considered only as two Hospitals built back to back, with the foul air in each intermingling by the doors."

Hospitals "back to back," and that it is without disputing such regulations and admitting such circumstances that the Hospital Commissioners are still compelled to declare the space actually given to have been not even in accordance with such regulations, but far below them—we think we may reiterate the term "frightful over-crowding" with, alas! no hope of contradiction.

"We have allowed in the wards five feet per man, according to the Hospital regulations of the service, except where the height of the rooms does not give, with that superficial measurement, the cubic space of 800 feet per man. In that case we have determined the number which can be accommodated by allowing that amount of cubic space to each person. Cumming Maxwell Report.

"The corridors of the Barrack and General Hospitals are at present occupied by sick and wounded. Those of the Barrack contain two rows of beds, and those of the General Hospital have a single row. We think it much to be regretted that they should be so occupied, for such occupation is not only injurious to the ventilation of the wards, but deprives the patients of the place in which they can most conveniently take exercise during their recovery. Making all due allowance, however, for the great demand for hospital accommodation which has existed here during this winter, and for future contingencies, we think that not more than a single row of beds should, under any circumstances, be placed in the corridors; and our calculation proceeds on the supposition that each man in that single row has five feet in width allowed to him."

Hoping that never again may be seen "allowed in the service five feet in width to each man," or about two feet between the beds, and especially not in war time, especially not in war epidemics, when it would be far better for the men, were they treated in the open fields than in such Hospital space, we take leave of this part of the subject.

2. With regard to the ventilation, scarcely anything had been done, up to the arrival of the Sanitary Commissioners, March 6, 1855, to improve its state in the Barrack Hospital, not even as much as breaking a pane of glass in the privies. 2. Bad Ventilation.

What they did shows its defects; and what the atmosphere was at night in that Hospital, especially in Corridor and Wards D, it is impossible to describe, or to remember, without wondering that every patient in them was not swept off by fever or cholera.

28

"On entering the Hospital, the first thing that attracted our attention was the defective state of the ventilation.

"Excepting a few small openings here and there, there were no means of renewing the atmosphere within the Hospital. The large cubic space above the top of the ward windows always retained a considerable amount of hot and foul air for which there was no escape. There was not even an open fire-place connected with the building, and the wards were heated by stoves, the pipes of which passed through a small hole at the top of one of the windows.

"There was no communication between the wards and corridors in the majority of instances, except by the doors, and hence that free circulation and perflation of the atmosphere, so necessary in military hospitals was impossible."

"The upper parts of the windows in the privies and in the galleries connecting them with the corridors were at once removed, so as to allow the emanations to escape into the external atmosphere."

"The rooms are large and lofty, and have generally three windows, much too small for their cubic contents, and the heads of these windows do not reach to within five or six feet of the ceiling. The window space in the corridors is considerable, and the heads of the windows come up much closer to the ceiling. The different flats of the building communicate by large roomy stone staircases.

"To remedy the defective ventilation, the Commission recommended that the upper portion of the windows should in all cases be opened, and the current of air modified by the insertion of perforated zinc plates, louvre boarding, or otherwise, that adequate space for the escape of foul air should be provided as near as possible to the ceiling of each ward, and that the staircases should be used for ventilating shafts by openings being made through their ceilings to the roof."

The ventilation in the General Hospital was much less objectionable.

"Both wards and corridors were used for the sick, but the disposable means of ventilation were such that the Hospital could hardly be said to be over-crowded."

Viz., March 6, 1855.

"Permanent and independent ventilating arrangements, by perforated zinc panes in the windows and ventilating openings at the ceilings, were directed to be introduced for the wards, the same as those for the Barrack Hospital.

"The upper window sashes in the privies and galleries were directed to be removed, so as to prevent, as far as practicable, effluvia from entering the corridors.

"The General Hospital, like the Barrack Hospital, is divided longitudinally all round into wards and corridors; the wards facing outwards, and the corridors facing towards the court-yard. But it differs from the Barrack Hospital in one important particular—namely, that the wards and corridors communicate not only by the doors but by numerous large lofty windows in the division wall, so that by proper management of the windows, by the introduction of perforated zinc panes, and by suitable ventilating openings at the ceiling of each ward, a thorough ventilation could be at all times secured."

3. With regard to want of drainage, so much has been said, that a few extracts from the diary of the Sanitary Commission are all that is necessary.

3. Bad Drainage.

"We found the whole of the Turkish sewerage belonging to the Barrack Hospital in a defective condition. The sewers and drains were badly formed, badly constructed, badly laid, and untrapped.

"It may be here stated generally, that all the buildings used as Hospitals were sewered. Turkish sewers are made of rubblestone or coarse brickwork. The bottoms are flat, rough, and uneven; there are no means of external ventilation, no means for cleansing or flushing, and the ends or mouths of the sewers at Scutari opened above the level of the sea, and were exposed to the action of the winds, which, in certain directions, blew into the sewer-end, and carried the foul emanations from the deposits within them through the pipe drains to the privies, and thence into the corridors and wards where the sick were placed. It was stated to us that a change of wind had been observed to be attended by an accession of fever cases from among the sick, and that existing fever cases put on a more aggravated form. We found that the winds to which these results were attributed blew in the direction of the open mouths of the sewers. These sewers were, in fact, cesspools of the most dangerous description, through which, and through the privies, the wind forced sewer gases directly into the wards of the Hospital.

"The exhalations escaping through the defective walls and covers of sewers, where they happened to pass close to or underneath occupied rooms, could in some instances be distinctly observed within the rooms, and there is reason to believe that fatal cases both of fever and cholera arose from this circumstance among the inmates."

"In order to diminish, as far as practicable, the injurious emanations proceeding from the sewers and privies, it was directed that the outfall sewers of the Hospital should be extended, and a canvas cover placed over their mouths to prevent the wind driving the effluvia into the Hospital; that three openings for ventilation should be made in each main sewer, between the Hospital and the outfall, with a water-trap at each ventilator, and a man-hoe for cleansing: water-tanks for flushing the sewers were also directed to be placed immediately outside the walls of the building. These tanks consisted of hogsheads, each having a large wooden valve, covering a pipe communicating with the head of each sewer. The inspector was directed to see that these flushing tanks were filled with water three times a day, and the valves opened by himself.

"All the privies, sewers, and drains, were directed to be thoroughly cleansed, and their contents deodorized and removed. It was further directed that peat charcoal should be freely used as a deodorizer for these purposes."

"The privies of this large building (the General Hospital) are situated in four square towers, built on the outside of the Hospital, instead of being within the square, as in the Barrack Hospital. One of the towers is situated at each angle of the main building, and communicates with the interior by means of a gallery opening into each corridor. The windows of these galleries were all closed at the time of our examination, and as the structure of the privies and the arrangement of the drainage were essentially the same as in the Barrack Hospital, the effluvia entered the corridors, and could be easily detected within them at some distance from the doors.

"This constituted the main sanitary defect of the General Hospital, but it was a very dangerous one, and neutralized, to a great extent, the advantages possessed by the building."

"On several occasions, both in the Barrack and other Hospitals, we saw the excreta of patients in utensils under the beds, instead of having been at once removed."

"The effluvia from the privies had free access to the corridors, and added materially to the impurity of the air."

"The first step taken by the Commissioners was to examine carefully the outskirts of the Barrack Hospital, to ascertain whether there were any external causes likely to affect the purity of the surrounding atmosphere.

"The site of the Hospital, as already stated, is open and airy, overlooking the sea on two sides, and on a third side facing the open country; on the fourth side it is contiguous to one extremity of Scutari, which, like all Turkish towns, we found to be in a bad sanitary condition. The paving was rough and badly laid, and the channelling very defective. The surface in many places was filthy, and had putrefying mud lying in hollows, and there were nuisances among the houses. The ravine to the south-east of the Hospital, contained offensive deposit, which tainted the air on that side of the building. There was some refuse, and several dead dogs lying close to the Hospital walls.

"The surface of the inner square was uneven, badly formed, imperfectly drained, and very dirty.

"Four detached buildings within the court-yard, one at each angle of the square, and communicating with the corridors, contain the privies. These buildings open into each line of corridors by two large doors, one on either side of the angle. By this arrangement each corridor in the circuit of the building communicates with the privies by eight doors. The privies consist merely of a marble slab with an opening communicating with a vertical pipe of red tile carried down into a drain at the basement of the building. The privies, and the galleries between them

31

and the corridors, are lighted by a number of glazed windows, which
we found were all closed, so that there was a direct communication
between the sewers, which were loaded with filth, and the corridors
and wards of the Hospital."

"The Turks, as it is known to those who have travelled in the East, House of
are remarkably decorous in their habits, and the necessaries on the Commons
side of these long Corridors were separated from the Corridor by an Committee
ante-room; the door leading into the ante-room was not opposite to Evidence.
that which led to the necessaries, so that it was impossible, even if the
door had been opened, for anyone to obtain a view of those places. The
Turks never use any paper, and therefore the soil-pipes were very
small; but there were, as it is a part of their religion to perform ablu-
tions after using these necessaries, small taps on the left-hand side.
When the army was at the Barracks in the summer, these taps were
by the soldiers broken off, and in consequence the supply of water was
stopped. When the Barrack was re-opened as an Hospital, no sufficient pains were taken to repair those pipes, or secure a flow of water;
and the pipes soon choked up; and the liquid faeces, the evacuations
from those afflicted with diarrhoea, filled up the pipes, floated up over
the floor, and came into the room in which the necessaries were,
extended and flowed into the ante-room, and were more than an inch
deep when I got there in the morning; men suffering from diarrhoea,
who had no slippers at the time and no shoes on, as this flood of filth
advanced, came less and less near to the necessary, and nearer and
nearer to the door, till at last I found them within a yard of the ante-
room performing the necessary functions of nature; and in consequence the smell from this place was such that I can use no epithet to
describe its horror."

The hideous state of the privies too truly described in this
last extract, which refers to the Barrack Hospital, continued
there, more or less, up to March, 1855, in which month it was
still occasionally at once our crime and our punishment.

A farther misery, and the cause of much disease, was, in the
autumn of 1854, the placing of tubs in those wards farthest
from the privies (in the absence of utensils), to hold the excreta of from thirty to fifty patients, afflicted with diarrhoea and
dysentery; it is easy to imagine the consequence of this frightful nuisance, and it often became Miss Nightingale's duty to see
these tubs removed and emptied by a couple of orderlies, who
carried one on a pole between them.

These tubs were, however, discontinued at a late period of the
winter of 1854-55.

"We directed the immediate removal of the excreta of the sick out of Sanitary
the Hospital." Report.

This was, however, not done, not even to the last.

And, again, we wish to allude to the fact, that in no Hospital is there less discipline than in a military one. It is unquestionable that there can be no safety for the sick, especially for cases of typhus and bowel disease, if their excreta are allowed to stand for twenty-four, nay, even twelve hours in the wards, excepting in the most perfectly constructed close stools,—perhaps not even then; they ought to be carried immediately and instantly away and emptied.

Yet it was found impossible, from first to last, to induce the orderlies to do this more than once, as a practice, in twenty-four hours; should they have accomplished it twice, they thought they had done wonders.

I have seen a zealous Orderly Medical Officer when going his rounds, open every close-stool (when we had close-stools) and, finding every one full, call up the orderly, and make him empty them.

I have heard the rule made over and over again, always to empty them immediately; but if Medical Officers, Sanitary Commissioners, Hospital Officers, think that it was done, i. e. with any regularity or as a rule, they are mistaken.

And is it fair to ask Medical Officers, to see to these details of drudgery? My own belief, founded on much experience, is, that it can only be effectually done by a woman; it is done in the Civil Hospitals by her; it has been done in Military ones by her.

And here, homely and sickening as is the subject, I must pay my tribute to the instinctive delicacy, the ready attention of orderlies and patients during all that dreadful period; for my sake, they performed offices of this kind (which they neither would for the sake of discipline, nor for that of the importance to their own health, which they did not know), and never one word nor one look which a gentleman would not have used; and, while paying this humble tribute to humble courtesy, the tears come into my eyes as I think how, amidst scenes of horrible filth, of loathsome disease and death, there rose above it all the innate dignity, gentleness, and chivalry of the men (for never, surely, was chivalry so strikingly exemplified) shining in the midst of what must be considered as the lowest sinks of human misery, and preventing instinctively the use of one expression which could distress a gentlewoman.

I return to the point, viz, that if it is thought that discipline in such matters as these is best enforced by Medical Officers and Ward Masters, it is a mistake. The Medical Officers should be strictly professional; the Ward Masters should enforce every rule except what pertains to the bedside of the patient; this last can only be done by women, not with their own hands, but by directing and training orderlies; it is an humble prerogative which no one will grudge them.

And now I take leave of this disgusting subject, only adding that, if it sickens us to read it, it was far more sickening to see it and go through with it, involving, as it did, disease and death to an unknown number of brave men.

"Connected with this question of over-crowding, we may state, that we found a considerable portion of the Barrack Hospital in use as a Depot. We considered that the presence of so many soldiers and other persons not necessary for the treatment of the sick, was a source of danger, from occupying cubic space within the building, and increasing the impurity of the air, from the defective privy drainage, of the truth of which opinion we had subsequently two striking confirmations.

"All the Hospitals had a water supply. That for the Barrack Hospital was found to be hardly sufficient in amount for so large a number of sick. The water was not so pure as could have been desired, and it was received into tanks within the barrack square.

"Speaking generally, we were of opinion that the walls of the Wards and Corridors were not so clean as they might have been.

"There were false floors in the Wards, which had been used as sleeping berths for the Turkish soldiers, and which had the bedsteads of the sick placed on them. There were also box seats along the walls of the Wards, for the use of the soldiers. We were of opinion that there ought to have been no such inclosed spaces capable of collecting dirt and foul air within the walls, and that it would have been advisable to have moved the whole of this useless woodwork before the sick were put into the Wards, had there been time and means for doing so.

"We directed the frequent use of quicklime-wash for the purpose of cleansing the walls and improving the atmosphere in the Wards and Corridors. This we considered one of the most important sanitary precautions which could be adopted. Experience has shown that all porous substances, such as the plaster of walls and ceilings, and even woodwork, absorb the emanations proceeding from the bodies and breath of the sick. After a time, the plaster becomes saturated with organic matter, and is a fresh source of impurity to the air of the Ward. It hence follows that unless the walls and ceilings of Hospitals be constructed of absolutely non-absorbent materials, it is necessary, at short intervals, to use some application capable of neutralizing or destroying the absorbed organic matter. Of all known materials, quicklime wash is the best and cheapest for this purpose. Its effect in freshening the air in crowded wards and rooms is immediate, and it is one of the most efficacious agents for mitigating the virulence of epidemic disease.

Sanitary Report.

34

"The following is a summary of the work done during the period of Mr. Wilson's inspectorship:—

    Hand-carts or large basketsful of filth removed   5,114
    Sewers and latrines flushed (times)   466
    Carcases of animals buried   35

WEEKLY ABSTRACT OF MR. WILSON'S DIARIES

Week ending March 24
"Thirteen men, on an average, employed in cleansing the surface of the ground in the vicinity of the Barrack Hospital and at Kulali, in removing the refuse, burying animals, &e. During the week there were collected and removed from the vicinity of the Barrack Hospital 202 hand-carts of baskets full of filth, rubbish, and offensive matter. Two tons of filth were removed at Kulali. The carcases of 15 dogs and 2 horses were buried, and the sewers of the Barrack Hospital were flushed three times.

Week ending March 31
"The cleansing operations were extended to the General Hospital and Palace Hospital this week. The number of men employed was 20 on the average. The ground about both Hospitals, and that portion of the village nearest the Barrack Hospital was swept clean. A large sewer within the barrack square was opened, by order of the Commissioners, and 42 hand-carts of filth removed from it. The sewers connected with the privies were opened and cleansed, and 26 hand-carts of filth removed from them. A sewer at the General Hospital was also opened and cleansed, and 14 hand-carts of filth were removed from it. Water was carried to the flushing tanks, and the sewers at the Barrack Hospital were flushed nineteen times in the course of the week. The total filth and refuse removed from the vicinity of Barrack, General, and Palace Hospitals during this week, was 354 hand-carts or baskets full, and the carcases of 7 dead animals were buried. Peat charcoal was used in the cleansing operations.

Week ending April 7
"The ground about the Barrack, General, and Palace Hospitals was swept as usual, also part of the village of Scutari; an offensive sewer at the Barrack Hospital was cleansed. The average number of men employed during the week was 25. There were 297 hand-carts or baskets full of filth removed. Water was carried to the flushing tanks, and the sewers and privies at the Barrack Hospital were flushed twenty-one times. The Hospital at Kulali was inspected. Peat charcoal was used for deodorizing the privies. The ground round the Hospital was cleansed and the privies flushed.

Week ending April 14
"The average number of men employed this week was 20. The ground about the Hospitals was swept as usual, and 215 hand-carts or baskets

full of filth were removed. Water was carried to the flushing tanks, and the sewers at the Barrack Hospital were flushed nineteen times during the week. The carcases of 2 horses, a cow, and 4 dogs were buried.

Week ending April 21

"Several large foul sewers were opened at the Barrack Hospital by order of the Commissioners; peat charcoal was applied to deodorize their contents, and above 100 hand-carts of filth were removed from them. The ground around all the Hospitals was cleansed. The filth and refuse collected and removed during the week, amounted to 417 hand-carts or baskets full. Water was carried to the flushing tanks, and the sewers and privies at the Barrack Hospital were flushed out twenty-four times. Peat charcoal was applied to the privies every day. A dead horse was buried. The average number of men employed during the week was 26.

"Similar cleansing works were carried out during the two succeeding weeks."

4. We come now to the fourth cause of our disaster at Scutari—want of cleanliness. *(margin: 4. Want of Cleanliness. Deficiency in washing.)*

(1) The Washing:

Dr. Smith's evidence upon the subject is as follows, in answer to the question—

(margin: A. Smith, Esq, M.D. 26 March, 1855.)

8853. "Then the state of things which has been described, the absence of washing and so on, occurred while Mr. Wreford was there?—I must say that there was not an absence of washing. Not long ago I called upon him to show me what washing had been done, and he sent me home a return, showing the washing that had been done for three months by contract, and the number of articles washed was very large; but I must say it was not what I considered sufficient for so large a hospital.

8854. "Did you observe whether that return included the early part of November?—I will ask permission to put the return in as evidence. I feel convinced that it did apply to that time; but it was done by contract, not in the hospitals.

. . . I was perfectly aware that females can see many things, in which there might be a deficiency of cleanliness and comfort, that men do not see, and even that men have not time to see; because the medical officers were overwhelmed with work—there might be a spot upon a sheet that a medical officer would not notice, and a woman would at once.

9504. "You thought that the hospitals were in that great state of cleanliness, that it would require the delicacy of a woman to find out the least dirt in the hospital?—I do not say that.

9505. "You spoke of a spot on a sheet?—I put that as an example. I spoke figuratively, and that a female would notice that when a man would not.

9506. You thought that there was no dirt or filth in the hospitals that would be readily noticed by men, and that there would on that account be an advantage in women going out?—I had no reason, from any

36

communications that I had received, to believe that there was that state of filth in the hospital that it would be readily noticed."

In order now to form an idea of what Dr. Smith considers as a "very large number of articles washed," it is, of course, necessary to compare them with the number of men washed for. A Return is annexed.

"Returns showing the total number of sick and wounded treated in the hospital at Scutari:

Months.				Total treated.
During November, 1854	..	..	..	16,846
" December, 1854	..	..	..	19,479
" January, 1855	..	..	..	23,076

A. Smith, M.D. D.-General.
"13, St. James's-place, 29th March, 1855."

The number of sick treated, although manifestly incorrect, is taken from Dr. Smith's return, Sevastopol Committee, 2nd Report, p. 705, where it accompanies the number of articles washed, in the same return, apparently for the purpose of comparison, and the result is as follows, viz., that, in the month of January, when 23,000 men were treated in hospital at Scutari,

11,600 shirts,
10,600 sheets,
9,200 blankets,

were considered to be a "very large number of articles washed" for them, or 1 shirt to each 2 men, and less than 1 sheet and 1 blanket to each 2 men.

The total number of pieces washed is 51,000, or rather less than 2¼ articles per man.

Yet this is the month in which the washing reaches the maximum of the three months under consideration.

At the same time, it is necessary to mention that the monthly "numbers of sick" returned as "treated in the Hospitals at Scutari," are the same as the monthly numbers in the return representing *not* the "sick treated in the Hospitals at Scitari," but the "total sick of Lord Raglan's Army."

Let us now take the evidence of the Cumming-Maxwell Report:—

Cumming Maxwell Report.

"Immediately connected with the subject of hospital furniture and clothing is the provision which has been made for the washing, both of bedding and personal clothing. This, we are of opinion, has not been satisfactory. At the General Hospital, indeed, eight or ten Armenians are employed for this purpose, and we have heard no complaints from the men there, except that they frequently get the shirt of another instead of their own from the wash; and this we may observe involves a greater evil than the mere loss of property. The washing is effected without boiling, and without this process it is impossible to get rid of animal matter. Under such circumstances the exchange complained of is peculiarly objectionable. The washing of the bed linen is very badly done there, the sheets which return from the wash being frequently found in a more filthy condition than those which they are intended to replace.

"From the following table, which has been furnished to us by the purveyor, it will be seen that 7,824 shirts were washed at that hospital during the month of January, which gives to every man about two shirts per week. The number washed at the Barrack Hospital during the same period was only 3,837; and as the average number of patients in that building exceeded in January 2,200, all the men did not even get one shirt in a fortnight from the public washing establishment."

It is thus to be deduced from the above, that the deficiency of washing in the Barrack Hospital was much more alarming than at first appears. Because the articles washed for the Barrack Hospital were 23,400, for the General Hospital, 28,000, whereas the average of Patients in the General Hospital was under 1,000, in the Barrack Hospital over 2,200.

9512. "Did they state whether the linen was washed or not, or whether it was in good order?—The purveyor himself reported to me that the linen was washed. I have a letter here now to that effect. A. Smith's Evidence

9513. "What letter is that?— I have a letter dated the 12th of February; this refers back to November and December; it was written in consequence of my having written out on the subject:—'Sir,—I have the honour to transmit for your information the inclosed return of washing done by the contractors, &c., for this hospital during November and December, 1854, and January, 1855. I may here be allowed to state, that in no instance have I known application made at the clean linen store for a fresh supply, or for an exchange of bedding, in which the same was not instantly complied with.' That is from Mr. Selkirk Stuart, purveyor to the forces.

9514. "CHAIRMAN: Is that dated Scutari?—Yes; 12th February, last month, and it refers back to November, December, and January. I may say, that Mr. Stuart was the purveyor in charge of the Barrack Hospital; then here is another letter to me from Mr. Wreford, dated the 12th of February:—'Sir,—I have the honour to acknowledge the receipt of your letter of the 26th ultimo, inclosing a list of washing machines, &c., and to acquaint you that the 'Eagle' arrived on the 9th instant, and the stores she brought out are in course of landing; the inclosed letter and return are the best reply I can give to your postscript; and to add, that I know nothing officially of the subsidiary washing establishment to which you allude, the necessity for which has never been made apparent to me.' Then this is a return (producing the same, v. p.

RETURN of ARTICLES OF BEDDING, &c., belonging to the GENERAL and BARRACK HOSPITALS, washed by the CONTRACTORS, &c., during the MONTH of JANUARY.

Scutari, February 8, 1855.

	General Hospital.	Barrack Hospital.	Total.
Palliasses..................	1,324	1,417	2,741
Bolsters	215	1,068	1,238
Blankets	3,254	5,984	9,238
Rugs......................	266	1,371	1,637
Sheets	4,844	5,797	10,641
Turkish Beds..............	. .	11	11
Turkish Pillows	. .	2	2
Turkish Coverlets	. .	26	26
Turkish Sheets.............	172	23	195
Great Coats...............	. .	367	367
Gowns, H.P...............	. .	329	644
Waistcoats, H.P...........	. .	189	440
Trowsers, H.P.	397	322	719
Shirts....................	7,824	3,837	11,661
Drawers..................	. .	193	193
Coatees	. .	685	685
Bandages.................	. .	811	811
Hair Beds	. .	86	86
Hair Pillows...............	. .	28	28
Flock Beds................	. .	40	40
Flock Pillows	. .	44	44
Haversacks	. .	121	121
Towels	1,-47	85	1,432
Regimental Trowsers........	. .	182	182
Pairs of Stockings	7, 24	. .	7,824
Pairs of Socks	. .	261	261
Nightcaps	. .	97	97
Fine Sheets	. .	4	4
Turkish Gowns	. .	2	2
Pads.....................	. .	7	7
Ship Mattresses............	. .	7	7
Turkish Curtains...........	. .	2	2
Handkerchiefs	. .	2	2
Total Pieces..........	28,033	23,402	51,435

(Signed) SELKIRK STUART,

Purveyor to the Forces.

103) of the washing done by contract (for there may have been other means of getting it done besides*), during the months of November,

* A glance at this Return, p. 103, will show that it comprises all the washing done by Purveyor, whether "by contract" or otherwise.

December, and January; there were during the month of November 4,832 pieces washed; during the month of December, 14,044 pieces washed; during the month of January there were 23,402 pieces washed. I will hand this return in. (The same was handed in.)"

"The washing at the Barrack is done by contract, and not only is the quantity washed in general insufficient, but the washing is very inadequately performed; Miss Nightingale states, in her evidence in February, that she had seen 'blankets come back from the wash torn and covered with stains.' She added, that she had herself 'sorted these blankets when taking in sick, and been compelled to throw away the so-called clean blankets till they could be carried away and destroyed.' Mr. Stuart gave us a similar description of the washing at an earlier period. We must add, that we heard of some shirts having been brought into the wards on one occasion as clean, which were found on examination with lice upon them; and Dr. Calder states in his evidence the same thing with respect to blankets. Naming Maxwell Report.

"With the view of meeting to some extent the want of proper washing, Miss Nightingale established a wash-house on the 30th November, which was provided with boilers, partly from the engineer office, partly from her own resources. The average number of articles washed weekly at that establishment during the month of January was 500 shirts and 150 other articles; but these figures, like the other returns which we obtained from the same quarter, do not indicate the whole extent of the evil sought to be remedied. We are glad to state, however, that washing, wringing, and drying machines have arrived from England, for the purpose of doing all the washing of these establishments."

Yet, after all this reporting, the Chief Commissioner being himself Inspector-General at Scutari, the establishment here promised, with its machines, did not come into operation till May 1, 1855.

" . . . In the first instance—indeed, till a comparatively recent date, I had no sheets; even blankets were scarce. I had frequently difficulty in procuring them, the men often requiring a change—such as were bleeding, or with profuse discharge. When I asked for blankets, I was told none were to be had, in consequence of difficulty of getting them washed. Rugs were in want also, but not to the same extent. If we had blankets we did not care so much for rugs. In more than one instance I had to send them back because they were filled with lice. These were isolated cases, and by no means general. Things were generally clean. Dr. Calder's Evidence.

"For a few days I had considerable difficulty in getting hospital utensils, especially bed-pans. This was especially felt in the case of men with stumps or fractures."

"13104. In going through the Hospital, did you notice the condition of the linen of the patients?—Yes. Commissioner Maxwell's Evidence.

"13105. What state was it in?—When I first arrived there, I found the men constantly without linen at all. I found them constantly with-

PAPERS delivered by A. SMITH, ESQ., M.D., 26th March, 1855.

RETURN of WASHING Performed by the CONTRACTORS, &c., for BARRACK HOSPITAL, Scutari, from 1st November, 1854, to 31st January, 1855.

	1854 Nov.	December, 1854.			January, 1855.			TOTAL.
		By whom Washed.						
	Mr. Ottoni.	Mr. Ottoni.	Mr. Parry.	Soldiers' Wives.	Mr. Ottoni.	Mr. Parry.	Soldiers' Wives.	
Palliasses	394	161	499	. .	712	705	. .	2,462
Bolsters...........	209	120	359	. .	564	504	. .	1,756
Blankets	2,488	902	2,920	. .	2,831	3,153	. .	12,294
Rugs	251	81	497	. .	694	677	. .	2,200
Sheets............	716	531	2,458	. .	3,116	2,681	. .	9,502
Turkish Beds.......	36	27	43	. .	7	4	. .	117
Turkish Pillows.....	2	10	. .	. .	. .	2	. .	14
Turkish Coverlets ...	32	1	52	. .	1	25	. .	111
Turkish Sheets	3	. .	163	. .	. .	27	. .	193
Turkish Gowns	. .	. .	. .	. .	1	1	. .	2
Turkish Curtains ...	. .	. .	. .	. .	2	. .	. .	2
Great Coats........	120	125	62	. .	223	144	. .	674
Gowns, I.P.	6	11	138	. .	120	209	. .	484
Trousers, I.P........	24	19	117	. .	128	194	. .	482
Waistcoats, I.P.	2	1	91	. .	79	110	. .	283
Shirts	6	310	398	2,446	1,758	1,458	621	6,997
Drawers	. .	8	23	41	82	111	2	267
Coatees	42	. .	44	. .	540	145	. .	771
Bandages	13	. .	319	74	12	764	35	1,217
Hair Beds	247	23	75	. .	43	43	. .	431
Hair Pillows	163	26	57	. .	9	19	. .	274
Flock Beds	48	5	35	. .	23	17	. .	129
Flock Pillows.......	4	. .	29	. .	17	27	. .	77
Haversacks	17	. .	9	1	2	119	. .	148
Towels............	. .	. .	3	44	18	63	4	132
Pairs of Socks	. .	. .	18	99	105	139	17	378
Night Caps	. .	. .	22	14	21	76	. .	133
Pads	9	. .	29	. .	. .	7	. .	45
Ships' Mattresses ...	. .	. .	1	. .	7	. .	. .	8
Handkerchiefs......	. .	. .	. .	. .	2	. .	. .	2
Regimental Trousers.	. .	. .	8	. .	112	70	. .	190
Russian Coats......	. .	. .	4	. .	. .	. .	. .	4
TOTAL PIECES ..	4,832	2,361	8,964	2,719	11,229	11,494	679	42,278
			14,044			23,402		

(Signed) SELKIRK STUART, *Purveyor to the Forces.*
10th February, 1855.

out sheets, and I found them constantly with shirts of the very filthi-
est description; and I thought it so important a matter to look into,
that one of the very first points to which we addressed ourselves was
to ascertain what had been done for the washing of the hospital.

"13106. What did you find had been done in that respect?—We found
that in the General Hospital the washing was done by a party of
Armenians, eight or ten in number. There was a wash-house there,
supplied with troughs, and the washing, as far as quantity was concerned, I never heard a complaint of. The men got their two shirts a
week, but I frequently heard them complain that they did not get their
own shirts. There was great confusion, and a man who sent his shirt to
the wash was never sure of getting it sent back; naturally, therefore,
those who had shirts were very often extremely reluctant to part with
them. I have been told of repeated instances (though I never found it
myself), of four or five shirts having been found under the pillow of a
patient, because he was afraid that if they went to the wash, they
never would come back, or that he would get others. In respect to the
Barrack Hospital, I found that the purveyor, shortly after that establishment was set on foot, had entered into a contract with an Italian,
or Levantine, of the name of Ottone; in that respect, I think, following
the regulations that have been referred to: but that contract was broken repeatedly.

"13107. How was it broken?—The man did not wash the things, so
the purveyor assured me. When I first examined the purveyor, he told
me that he was then about to enter into a contract with another con-
tractor; and when I left, the washing of the Barrack Hospital, so far as
it is done (I do not say that it is well done, very far from it), is done by
those two contractors, Ottone, and a gentleman of the name of Parry.

"13109. What was about the average number (viz., of Patients in
Hospital):—In the Barrack Hospital, in the week ending the 4th of
November, there were 1,500 patients; in the week ending the 11th,
there were 2,062. On November the 18th, there were 1,958; and on the
25th of November, there were 2,183. I think that shows the average
sufficiently.

"13112. Speaking generally, what should you say was the condition of
the men with regard to their linen in the two Hospitals?—Generally
speaking, I should say that they were in a very unsatisfactory condition.

"13113. Including linen sheets as well as their shirts?—Yes. The
washing has been very badly done throughout, simply for this reason,
that they do not understand boiling clothes out there, and in order to
get rid of animal matter, it is indispensable, so I am assured, that the
clothes should be boiled. In the next place, the men came down sometimes with vermin, and the vermin could not be got rid of unless the
clothes were boiled. There have been cases in which shirts have been
brought back from the wash with vermin; one was mentioned to me in
conversation, of about a dozen shirts, I think, that were brought back
into the wards of the Hospital with vermin upon them, although they
professed to be clean."

Mr. Stafford's
Evidence.

"7590. In what state were the clothes of those men?—The clothes of those men were swarming with lice, as thick as the letters on a page of print; and when I have been undressing the men, to put them to bed, when they had not strength to undress themselves, they have asked me not to come near them, knowing the state in which they were. My own clothes were never free when I was in the Hospital."

ABSTRACT of Weekly States of SICK and WOUNDED from October 1
January 31.

Date.	OFFICERS.					MEN.				
	Remained.	Admitted.	Discharged.	Died.	Remained.	Remained.	Admitted.	Discharged.	Died.	Remained.
1854										
1 to 7 October	70	3	..	1	72	2,277	61	403	67	1,868
8 to 14 "	72	23	9	2	84	1,868	307	295	46	1,834
15 to 21 "	84	12	20	..	76	1,834	386	151	29	2,040
22 to 28 "	76	8	47	..	37	2,040	350	370	56	1,964
28 Oct. to 4 Nov.	37	11	2	1	45	1,964	952	384	52	2,480
5 to 11 "	45	34	10	..	69	2,480	850	469	36	2,825
12 to 18 "	69	49	4	3	111	2,825	1,045	557	94	3,219
19 to 25 "	111	9	..	..	102	3,219	438	144	67	3,446
26 to 2 Dec. ..	102	10	5	..	107	3,446	436	315	70	3,497
3 to 9 "	107	..	12	..	95	3,497	263	388	70	3,302
10 to 16 "	95	..	8	1	86	3,302	299	521	85	2,995
17 to 23 "	86	..	2	1	83	2,995	1,321	402	130	3,784
24 to 30 "	83	1	35	1	48	3,784	1,091	770	108	3,997
1855										
31 Dec. to 6 Jan.	48	16	6	1	55	3,997	1,044	367	249	4,425
7 Jan. to 13 "	55	18	13	..	60	4,425	727	444	277	4,431
14 to 20 "	60	16	8	1	67	4,431	667	346	270	4,482
21 to 27 "	67	29	30	1	65	4,482	1,243	984	274	4,467
28 to 31 "	65	29	16	..	78	4,467	619	127	165	4,794

R. W. LAWSON, *Dy. I. Gen., P.M.O.*
Principal Medical Officer's Office, Scutari, *February* 1, 1855.

Upon all this evidence, it is to be observed that, whereas the great deficiency in washing chiefly relates to the Barrack Hospital, the total admissions are not given with regard to that Hospital separately. It is obvious, upon a moment's reflection, that the "average weekly number" of patients, although a fair way of judging in matters which refer to consumption, cubic feet of space, &c., does not give a fair statement with regard to washing; since a man does not eat or breathe in hospital after he is dead or discharged, but his dirty shirt or sheet, it is to be presumed, is not to be worn or used by his successor. And when the state of the blankets and shirts, if any there were, of the men entering Scutari Hospitals from the Crimea, is remembered, too filthy for description, it is not to be supposed that the men were intended to be left in these.

"Two shirts per week" is a fair average per bed, if that bed be occupied by one inmate, but how, if it should be successively occupied by three or four in one week?

Yet the number of shirts washed for the Barrack Hospital in November, 1854, was 6 per month, for the whole of the Patients; of total pieces of all kinds, 4,832; the average number of patients being 2,000 after November 9.

Miss Nightingale never succeeded in washing more than 2,000 shirts per month in her small subsidiary washing establishment, a miserable number, even as a subsidiary for so many. But it was intended to supplement the Barrack Hospital washing only, that of the General Hospital being, as has been stated, tolerably sufficient.

(2) Another evil, less apparent, but no less deadly, was the state of the floors, walls and ceilings of the Wards and Corridors. The former were, in many cases, so much out of repair, that it was impossible to keep them clean. The wooden divans raised round some of the Wards in the Barack Hospitals, on which the men were laid on their mattresses, were receptacles of filth underneath, and were a hiding place for rats, the smell of which was abominable. The walls were saturated with organic matter, from the long continuance of patients with Hospital gangrene, typhus fever, and every worst kind of Hospital disease within them; and lime-washing was very imperfectly practised till the spring of 1855, at first not at all. Bugs, lice, and fleas, were inexterminable. The men were allowed to bring in their blankets with them from the Crimea till February, 1855, which were unavoidably covered with vermin, as there was no possibility of washing in the camp.

Filthy state of Floors, Walls, and Ceilings.

Yet Dr. Smith says in evidence:

"I have no proof, beyond Mr. Stafford's opinion, that disease was caused by any thing in the Hospitals."

And Mr. Wreford, Purveyor-General, writes to Dr. Smith, February 12, 1855:—

"The necessity for a subsidiary washing establishment has never been made apparent to me."

Had not the matter been too destructive of life, health, morality, and discipline, to be fit subject for a joke, one would be
tempted to think that one authority at least had been in jest
when he said that the use of the Female Nurses going out was
to see "a spot upon a sheet." At that time, sheets were not, at
least such as could be used.

Personal
Cleanliness. (3) With regard to the personal cleanliness of the men, it has
been said elsewhere both how eager they were for it, and how
impossible it was for them to attain it.

It may be added here, in confirmation, that the sum of the
towels washed by the Purveyor during the three months of
November, December, 1854, and January, 1855, for the Barrack
Hospital, containing in those months 2,000-2,400 patients, was
132! and that no basins or soap were provided officially. Nor are
either towels or basins to this day provided sufficiently in the
British Military Hospitals, the men and Doctors being still
expected to bring in their own, except one basin and one jack-
towel to each ward. The stone-floored lavatories on the ground
floor are still all that exists in our Military Hospitals.*

One of the first purchases made by Miss Nightingale, on her
arrival, was 200 Turkish towels at Constantinople. These were
accidentally delivered at the Purveyor's Office at the General
Hospital, and put into use by him among the patients there. She
was of course too glad that this should be done among the patients
anywhere, as the still greater want in the Barrack Hospital could
be supplied in the same manner. She therefore never reclaimed
them, and they were incorporated as Purveyor's stores.

But it might be as well to notice what, so late as February
1855, was the Return of Purveyor's Stores in use at the Barrack
Hospital, a time when the patients averaged 2,043.

194 towels. No basins. 14 baths.

5.Want of
Hospital
Comforts. 5. We have only one thing more to notice, as the fifth cause of
the mortality at Scutari; and that is the want of Hospital com-
forts.

This has been denied, will be denied again; a few official
records are therefore annexed.

(1.)   Bad cookery. The evidence annexed is that of
Commissioner Maxwell;—

---

* In Barracks, till lately, the pump and the urine tubs were all that soldiers
had to wash in; some insufficient lavatories have been now, I believe, provided
for the men in some Barracks.

RETURN OF PURVEYOR'S STORES IN USE AT THE BARRACK HOSPITAL, SCUTARI.

Articles.	No. of each.	Remarks.
Palliasses	2,894	
Bolsters	3,338	
Blankets	4,956	
Sheets	4,490	
Rugs	4,300	
Boards	7,185	
Tressels	4,551	
Gowns	2,120	A certain number of articles of
Trowsers	1,958	bedding, dresses, towels, &c. at the
Waistcoats	1,540	wash, are not included in the num-
Towels	194	bers stated in this Return, although
Stockings	1,072	it may be said they are in use at this
Tin plates	1,110	hospital, being required to keep the
Knives and forks	674	thing working, and supplying clean
Spoons	233	linen, &c.
Chamber-pots	992	
Close stools	276	
Bed-pans	204	
Urinals	36	
Tubs	19	
Baths	14	

Barrack Hospital, Scutari,
    February 12, 1855

SELKIRK STUART,
    Purveyor to the Forces.

"With respect to the kitchen, I may state, that in the lowest floor of the Barrack Hospital there is a kitchen which is only used for a depot; the Hospital has nothing to do with it. In the quadrangle there are two kitchens of considerable dimensions, one of which is used, and the other has never been fitted up, owing to some difficulty in getting coppers.

P. B. Maxwell Esq. 30 March, 1855.

"13092. CHAIRMAN.] Was there any difficulty in getting coppers in Constantinople?—I do not say there was any difficulty; I inquired why it was not so employed, and the answer from the engineer's department was that there was some difficulty in getting coppers.

"13093. MR. LAYARD.] Did you ever go into the bazaars at Constantinople?—Yes, often.

"13094. Did you never see any large coppers there?—I cannot say that I did; I may have seen them.

"13095. Do you not know that in every Turkish house there are large coppers?—They all cook in them. The other kitchen was fitted up as a Turkish kitchen, and was supplied with 13 copper boilers, containing about 56 gallons each.

"13096. Was that enough for the wants of that large Hospital?—For cooking the ordinary diets it was, but for cooking extras it was not enough. It was not at all adapted for cooking extras. To do that there were, I think, three or four supplementary kitchens attached to the Hospital; four supplementary kitchens have been constructed since we arrived there.

"13097. CHAIRMAN.] Had you any evidence while you were there of irregularity in cooking the food of the patients?—Yes, I noticed that myself.

"13098. What did the irregularity arise from?—I think it arose from a radically wrong system in the issuing and distribution of the food.

"13099. You thought that the system was wrong?—Utterly wrong, as it seemed to me.

"13100. In what respect?—In issuing the provisions for the different meals to the orderlies, and giving it to them to be carried out. The meat was taken, for example, raw to the kitchen by the orderlies, and there it was cooked; then the orderlies came back for it, and they had to carry it back to the wards and cut it up; all depended upon those orderlies. If the Committee will allow me, I will give a full account of it.

"13101. Did you observe that the food was not sufficiently dressed?—Sometimes it was done to rags, and sometimes it was insufficiently dressed.

"13102. Then do you attribute that to the system?"—Yes.

"13103. How?—I had better explain what the system is. The diets, ordinary and extra, are issued and distributed in the Barrack Hospital in the following manner, according to the evidence of Clifford, the steward; Hill, the cook; and Jennings, an orderly, whom we examined upon the subject. The Medical Officer prescribes daily in his morning visit the diet and articles of medical comfort which he thinks suitable for each patient for the following day. This diet-roll is, as we have already observed, submitted to the Surgeon of the division, who revises and returns it to the ward-master, in whose custody it remains until the following morning. At 6½ a.m. an orderly from each mess, which consists of about 25 men, attends at the purveyor's store with his diet-roll, and produces it to the steward, who delivers the quantity of bread required for breakfast, and at the same time makes a memorandum in his book of the number of full, half, low, spoon, and milk diets on the diet-roll.' That takes up a considerable time, and it is an inconvenient moment for the steward to make those returns when he is actually engaged in dealing out the bread. 'This is done because the book containing the diet-roll is not available after breakfast, being in use for marking the diets for the next day. As the number of orderlies thus engaged is necessarily considerable, an hour or an hour and a half is employed in this manner. The bread is delivered, not in portions, but in loaves. The tea is obtained by another, or sometimes the same, orderly from the kitchen. As soon as breakfast is concluded, that is, between 9 and 10 a.m., the orderly returns to the store, and obtains from the steward the proper quantity of meat (which is weighed and delivered to him raw, and in bulk), bread and salt for dinner. This process engages the time of the steward till 12½ p.m., or even later. The orderly carries the meat to the kitchen, ties it up, puts a skewer through it, and marks it with a tally, for the purpose of distinguishing it from the numerous other messes to be boiled in the same copper. The men arrive at the kitchen for this purpose, in slow succession, from about 10½ to 1½ p.m.' How can any one expect regularity, or that the dinner can be properly cooked? 'While the ordinary diets are in process of cooking, the orderly goes to his ward, and as soon as the Medical Officer has finished his round, and no longer needs the book in which the diet-rolls are bound up, takes that document, and returns again to the steward, from whom he now obtains the due allowance of porter, which he forthwith distributes; he then returns once more, and obtains the other articles of extra diet, such as chickens, wine, lemons, eggs, arrowroot, sago, brandy, &c. By this time the dinner is cooked; and notwithstanding the tallies, and the best efforts of the cook to see that the messes are issued fairly, mistakes occur, and the diets of one ward are sometimes taken to another. According to the evidence of John Hill, the cook, the distribution of this meal, including soup, occupies an hour and a half. The orderly carries up the dinner on a round wooden tray, which he places on the floor, and divides the meat into as many portions, assigning to each its due allowance of bone, as there are patients. To eat this meat the men are but imperfectly supplied with plates, knives, and forks; as soon as it is concluded the orderly goes for the extras which have been prescribed for the more weakly patients. They are now prepared by the cooks attached to the extra-diet kitchens; but before these were opened they used to be cooked by the orderlies themselves, sometimes in the kitchen coppers, but more commonly in their own tin canteens, and either in the house, or in some of the sheds in the barrack square, and not unfrequently in the stoves of the wards,' where I have found them constantly cooking. 'When the articles in question are cooked the orderly delivers to each patient all the extras prescribed for him for the day, without regard as to whether the food is to be administered at one or several times; he then cooks his own dinner, and afterwards gets the tea of his mess' This is the account which I have to give."

In speaking of the distribution of food, it is necessary to make one last remark on the want of discipline in Military Hospitals.

At Scutari, the food came up in messes to each ward, there to be divided either by the Orderly, or more often by the patients themselves. The practice was various. Sometimes the Orderly divided it upon his own bed, and the patients all ate it on theirs. The table in the ward, when one had begun to exist there, was generally covered, and the patients therefore rarely, if ever, dined there.

In the Barrack Hospital, it was at last attained, that convalescents should dine at a table in the corridors.

In one of the other General Hospitals, the Orderlies and Wardmasters, after they had brought up the patients' dinners, retired to eat their own. Many zealous Orderly Medical Officers always made a point of being present at the patients' meals, and seeing them properly distributed, and properly eaten at the table, if the patient were able to leave his bed, instead of on his bed. But this was never done as a rule even at the Hospital, without the intervention of the Medical Officer.

The meat is and always must be cold, before it is served to the Patients, both at the War Hospitals and at those Army Hospitals at home, which I have seen. For there are no means of keeping it warm.

I would suggest the following:—

That it should be always divided in the kitchen, which saves the (now) invariable scramble in the wards, upon a hot-water dish or table.* It may be also carried to the wards if there is far to go, upon hot-water dishes, for more precaution. It would then always arrive nicely served, instead of, as now, even if twenty minutes only elapse between the beginning of cutting up the food and its arriving at the Patient's hands, always cold.

Large hot-water tins were provided, by private means, at Scutari for carrying up the food, but were, I believe, rarely used.

Want of Shirts and Utensils for Eating.

(2.) Want of shirts and every kind of utensil for eating, drinking, &c.

The annexed is Dr. A. Smith's evidence:—

A. Smith. Esq. MD. 22 March, 1855

"8827. Do you consider that, for the proper treatment of the wounded and sick in that Hospital, it was necessary that there should be linen sheets and linen clothing for the men?—Yes.

"8828. Are you aware, and do you now believe, that they had not that necessary?—They had sheets† in abundance, and linen. I must explain, that about the year 1817 a new arrangement was established in the army: previously to 1817, every General Hospital was supplied, or the purveyor of every General Hospital was supplied, with what was called hospital clothing; that hospital clothing consisted of bedding, shirts, and stockings, and flannel shirts, and other things necessary to sick men in the hospital. That system, however, upon the idea that it would be more economical, was changed; and, instead of the purveyor being supplied with those articles, a regulation was issued that each

---

* When discipline has been introduced into Military Hospitals, then it will be better divide and weigh the food in the presence of the Patients, in the Ward itself, where there should be an oven, in which to keep the plates warm.

† They had virtually no sheets; for the sheets were of that excessively coarse canvas that the men begged to be laid in the blankets, which was necessarily done.

soldier coming into hospital should bring his pack along with him, and in the pack he must take care that there were two shirts, a set of shoe brushes, a knife and fork, and spoon, and a certain number of other things; the two shirts, knife, and fork, and spoon, shoe brushes, and whatever he was likely to require for constant use, were removed, and placed under the purveyor for the use of the patients in the Hospital, instead of being, as formerly, provided by the Government; that system has continued to this moment; and, therefore, I had no means of providing shirts for the soldiers, because I had to assume that the soldier's pack would be brought with him to Scutari, and there his two shirts would be available for his use, as well as his knife, fork, spoon, &c. Those, under the circumstances of the case, were not forthcoming, there was, for a time, no doubt, a very great want of shirts; the moment I knew there was a want of shirts, I made a requisition for 60,000 cotton shirts, which were purchased and sent out.

"8829. When did you first receive that information?—I think about October.

"8830. You received that information in October?—Yes."

With regard to Shirts the Cumming-Maxwell report states:—

"It will be noticed, upon examining Miss Nightingale's return of hospital furniture and clothing, that in the course of about three months that lady issued 10,537 cotton and 6,823 flannel shirts, of which only 400 and 400 respectively were obtained from the public store. Besides these, 11,234 more have been furnished from the purveyor's store between the 1st October and the 16th February. This enormous supply, co-existing with constant complaints of the want of the articles in question, needs explanation. Under ordinary circumstances, shirts form no part of hospital clothing. Every soldier is required to have three shirts, and these are used by him when in hospital, and are deemed sufficient in quantity. Upon the invasion of the Crimea, however, the men, as we have already mentioned, left, in obedience to orders, their knapsacks in the vessels which had carried them to Kalamita Bay, and many did not recover them for long after, and many did not recover them at all. The sick and wounded, who arrived at the hospitals immediately after the battle of the Alma, were, we believe, destitute of all clothing, except that which was on their persons; and the majority of those who subsequently arrived from the Crimea have been, until recently, in a similar destitute condition. Even the shirts which are found upon them on their admission into hospital are often in so filthy a condition that it is necessary to cut them off.

"Under these circumstances, it became necessary to provide them with shirts, and when they leave the hospital they are permitted to take with them the one actually in wear.

"On the other hand, it must be observed that a considerable number of the articles furnished by Miss Nightingale form no part of the ordinary hospital furniture. But further, confining ourselves to such goods

Cumming Maxwell Report.

50

as do, according to the hospital regulations, form a part of such furniture, the list must not be regarded as conclusive proof that the articles mentioned in it were invariably wanting in the stores, for goods have been refused, although they were, to our personal knowledge, lying in abundance in the store of the purveyor. This was done because they had not been examined by a Board of Survey. On one occasion, in the month of December last, we found that this was the case with respect to hospital rugs, and it is probable that this has not been the only instance of such an occurrence."

MAJOR SILLERY.

Major Sillery
Evidence.
Cumming
Maxwell
Report, p. 318.

"I was Commandant from the time the army left till within ten or twelve days. When convalescents or invalids leave the hospital, they come under my command. *Many of the sick and wounded men arrived with little or no clothing. From the want of any establishment for the purpose at this depôt, there is the greatest difficulty in supplying such men with necessaries.* There is a non-commissioned officer of each regiment here in charge of the men of his own regiment. It is the duty of that non-commissioned officer to meet the wants of the men if possible, getting the money for the purpose from the paymaster, who stops the amount from the soldier's pay. The corporal must get the shirts when he can. In the case of boots, which are a heavy article, there is more difficulty. We cannot get the regimental boots here. For men going up to the Crimea, we look very closely as to boots. Till the last draught we sent up about a fortnight ago, we generally got boots from the commissariat for men going up; but I do not know if we got any for invalids. Every man is examined before he goes to the Crimea or home but not when he comes out of hospital. We endeavour to complete the outfits as much as we can. This is done partly out of commissariat stores and dead men's effects. In the same way we give the red coatees of dead men.

We want a quartermaster's establishment,—a large store with necessaries of all kinds. The complication of accounts with so many soldiers of different regiments requires a large staff. In a regiment, a soldier who wants anything is supplied by his captain, who inspects him and draws the article wanted from the quartermaster's stores. Here we have no officer who discharges the duty of a captain."

The want of shirts, and indeed of almost all clothing, on the part of the men, being here proved beyond the possibility of dispute by the statement of almost every official,—in General Airey's short and pithy words, "the Army was almost without clothes,"—let us see what was the "enormous supply" which, as Commissioner Maxwell truly states, "co-existed with constant complaints of the want of the articles in question."

According to Dr. Lawson, the number of Admissions, Oct. 28, 1854, to Jan. 31, 1855, was 10,995.

The number of shirts issued from the Quartermaster-General's store was, up to 15th February, 4,387, a number equal to the men discharged from Hospital between December 5, the period when these issues commenced, up to January 31, viz., 4,349.

The Purveyor states that he issued from October 1 to February 15, 11,234 shirts, of which he says 2,500 were delivered to Miss Nightingale. Now, 800 only were delivered to her, as appears by the Extract from the Cumming-Maxwell Report, p. 356. The 2,500 she indeed made requisition for, but 800 only were received, because the rest were not forthcoming. Another example of the fallacy of requisitions as vouchers for receipt, although there is not the shadow of a suspicion of any dishonesty.

The 800 appear again in Miss Nightingale's schedule; therefore deducting from 11,234

                 2,500
                 ─────
            8,734 remain.

Miss Nightingale issued from November 10, 1854, up to February 15, 1855,—

            10,537 cotton shirts
             6,823 flannel shirts
            ──────
            17,360

Of which 400 and 400 respectively were, as just stated, from Purveyor's store, deducting which, the issue from her own stores was 16,560.

Therefore, to 11,000 men admitted into Hospital were issued—

SHIRTS.

4,387 from Quartermaster-General

8,734 from Purveyor

  800 ditto, through Miss Nightingale
─────

13,921, or little more than 1¼ shirt to each man.

Up to December 4, it appears that the number found in patients' knapsacks was 22!

52

Surely, in Miss Nightingale's issues of 16,560 shirts additional, there can be found nothing extravagant or unnecessary, but, on the contrary, they must be thought even insufficient. For no mention is here made of the 2,040 men in Hospital on Oct. 28, 1854, or of the Admissions after Jan. 31, 1855, or of the great want of washing, which, of course, made a greater supply of linen necessary.

Cumming
Maxwell
Report, p. 273.

NUMBER of SHIRTS found in Patients' Knapsacks that were deposited in the Pack Store of the Barrack Hospital at Scutari.

Twenty-two.

SELKIRK STUART,

4th December, 1854 *Purveyor to the Forces.*

Cumming
Maxwell
Report, p. 273.

RETURN of the NUMBER OF SHIRTS ISSUED from the Purveyor's Stores in the GENERAL HOSPITAL and BARRACK HOSPITAL at SCUTARI, from 1st October, 1854 to 16th February, 1855.

Issued.	To General Hospital.	To Barrack Hospital.	To Kululi.	To Haidar Pasha.	To Miss Nightingale.	Total.	Remarks.
From Store at General Hospital	4,203		..	512	1,000	5,715	
From Store at Barrack Hospital	..	3,019	558	442	1,500	5,519	
Totals issued	4,203	3,019	558	954	2,500	11,234	

Barrack Hospital, Scutari, SELKIRK STUART,
22nd February, 1855. *Purveyor to the Forces.*

With regard to all kinds of utensils, that there was a great want of these cannot now be denied, for it is proved by the Requisitions of the Medical Officers, an abstract of which is given, p. 149. A very insufficient Requisition for such was made upon the Ambassador, which was very insufficiently replied to.

Some further extracts are given, to establish not only the want of stores, but the great defect of system in issuing and receiving them, at Scutari. It will be proved—

1. That the system of Requisitions is a vicious one.

2. That there was a great want of store-room, and of all convenience for landing stores.

Bad Effects of
the System of
Requisitions.

1. That the system of Requisitions is a vicious one.

The Cumming Maxwell Report says—

ACCOUNT OF CLOTHING RECEIVED into QUARTERMASTER'S STORES at SCUTARI.

Cumming
Maxwell
Report, p. 274.

Date.	Shirts.	Drawers.	Socks.	Mitts.	Trowsers.	Boots.	
1854							
Dec. 5	589	1,173	4,628	. .	. .	. .	Received from Constantinople, purchased by Captain Wetherall.
16	3,588	1,817	4,597	. .	. .	. .	
1855.							
Jan. 14	3,092	. .	. .	. .	. .	1,600	From Quartermaster-General
„ 26	. .	. .	. .	. .	600	. .	Purchased by order of Lord William Paulet.
Feb. 2	. .	. .	2,081	4,086	. .	. .	From Constantinople, purchased by Captain Wetherall.
„ 3	. .	1,000	. .	. .	. .	. .	Purchased by order of Lord William Paulet.
„ 5	2,000	4,000	. .	. .	. .	360	From Quartermaster-General.
Total	9,269	7,990	11,306	4,086	600	1,960	

Of the above clothing there has been served out to the men of the General Depôt, and to invalids proceeding to England, since the 5th December, as follows:—

Shirts	Drawers.	Socks.	Mitts.	Trowsers.	Boots.	Blankets.
4,387	3,088	6,703	1,500	300	1,930	1,530

JASPER HALL,
Captain 4th K.O. Regiment,
Qr. Mr.

Scutari, 15th February, 1855.

The Store was established when the first articles of clothing were received, viz., on the 5th December, 1854, as above.

JASPER HALL, *Captain, 4th Regiment, QR. Mr.*

"In support of the practice of issuing upon requisition, it is said that those documents are necessary, or at least convenient, as vouchers to prove that the articles mentioned in them have been supplied; but we think that in this respect their value is worthless, because it must constantly be optional with the purveyor or clerk receiving the requisition whether he shall or not draw his pen or pencil through those articles which he is unable to supply. In this respect a receipt by the recipient after the article has been furnished is of far superior value and effect. We think it right, after making this observation, to add, that we have

Cumming
Maxwell
Report.

not the slightest ground for suspecting that any such fraud as we have alluded to as of possible occurrence, has even been attempted; but, in pointing out the evils of the system, we do not think it right to omit all notice of such a defect as this. For the reasons above set forth, we think that the practice of issuing on requisition is vicious, and should be limited as much as possible."

It is vicious both ways, for that which it has not, it pretends to supply, and that which it has, it does not supply.

Cumming Maxwell Report.

"From the neglect to file those requisitions which altogether rejected, coupled with the practice of never issuing articles except upon written demands, it sometimes happens, that while wards are in want of articles, a quantity of these is lying in store, and might be had upon application. We found this to be the case on more than one occasion in the course of our inquiry. The following instance may be mentioned. It may be seen, upon reference to the list of furniture in the purveyor's store on 31st January, which will be found below, that there were on that day a number of boards and trestles in store, and yet, upon inquiring, a few days later, we ascertained that there were still wanting in the Barrack Hospital alone 289 bedsteads, viz., 142 in the first division, 87 in the second, and 60 in the third, to complete its furniture; while in Haidar Pasha a considerable number of patients was still unsupplied.

"It is not to be inferred that the surgeons neglect to make the wants of their wards known. This state of things is the result of the omission to make a note or memorandum, when a requisition is not answered, of the article demanded, and of the person demanding it—an omission which leaves the purveyor without the means of furnishing the goods when his store is replenished, but compels him to wait for a fresh requisition. We have been assured that steps are taken to give due notice of the arrival of goods which have been in demand; but we believe that those steps have been very ineffectual. We have found that surgeons whose requisitions were not complied with when they were made, have remained long in ignorance that their demands might be supplied if repeated. On the other hand, the refusal which they have met becomes generally known, and requisitions for the article in question cease to be made. We believe that many deficiencies which have been at different times observed in the furniture of the wards is to be attributed to the practice of issuing only upon requisition, and to the neglect to supply at a subsequent time those requisitions which were not immediately answered.

Want of Store-room.

2. That there was a great want of store-room, and of the necessary conveniences for landing stores, owing to the dependence of Purveyor upon Commissariat.

December 25th.

MR. WREFORD.

"Dr. Menzies showed me a letter from the Ambassador some six weeks ago, and in consequence conferred with me as to the expediency of accepting the offer which it contained. After deliberation, as we expected hourly stores from Varna, we thought it best to decline the offer. We had not then heard of the disaster that had happened to the "Courier," the vessel which had been sent to that place for the purpose of bringing them down. On about the 16th or 17th November, I was given to understand, the offer was repeated; and then we agreed to ask for certain utensils and 200 sets of bedding. The bedding was sent, but unfortunately in the wet weather. We had asked for the bedding, from having received a communication from Dr. Hall, to be provided for the reception of at least 1,000 wounded, who were already on their way to Scutari. The 200 sets of bedding would, I think, have sufficed, or, at least, would have aided us. We did not like to ask for more, because I thought it would have sufficed. The wet did not spoil the bedding, and it came in very useful. We got a few chairs and tables, also, for the officers' quarters. All these things were applied for by Dr. Menzies to the Ambassador. I had been to the Pacha of this place, and asked him to get me the bedding, but they were obtained from the Ambassador. The offer of the Ambassador was not accepted for anything except these things mentioned—bedding, chairs, tables, and other things, of which I will furnish a list. Several of the articles have not yet been sent.

"As assisting Mr. Ward, I went to the bazaar to buy slippers. I passed several hours there, and could only get 50 pairs on that occasion. I have purchased altogether about 600 pairs. From an apprehension of running short, and to meet every possible contingency of non-arrival of ships, I purchased nearly 350 dozen of port wine from several houses in Constantinople. Nothing could be more timely, however, than the arrival of the supplies sent from England, both as to the time and the quantities sent. I have had great difficulty in getting stores landed here—not owing to the neglect of the Commissariat, but to the state of the elements. The Commissariat land for us. I know that our stores have sometimes gone to Balaclava, in consequence, I suppose, of improper stowage. It is the duty of the Commissariat to store for us, but they have not the means of storing. We are, to a certain extent, limited for storage in the Barrack hospital, but heavy bales are, I think, safe in the passage. There is a sentry there. It would be a great security if they were under lock and key.

"In England, the patient brings with him inventories in duplicate of his necessaries; one is signed by the pack storekeeper, and the other by the non-commissioned officer who brings the necessaries, and is attached to the man's kit. At the General hospital Mr. Ward has established the old practice of having a book with the man's name, and the articles written opposite.

Mr. Wreford's Evidence.—
Cumming Maxwell Report.

"When I came out matters were in arrear. They are now working gradually, but slowly. We have by no means a sufficient supply of clerks. Our great work has been with the hospital stoppages. That involves an account with every individual soldier. The stoppage is $4\frac{1}{2}d.$ a day. The Principal Medical Officer gets a daily return of the number of the patients admitted, discharged, and died, and names of each patient. He adds up the whole, and forwards it to the purveyor.

DR. MENZIES.

" . . . Did you give him that list?—I did.

"9819. When was that?—I think it must have been on or about the 14th of November.

"9820. Have you got it there?—Yes, I have; this is the list, with a note from Mr. Wreford, explanatory of the articles still wanting. This was sent in in November; but many of the articles were not supplied up to the 5th of January, when Mr. Wreford writes to me on the subject; I wanted to have some information as to the reason why those things had not been supplied.

"9821. Are the Committee to understand, that in the beginning of January you inquired why things that ought to have been provided in November had not been supplied?—I wanted to know what things he had got upon the requisition that was sent in about the 14th of November, and this is Mr. Wreford's explanation:— 'Dear Sir,— I herewith enclose a copy of the list of articles which accompanied my letter to you of the 19th November, which was prepared in compliance with a letter which you had consulted me upon, then recently received from Lord Stratford de Redcliffe, offering his kind assistance to procure for the use of the hospitals here any articles of which we might stand in immediate need. I beg to add, that having occasion to call at Messrs. Black's a few days afterwards, in search of port wine, I was shown the original list, and my opinion asked as to the description of articles we required, which I gave, and further urged upon them the necessity of their being procured with as little delay as possible. Now I may mention that the mercantile establishment of Messrs. Black is one of the oldest and one of the most respectable in Constantinople, and consequently having large and extensive ramifications, and yet even they have been unable to complete this list, the articles having been sent in in the quantities and at the intervals stated, the whole being as yet far from completion; and I have been more than once informed at the house that they cannot get the people to work, and to find all the articles ready made is impossible. I mention this to show the difficulties that surround us here; for if a merchant like Mr. Black cannot procure these things, how much less practicable is it for strangers to do so.' "*

[The following list was handed in.]

* How then were "these things" procured, in Constantinople, by others, although also strangers?

STATEMENT of ARTICLES RECEIVED, in accordance with a List to the AMBASSADOR, about the 20th or 21st November, 1854, from MR. BLACK, and of those yet to be supplied.—2nd January, 1855.

DESCRIPTION OF ARTICLES.	Quantities Ordered.	Supplied 28 Nov. 1854.	Supplied 5 Dec. 1854.	Supplied 28 Dec. 1854	Supplied 31 Dec. 1854.	TOTAL Supplied	Yet to be Supplied.
Hair brooms, &c.	200						
Turkish brooms, &c.	..	..	196	..	..	196	
Tin cans, 2 gallons	100	..	..	..	..	..	109
Bed-pans	200	..	..	15	15	30	170
Close-stool frames	150	..	..	..	26	26	124
Spitting-boxes	300	45	58	..	..	103	197
Mop heads	500	..	..	..	..	..	500
Mop handles	100	..	..	..	..	..	100
Hand scrubbing brushes . .	100	..	..	..	..	..	100
Tin plates	1,000	190	794	..	..	984	
Drinking cups, pint: Goblets . . . . } Tin cup	1,000	283	419	..	..	702	298
Buckets (2 gallons)	100	..	..	..	..	..	100
Washhand-basins	200	197	..	..	..	197	3
Door-mats	36	..	35	..	..	35	1
Urinals	700	..	..	..	..	..	700
Spoons, iron	200	204	..	..	..	204	
Soup-ladles	40	..	39	..	..	39	1
Frying-pans	12	12	..	..	..	12	
Slippers	1,000	..	..	..	341	341	659
Woollen socks	2,000	..	..	..	2,000	2,000	

B. SELKIRK STUART,
Purveyor to the Forces.

The representations as to the satisfactory state of Scutari Hospitals, given below, were exactly the same as those made to me when I left England for Scutari, October 1854, (including the singular and misleading expression, that "the Medical Officers would not object to" my "giving the men a nice drink of Capillaire Syrup,") *vide* p. 131; but, nevertheless, they seem to have been altogether at variance with even that evidence which had been already at this date, October 1854, received at home, and which tended even then to throw light upon the real state of the men.

Dr. Smith's representation of the case.

"8785. Have you ever had any reports from Dr. Hall as to the insufficiency of the clothing of the men?—Not of the insufficiency of the clothing of the men after the winter clothing was issued.

"8786. Have you any such reports at all?—In a letter latterly received from him, when I called upon him to explain the causes of the

Dr. Smith's Evidence.

great sickness, he stated that the causes of the sickness had been very various that the men had been over-wrought and over-fatigued in the trenches, sometimes for 10, 12, and 14 hours a day, often up to nearly their knees in mud, and wanting any covering when they were away from duty, trying to get rest in the mere tents.

"8787. Have you had any reports either in those letters, or otherwise, of the insufficiency of the clothing of the men?—Not specific reports.

"8788. Up to what date have you any reports?—Dr. Hall informed me that the want of sufficient clothing was one of the causes of the sickness.

"8789. When did Dr. Hall's reports cease stating that the men were suffering from the want of sufficient clothing?—They have only ceased very lately; that is to say, he used to complain that the abundance of warm clothing which was at Balaklava, would have saved many men from sickness, if they could have got it up to the camp.

"8790. Has the Principal Medical Officer, Dr. Hall, been sufficiently consulted as to the state of the health of the army, and its fitness for the duties required of it?—I cannot exactly answer that question. I think that, looking at it as a medical man, he would probably have advised some little modification; but whether he was consulted or not, I cannot positively say.

"8791. Has he sent you any of the reports that he made to the Commander-in-chief as to the state of the men?—I think that the only report he wrote to me was in answer to a letter in which I asked whether he had taken sufficient precautions to endeavour to get a proper place in which the men might sleep and rest in winter;—he stated, in the first place, that he had no knowledge till a very late period, that there was any probability of the men remaining in the front of Sebastopol during the winter, but when he did get that knowledge, he suggested that they should endeavour to imitate the practice of the Russians by digging places in the ground, and throwing spars over them, so that they might put earth upon them, and in that way gain a mode of shelter better than tents. But then the question came to be, would they be able to do it? .

"8182. . . . It has been represented to this Committee by competent witnesses, who have themselves seen the facts upon the spot, that nothing could be so horrible or so disgusting, or in every way so calamitous, as the state of those Hospitals from the time of the arrival of the sick from the battle of the Alma, and for a considerable time afterwards. It has also been stated by Mr. Macdonald, the witness who was sent to distribute the charitable fund collected by the "Times" newspaper, that he applied to you upon the 5th of November, for a letter of introduction, and for information with respect to the state of the Hospitals in the East, and that you at that time told him that his mission was a very supererogatory one, and not required at all, inasmuch as ample means had been provided, and every precaution taken to supply everything that was necessary for the comforts and the care of the sick in the Hospitals at Scutari; what reports had you at that time from Constantinople, to justify that representation?—I had no reports to have justified me in saying anything else.

"8183. What reason had you to believe that the state of things at that time known to the public, or published to the world, was false?—In the first place, I was aware that I had despatched from this country ample provision for every want; and in the next place, it was considered by the medical authorities out there, that they had what was wanted.

"8184. CHAIRMAN: What evidence have you got of that last proposition?—I ought, to a certain extent to comment upon the last part of what I said; when the medical authorities wrote to me to that effect, they were daily in expectation of receiving from Varna, all that had been left at Varna. When the army moved from Varna they left the entire equipment of their General Hospital behind them, and the Inspector-General of Hospitals gave positive directions to the authorities that remained, to forward everything directly to Scutari, where the sick and wounded would be sent. Those authorities made every effort that they could to do so, but they failed. The authorities at Constantinople, who were communicating with me, were also exerting themselves to the utmost of their power, to induce the transport department to send vessels to Varna to bring away the stores; and day after day were those efforts repeated, but without success; the supply had not arrived on the 10th of November; but I was not aware of that.

"8185. MR. ELLICE: What letters or reports had you from those medical authorities at the time?—I had regularly letters by each mail, reporting what had happened.

"8186. Will you state to the Committee upon what grounds you formed that opinion, which you expressed to Mr. Macdonald, that there was an ample supply of everything required for the sick and wounded in the Hospitals at Scutari?—What I expressed to Mr. Macdonald was this: he brought a letter of introduction, asking for an introduction to the Principal Medical Officer at Scutari; and I said I should be happy to give him one; his reply was, that as he was going on a special purpose of this kind, he would like to consult with me. I said, 'If you will state to me on what principle this fund has been raised, and in what way it is intended to distribute its means, I will give you what information I can.' He did not immediately reply to that, and I said, 'Perhaps you may not yet have established a principle, therefore I will volunteer to give you what information I can.' I said, 'The Medical Officers of the army are held by myself and the Government responsible that every man in the hospital is supplied with whatever he requires for his welfare, irrelevant of expense; it does not matter what it is, if he requires it, the Medical Officer has the power of ordering it; on the other hand, the Medical Officer is equally bound not to allow anything to be administered to a man in the hospital that can in any way conduce to his injury. Those two points are to guide the Medical Officers.' Then I said, 'Under those circumstances, and assuming as I do, that the Medical Officers are supplied with what is necessary for the first, and that they do not want to be supplied with what is necessary for the second, anything that you will have to distribute will be of a neutral description, that neither do good nor harm, but may please the palate of the men. For instance, a medical man knows best what is useful for the sick, and he will probably give barley water, in a case of fever, in preference to giving capillaire syrup (v. p. 127). I do not know that the Medical Officer would object to your giving the man a nice drink of capillaire syrup; such things, I think, you may give out advantageously, without being interfered with; but I think your main object will be to distribute this fund to the poor men who may have been discharged from the Hospital, and who may have many wants to be supplied which the Government are not in the habit of providing for. Let me give you one piece of advice, not to give them money; or else you will give them the means of obtaining drink, and only send them back to the Hospital.'

"8187. The department of the Government must have been under the same impression; the Duke of Newcastle stated the same thing to Mr. Macdonald, but that impression, or that opinion, must have been founded upon some report you had received; that what you have stated to be the duty of the Medical Officers had been performed efficiently, and that every comfort and every necessary had been supplied to the Patients?— I certainly understood that from the correspondence. The Medical Officer in correspondence with me, was every moment expecting arrivals from Varna, which would make them independent of everything.

"8188. The facts of the case have been represented to the Committee by two witnesses, Mr. Stafford and Mr. Macdonald, to be these: that there were very few beds; that the poor soldiers were brought down with scarcely any clothes, their clothes having been worn off their backs, were placed upon paillasses, and their clothes, or at least the remnants of them, full of vermin, taken off their backs and put under the paillasses; that no washing had been performed in the hospital, nor the floor washed for six weeks; that no washing of linen had been performed; that there were no hospital dresses; that there was neither cooking, nor comforts of any kind provided; and as to the whole state of the Hospital, that it was pestiferous and infectious, the privies being in such a state that nobody could approach the place; this is the description that has been given before this Committee of the state of the Hospitals at that time. You state that it was the duty of the Medical Officers to have provided everything for the comfort and convenience of those Patients; can you tell the Committee how you account for the difference between the state of things as described to this Committee by some of the witnesses, and that which you supposed to exist at the time of your conversation with Mr. Macdonald?—It is difficult for me to say how it happened, because I must assume that what has been stated in evidence is correct. I can only say, that there was a very large proportion of stores left behind at Scutari when the army proceeded to Varna, and those stores must have been available for immediate use. Then the only way that I can account for their not having ample of everything is, that it had not been possible to move the transport department to bring from Varna, a distance of only eighteen hours, the articles absolutely necessary for the requirements of the hospital. On the 3rd of September, an application was made to have those stores forwarded down from Varna to Scutari; and I know from a letter that I received, that the Principal Medical Officer had not been successful up to the 10th of November in getting them down.

"8189. Supposing that to be the case, and supposing the state of affairs that I have described to have arisen, either from the want of transport, or the neglect of the different authorities when those hospital articles were at Varna, or from whatever cause this state of things arose, it was the duty of the Medical Officers to remedy this state of things by any means that they had in their power?—Yes, if they had the means; but the question is, had they opportunities of making immediate purchases to the extent necessary to supply an equivalent to that which Varna would have supplied, had they prepared to spend any amount of money.

"8190. To take a common illustration of that, the 'Times' Commissioner had no difficulty in purchasing shirts for the poor patients in the Bazaar at Constantinople; why then could not the Medical Officers, or some authority, have purchased those shirts?—I see no reason why.

After all that has been stated, as to the

> Overcrowding,
> Want of ventilation,
>   „   drainage,
>   „   cleanliness,
>   „   Hospitals comforts,

Conclusions as to the Condition of the Hospitals at Scutari.

it will no longer be matter of surprise that the mortality at Scutari was so great. On one occasion, I remember our losing 39 out of 40 secondary amputations consecutively.

The Return below gives a melancholy corroboration.

Out of 44 secondary amputations of the lower extremities, 36 died!

During November 1854 we had 80 recorded cases of Hospital Gangrene, and many, many more were unrecorded. The causes of Hospital Gangrene are well known.

The Report below is only given to show that opinions, when substituted for facts, are of no value in enlightening the governing authority as to the true state of things, and may even represent a place where disease and death were being generated wholesale, as one to be "reported of favourably," and as "con-

Dr. Menzies' Favourable Report.

ABSTRACT of the NUMBER of AMPUTATIONS treated in the GENERAL and SUPPLEMENTARY HOSPITALS from the 26th September to the 27th November, 1854.

Description of Amputation.		Primary.	Result.				Secondary.	Result.			
			Died.	Under Treatment.	Discharged Convalescent.	Sent to England.		Died.	Under Treatment.	Discharged Convalescent.	Sent to England.
Upper Extremities	Shoulder	6	1	5	...	...	...	...	...	...	...
	Arm ...	61	2	54	4	1	15	4	9	2	...
	Hand...	1	....	1	....	....	1	...	...	1	...
	Finger..	1	....	...	1	...	...	....	...	...	...
Lower Extremities	Thigh ..	37	6	28	...	3	33	28	2	3	....
	Leg	39	5	31	....	3	11	8	3	...	....
	Foot ...	4	1	1	....	2	....	....	...	...	...
	Toe	1	...	1	...	...	....	....	...	...	...
Resection of Joints ...		1	1	...	....	...	...	....	...	...	...
Total		151	16	121	5	9	60	40	14	6	....

Total Cases treated, Primary and Secondary ... 211

venient for the reception of the sick and wounded." The one fact, however, relating to the drainage ought to have awakened the attention of authorities at home, as to the state we were in at Scutari.

GENERAL REMARKS ON THE PREVAILING DISEASES, &C. &C. IN THE BRITISH MILITARY HOSPITALS AT SCUTARI, FOR NOVEMBER, 1854.

'The prevailing diseases have chiefly been bowel complaints in the form of diarrhoea, which merged into a chronic form, although not of a fatal character. Notwithstanding that the climate of Scutari had been generally speaking healthy during the above period, the weather had been very changeable, stormy, wet, and cold, which conditions must no doubt have tended to aggravate the affections to which I have alluded, and which have chiefly come from the Crimea.

"I have to report favourably of the buildings now denominated the General and Supplementary Hospitals, the former having been built for the purposes for which it was intended, but the latter as a barrack for troops, but which has lately been given over for the use of the sick and wounded of the British Army, reserving a small portion only for the troops and garrison staff. These buildings may be pronounced convenient for the reception of the sick and wounded, being roomy, well ventilated, and supplied with excellent water, out-offices, and other necessary conveniences. There are, however, no doubt various improvements required, such as the construction of an additional kitchen for the General Hospital, and a wash-house and dead-house at the Barracks. There is also required in both buildings appropriate rooms for the accommodation of the nurses who have recently been sent out by the Government, those occupied by them being much too small, and without conveniences for a separate cooking establishment, without which their efficiency must necessarily be impaired.

"Some parts of the General Hospital require repairs, some of the rooms being very leaky. The quarters for Medical Officers are also inadequate for the present number doing duty there. The drainage and privies are at times greatly out of order, and when the south wind blows there is a very offensive odour wafted up through the building from these reservoirs. It is my opinion also that the close proximity of the burial-ground which lies between the sea and the Hospital, may prove hereafter a source of unhealthiness in this locality. I beg to recommend that the site of the burial-ground be therefore changed, and no more bodies be placed in the immediate vicinity of the Hospital.

"DIET.—I have very little to say on this subject. Provisions are supplied by contract. At one time the supplies for the Hospital were by no means of the best quality, but much improvement has of late taken place in this respect. The articles of diet are those pointed out in the Hospital regulations, and which are in my opinion quite sufficient.

"The extras and medical comforts are allowed to any extent considered necessary for the particular cases by the Medical Officers.

"With respect to the hospital bedding, we have been indebted to the Turkish authorities for a large supply for the General Hospital, during the time that our own bedding was deficient in consequence of its being detained at Varna, and what was left with us here being insufficient for the large number of sick and wounded carried at different times from the Crimea. The boards and tressels sent from England are too low for the comfort of the Patients, and inconvenient during surgical appliances to cases of severe wounds, to say nothing of their closeness to the cold stone floor of the corridors and some of the wards, and the insufficient ventilation necessarily inseparable from them. I have no doubt that neat iron bedsteads would be in every respect more desirable, and they would moreover give an appearance of order, cleanliness, and regularity to an hospital, and the expense would not, I presume, be great.

"DUNCAN MENZIES,
"*Deputy Inspector-General of Hospitals.*"

Lastly, we append two letters of the Hospital Commission to the Commandant of Scutari, which, however, were but little attended to, notwithstanding that they give but so small a portion of our miseries.

64

Copy of a Letter from Dr. Cumming, P.B. Maxwell, Esq., and P.S. Laing, Esq., to Lord W. Paulet.

"My Lord,   "*Scutari, January 26th.*

"Having recently received instructions from his Grace the Duke of Newcastle to report to your Lordship all practical alterations which we recommend with a view to the better organization and working of the Hospital here, we hasten to submit for your consideration some points which have occurred to us in the course of our inquiry, and upon which we are all agreed.

"1. It appears to us that the first step towards the due organization of the Barrack Hospital would be the total removal of the depot* from its precincts. As long as the building, which is now chiefly devoted to the accommodation of the sick, is partially occupied by duty men, convalescents, and a large number of soldiers' wives, and is consequently frequented by a variety of other persons, either connected with the canteen which is established in the place, or otherwise, we are of opinion that great difficulty will continue to exist in establishing order and regularity in the hospital.

"2. It appears to us that one of the most obvious defects in the organization of our hospital establishments, is the utter absence of a trained body of orderlies. The task which devolves on these men requires that persons of intelligence and respectable character, good constitution, and active habits, should alone be employed; and, further, that they should have undergone some training in their duties before they are placed in this responsible situation. Your Lordship is probably aware that our hospital orderlies seldom fulfil these conditions. In order to form gradually such a corps as we suggest, we would beg to recommend that the Medical Officers in charge of wards should be requested to report at once, and from time to time in future, to the Commandant, such of their orderlies as may be, either from ill-health, inaptitude, habits, or character, unsuited for their situation; that these men should be removed; that their places should be filled only by men, who upon due inquiry should appear to possess, as far as possible, the qualifications which we have mentioned; and that those who prove themselves duly qualified should not be removed except for misconduct or incapacity, but should be retained in their situation as long as their services were needed and useful.

"3. We would offer a similar recommendation respecting the selection of hospital serjeants, wardmasters, and cooks.

"4. It appears to us extremely desirable that the clothing of every patient should, on the eve of his leaving the hospital, be inspected by a Medical Officer, and that every article of dress essential to his health should be supplied before he be discharged. This recommendation, if adopted, would necessitate the establishment of a clothing store in the

* This was not effected till May, 1855. Consequently, this fruitful source of disease was left festering in the Barrack Hospital during the whole time of our greatest overcrowding.

hospital; but any inconvenience arising from the introduction of an additional element into the already complicated organization of our hospitals would be more than compensated by the beneficial effect which it would have on the well-being of our soldiers. Owing to the want of such a store, men have either been exposed to a recurrence of sickness from insufficient clothing, or have been permitted to carry away shirts, flannel waistcoats, drawers, and other articles of hospital clothing. This practice has, we learn, been carried to an extent seriously detrimental to the comfort of the sick in hospital, as it has been found practically impossible to supply the constant drain thus kept up on the purveyor's store.

"We have, &c.,

"(Signed)	"A. CUMMING, I.G.H.
"Lord William Paulet,	"P. BENSON MAXWELL.
"Commandant, Scutari.	"P. SINCLAIR LAING."

February 9th.

COPY OF A LETTER FROM DR. CUMMING, P.B. MAXWELL, ESQ., AND P.S. LAING, ESQ., TO LORD W. PAULET.

"My Lord, *"Scutari, February 9th.*

"In pursuance of our instructions from the Duke of Newcastle, to report to your Lordship all practical alterations which we recommend with a view to the better organization and working of the hospital, we beg to recommend that further hospital accommodation should be at once provided for the sick and wounded of the army.

"We are of opinion that the Barrack Hospital is at present much overcrowded. From calculations which we have made, based upon the superficial measurement of the ward and corridors at present occupied by the patients, we think that not more than 1,913 men should be admitted into this hospital. The number of men, exclusive of orderlies, in the wards and corridors devoted to the sick is, this day, 2,107, and amounted, within the last month, to 2,400.

"The over-crowding is altogether in the corridors. It is much to be regretted that any patients should be placed in them, but we think that under no circumstances ought they to contain more than one row of beds. If the second row were removed, the corridors might still afford accommodation for 725 men. The wards may contain 1,188 more, making a total of 1,913, from which, if 192 orderlies—taking their number at the rate allowed by the regulations of the service—be deducted, it will appear that the wards and corridors now occupied as an hospital ought not to contain more than 1,721 patients,—about 400 less than the number actually in the building on this day. Our estimate is perhaps larger than it ought to be, when it is considered that many of the patients are suffering from fever of a very dangerous character.

"The General Hospital, the stables adjoining the Barrack Hospital, and the buildings at Haidar Pasha in our possession, are full. The hospitals at Kululi are already more crowded than they ought to be, and the huts in course of erection in the Barrack Square will not, we believe, suffice, when completed, to accommodate the number of men at present in excess in the Barrack Hospital.

"Under these circumstances, we deem it our duty to suggest to your Lordship the expediency of providing further hospital accommodation for the reception of any sick or wounded men who may be sent hither from the Crimea, and also of the large number who at the present time over-crowd the Barrack Hospital.

"We must add, that the crowded state of the barrack rooms in which the soldiers of the depot and soldiers' wives are quartered is extremely injurious, not only to their inmates, but also to the sanitary condition of the hospital.

"The prevalence of fever at the present time renders it necessary that we should also earnestly recommend that your Lordship should provide the Medical Officers employed in the hospital with quarters out of the building. Four Surgeons have died within the last month of fever caught in the hospital, and three more have narrowly escaped the same fate from the same cause.

"We have, &c.,

"(Signed)

"A. CUMMING, I.G.H.

"P. BENSON MAXWELL.

"Lord Wm. Paulet,

"P. SINCLAIR LAING."

"*Commandant, Scutari.*

IV.

RESUMÉ OF THE EVIDENCE AS TO (1) THE CRIMEA, (2) THE SICK
TRANSPORT, (3) THE SCUTARI HOSPITALS IN THE WINTER OF
1854–5.

Has it not been too sadly proved by the above evidence, that
the excessive mortality in the winter of 1854-5 cannot be attributed to any one single cause, but to the combined action of
three distinct and successive conditions?

1. The Army was ill-provided in the Crimea, and disease was
generated there.

2. The Sick Transports were in a state fatal to the Sick, and
absolutely unhealthy for all; and the Sick were from 6-27 days
on board. Up to February 13, only one voyage appears to have
been not longer than 3 days—only 5 not longer than 4—only 1
of 5 days. Up to this date, eight per cent. of all the sick
embarked from the Crimea perished on board between
Balaclava and Scutari.

3. The sanitary state of the Hospitals at Scutari was such
that the sick had not a chance. It appears vain to heap evidence
upon evidence that this was so: if the evidence already given is
not enough to make people believe it, "neither would they
believe if one rose from the dead!"

The Mortality per cent. rose as rose the number of Patients—
a sure proof always of sanitary defects in the construction of
the buildings. Mortality may be high from the state of the
Patients admitted; but, if the *percentage* be higher as the number of those Patients increases, then it proves that there is
something destructive in the building itself. Now every admission of Patients at Scutari not only made every sanitary evil
worse for these Patients themselves, but for those who came
after them. The consequence was that there was always an
excess of mortality a little after each in-road of Patients, then
a disproportionate rise.

Statistics tell nothing without conditions. But the whole history of Scutari may be read at a glance in our Statistical
Records, an analysis of which I here annex, if we compare them
with our conditions, which I have enumerated:—

Note.—After consulting the best Statistical authorities, I find
that the mortality of Hospitals can be compared in two ways,
which mutually check and confirm each other: (1), by dividing
the deaths by the mean "strength" of the sick in Hospital, and

The Excessive
Mortality was
owing, 1, to
the Sufferings
and Privations
in the Crimea;
2, to the
Wretched
Condition of
the Sick
Transports; 3,
to the utter
Unhealthiness
of the
Hospitals at
Scutari.

The *per-
centage* of
Mortality in
the Hospitals
rose with the
Number of
patients, but
did not fall
immediately
with its
decrease.

ANALYSIS of WEEKLY STATES of SICK and WOUNDED, from October 1, 1854, to June 30, 1855, in the Hospitals of the Bosphorus.

Date.	No. of Days.	Sick Population of the Hospitals (mean of weekly numbers remaining).	Cases Treated (mean of Admissions and Discharges, including Deaths).	Deaths.	Mortality.	
					Rate per cent. per annum on Sick Population.	Per cent. on Cases Treated.
1854. Oct. 1—Oct. 14	14	1,993	590	113	148	19·2
Oct. 15—Nov. 11	28	2,229	2,043	173	101	8·5
Nov. 12—Dec. 9	28	3,258	1,944	301	121	15·5
Dec. 10—Jan. 6, 1855	28	3,701	3,194	572	202	17·9
1855. Jan. 7—Jan. 31	25	4,520	3,072	986	319	32·1
Feb. 25—Feb. 28*	28	4,178	3,112	1,329	415	42·7
Feb. 25—Mar. 17	21	3,779	1,621	510	235	31·5
Mar. 18—Apr. 7	21	3,306	1,650	237	125	14·4
Apr. 8—Apr. 28	21	2,803	1,190	127	79	10·7
Apr. 29—May 19	21	2,018	1,350	70	60	5·2
May 20—June 9	21	1,504	996	48	56	4·8
June 10—June 30	21	1,442	1,266	28	34	2·2
* Koulali, 1855. Feb. 1—Feb. 28	28	648	581	302	608	52·0
Compare (i. e., omitting the worst time, viz., February) { 1854. 1855. Oct. 1–Jan. 31	123	3,140	10,843	2,145	203	19·8
1855. 1855. Feb. 25–June 30	126	2,501	8,073	1,020	118	12·6

reducing the mortality to that which would obtain, were the time of observation a year. By this method, it will be seen in the Table I give, that the mortality in the Bosphorus Hospitals fell from
415 per cent. per annum in February

to   235   „   „   { in the three weeks ending March 17, 1855,

to   125   „   „

79   „   „   in five successive periods of

60   „   „   *three weeks* each.

56   „   „

and   34   „   „

By the second method the *deaths* are divided by the number of *cases treated*. Where the number of sick is stationary, the numbers (1) admitted and (2) discharged (including deaths) must be equal in a given time. The number of cases treated will be represented by the numbers either admitted or discharged, as they are equal. Then the number of sick increases or decreases, the numbers admitted and discharged will differ; but the number of *cases treated* will, in all ordinary cases, be nearly represented by taking the mean of the numbers admitted and discharged. Thus, 6,751 Patients were *admitted* into the Bosphorus Hospitals in the 126 days, February 25—June 30, 1855, and in the same period 9,392 patients were discharged. The cases treated are represented by

$$\frac{6,751 \ + \ 9,392 \ = \ 16,143}{2} \quad \frac{}{2} \ = \ 8,072.$$

As the deaths were 1,020, the mortality on the cases treated was 12·6 per cent.

By this method the mortality of the cases was at the rate of 31·5 in the first three weeks, and fell progressively

$$\left. \begin{array}{l} \text{to } 14\text{·}4 \\ \phantom{\text{to }} 10\text{·}7 \\ \phantom{\text{to }} 5\text{·}2 \\ \phantom{\text{to }} 4\text{·}8 \\ \phantom{\text{to }} 2\text{·}2 \end{array} \right\} \text{ per cent. of cases treated.}$$

As 2,501 were under treatment 126 days, the days of sickness were

$$2,501 \ \text{x} \ 126 \ = \ 315,126 \ \text{days}$$
$$\text{That is} \ \ 315,126$$
$$\frac{}{8,073} \ = \ 39 \ \text{days}$$

to the treatment of each case on an average.

In the first period, the cases were under treatment about 49 days; in the last 24 days.

While the mortality fell from 31·5 to 2·2, the duration of the cases fell from 49 to 24 days.

At Koulali, the worst of all the hospitals, in February 1855, the mortality was 52 per cent. on all the cases treated in Hospital during that month! At Scutari and Koulali, it was nearly 43 per cent. during February on the cases treated!

In other words, had the rate of mortality at Koulali continued,—in two months, the troops in Hospital there would have been swept away. Had that at Scutari and Koulali continued at what it was in February, in three months its Hospital population

70

would have been annihilated; that is, the mortality there was 415 per cent annually, on the sick population,—at Koulali, it was 608 per cent. annually.

On comparing the cases treated with the rate of mortality, by the aid of the Table, it will be seen that the per-centage of deaths rose at the rate of more than twice the increase of Patients: that is to say that, when the Patients increased in number by one half, the mortality per cent. was double what it was before. We reiterate the words. It was not the absolute number of deaths which was doubled. It was the per-centage of deaths among the Patients, which became about 32 per cent. from 15½ per cent.

But, in February, when the *number* of Patients stood still, the *mortality* still continued rising by one-third of the per-centage!

Decrease after the Sanitary improvements and with the decrease in crowding. Again, when the number of cases treated was diminished by one-fourth, the per-centage of mortality fell to about one-fifteenth. This was after the improvement of the sanitary conditions of Scutari, effected by the Sanitary Commission. We attribute one-half of the decrease of mortality to this improvement—the other half to the cessation of the over-crowding, and to the improvement in the condition of the Patients admitted.

It must not be forgotten that the evils arising from over-crowding, together with bad sanitary conditions, are an ever accumulating ratio.

If nothing is done to the drainage, every excess of Patients leaves it in a worse state for the next. If nothing is done to the walls of wards, the respiration and exhalations from Patients contaminate them with a still greater impregnation of organic matter for the next series of inhabitants. If nothing is done for the ventilation, the Hospital atmosphere becomes more and more fatal.

This is what took place at Scutari.

Now mark the decrease in terms of three weeks. In the three weeks ending March 17, the ratio of Deaths to cases treated had fallen, at Koulali and Scutari, to 31½ per cent. In the three weeks ending April 7, at Koulali and Scutari, to 14½ per cent. In the three weeks ending April 28, at all the Hospitals, to 10·7 per cent. By May 19, to 5·2 per cent. By June 30, to 2·2 per cent.

The Sick Population of the Hospitals, i.e., the mean of the numbers remaining at the beginning and end, fell in that time from 3,800 to 1,400—the number of cases treated from 1,600 to 1,200. That is to say, that, while the mortality fell from 31·5 to

2.2 per cent. of cases treated, the duration of the cases fell from 49 to 24 days.

It has been continually stated, and lately in evidence, by the Principal Medical Officer of the Army in the East, that the reduction of mortality at Scutari, *after* those Hospitals were put under good sanitary conditions, was due, not to these, but solely to the improved state of the Army in the Crimea.

The Decrease of Mortality was not owing to one but to several causes.

Has it not been sufficiently proved that the condition of the Army in the Crimea, the condition of the Sick Transports, the condition of the Hospitals on the Bosphorus were all concerned in producing our fearful mortality? What more could we have of proof?

Put healthy men, sick men with good constitutions, sick men with ruined constitutions into buildings in the state of those at Scutari, during the winter of 1854-55, and there will be seen a certain amount of mortality among the healthy men, as was illustrated by that among our Orderlies and troops in Depot, a greater amount of mortality among those with ruined constitutions.

But what is it that we wish to prove? That it was no use trying to do anything for these poor disabled men, already condemned to death? Rather prove how much more they ought to have been cared for and placed under the best conditions for recovery.

There was nothing new to history in the sanitary results of our campaign.

There was nothing different from the Irish famine fever in that among the starved Crimeans, except the strong scorbutic character impressed by the use of salt rations. There was nothing different from the old Gaol fever, familiar to us from Howard's researches, in the Hospital fever of Scutari, except that it was in a somewhat milder form.

Beautiful and "convenient" as were the buildings of Scutari to an unpractised eye, to one accustomed to look at gaols, hospitals, poor-houses, with a view to their sanitary condition, these Scutari buildings were, in their unimproved state, like the Gaols of old, pest-houses of Typhus Fever. The five conditions generating this plague have been enumerated above.

Let us not deny them, but let us set to work to ascertain what is the education, what the organization, what the system of Medical and other Departments, which will prevent the recurrence of such a fearful loss of life?

72

HOSPITAL KIT

Note as to
Hospital Kit.

After a narrative of the privations of the sick in the Hospitals at Scutari, one question naturally occurs. Independently of the neglect of repairs in the fabric and the want of medical comforts, why should there have been so entire a deficiency of such common articles as shirts, stockings, shoes, towels, or knives and forks? Whose duty was it to supply these, and why was it not performed?

The answer is that it was not the duty of any one. No one of the officials attached to the Hospital was bound to supply them. The soldier himself was bound to bring them with him (from the Crimea) into Hospital (at Scutari).

What the Warrants of the War Department require the Soldier to bring into Hospital.

The warrants of the War Department, still existing, although their power was for a time overruled by General Letters, (these, however, but partially obeyed) require each soldier to use in the Hospital the following articles, which his kit contains—

ARTICLES GIVEN OVER TO THE MAN FOR HIS USE WHILE IN HOSPITAL.

Stock or Neckerchief.	Towels.
Braces.	Shoes or Boots.
Shirts.	Brushes.
Waistcoats, Flannel.	Blacking.
Drawers.	Knife, Fork, and Spoon.
Belt, Flannel.	Comb.
Handkerchiefs.	Pocket Ledger.
Stockings or Socks.	

And this is the consequence of the General Hospital being nothing more than the copy of the Regimental Hospital, to which the soldier can easily bring his kit, out of his neighbouring Barrack room or tent, as the case may be.

He is thus expected to use his own knife, fork, spoon, comb, shirts, socks, towel, and though mess-can and soap are not specified in the list, if, in the late War, he did not bring these articles, he was without them.

These Articles the Purveyor refuses to issue.

The Purveyor, therefore, refuses to issue what appears a second supply of these and such like articles.

Some of these articles may be wanting in peace—the man can therefore only borrow from his comrades—or be supplied on stoppages; i.e., at the soldier's expense.

The Soldiers at Scutari came with nothing.

But, in the late War, during the first winter, the soldier came into Hospital without his kit at all, sometimes abandoned by order of his Commanding Officer, sometimes lost on his voyage to Hospital, or its contents, exhausted by the wear of the Campaign.

Many men came into Hospital with nothing on but a pair of old regimental trowsers, a blanket, and a forage cap. I scarcely remember a single instance, during the winter of 1854-55, of any of the articles enumerated in the list being brought into Hospital by the man, or being in his possession at all.

On leaving Hospital, in some cases, at least after December 5, 1854, the clothing was supplied; but, during the man's stay in Hospital, the contents of his kit, as they could not be replaced under the existing warrants, were not supplied at all. Hence the great number of these articles supplied by Miss Nightingale (*vide* list,) besides the articles supposed not to be of necessity, and never mentioned in warrants, such as benches, tables, lamps, cans, &c. A restricted quantity of these things is however furnished at home by the Barrack-Master.

After the supplies of Miss Nightingale there were, however, small and inadequate requisitions replied to by the Purveyor, who appears to have been ashamed of carrying out his own refusal.

Although, on leaving, in some cases, as above stated, the clothing was supplied to the soldiers who had come in without, vast quantities were carried away by them for their Regimental use, which had been supplied by Miss Nightingale, as above, for Hospital use.

The extreme exigency of the service and the destitution of the troops before Sebastopol, previous to the distribution of the winter supplies, made this necessary.

Although the destitution was notorious, and known to hundreds of Officers as well as to the men themselves, and although the articles were supplied on the requisitions of the Medical Officers, yet the Commandant, having no official report of the fact, never issued any official order upon the subject.

Thousands of articles therefore went through the Hospital to the Army, or to the men invalided home, which had their origin in private supply. And although that portion of this private supply, charged to the War Department, was repaid, other portions being derived from two well-known funds, yet the supply does not enter into any Report of the Commandant of the Hospital, and still less into any Regimental Report—whereby this supply which was patent to every one, as well as its cause, is ignored officially; and consequently may be made to appear officially as an act of unnecessary and ostentatious benevolence.

Supply from Private Sources.

List of
Articles
Supplied
Privately,
upon the
Requisition of
Medical
Officers.

An abstract of some of the principal articles thus supplied in the Crimea and at Scutari, upon the requisitions of Medical Officers, is therefore here annexed:—

Shirts (flannel and cotton)	. . . . . .	50,000
Pairs of Socks and Stockings	. . . . . .	23,743
Pairs of Drawers . .	. . . .	6,843
Towels . .	. . . .	5,826
Handkerchiefs	. . . .	10,044
Comforters . .	. . . .	9,638
Flannel . .	. . . . . . yards	1,384
Pairs of Slippers	. . . .	3,626
Knives and forks	. . . .	856
Spoons . .	. . . .	2,630
Night caps . .	. . . .	4,521
Gloves and Mits	. . . . . . prs.	4,545
Drinking cups	. . . .	5,477
Tin plates . .	. . . .	2,086
Basins, zinc, &c. . .	. . . .	624
Dressing gowns	. . . .	1,004
Air Beds and Pillows	. . . .	232
Thread and Tape	. . . . packages	74
Lanterns, Candle Lamps, and Lamps	. . . .	168
Preserved meats . .	. . . . . . cases	253
Meat Biscuits	. . . . . . .barrels	2
Isinglass and Gelatine	. . . . . . lbs.	148½
India-rubber sheeting	. . pieces, 325 yds.	26
Camp Kitchen Cooking Stoves and Canteens	. .	55
Boilers and Stewpans	. . . .	68

Tables and Forms,
Baths,
Soap,
Games,
Brooms and Scrubbers,
Bedpans,
Tin pails,
Combs, Scissors, &c., &c.,

were supplied with and without Requisition.

The above is independent of the Extra Diets, including Wine, and of the innumerable minor Surgical appliances, such as Arm-Slings, Bandages, Eye-shades, Old Linen, supplied as they were wanted. Both descriptions of things ought to be, and it is trusted always will be, in future, under the charge of women. These do not, therefore, strictly belong to our example.

The conclusion which must necessarily be drawn from this unhappily large example is, that the soldier ought to be supplied with Hospital clothing and necessaries, and that his own kit should be placed under charge in a regulated Pack-store, there to await his recovery or death.

In the last event it would be, as now, sold, and the proceeds delivered to the Purveyor or Governor, for transmission to the Regiment, and from thence to the War Department, which answers the application of relatives.

Among the unhappily neglected Departments, the Pack-store at Scutari showed a greater confusion, perhaps, than any other. Hundreds of men's knapsacks were thrown into it, promiscuously, and lay for months unsorted—were, indeed, not unfrequently plundered. These knapsacks belonged partly to the Sick who came into Hospital, partly to those who died on the passage. Consequently those who could claim the knapsacks, whether the soldier who recovered, or the widow of him who died, had no means of discovering them in the confused heap. And it was not till April 1855, when thousands of men had gone away, that the Pack-store was reduced to order.

76

PREFACE

TO

PART III
NOTES ON THE CAUSES OF
DISASTER AT SCUTARI

The Scutari disaster was a separate problem and must be considered by itself. It was the case of thousands of sick removed 300 miles from the causes which had occasioned the sickness and exposed to another class of risks in the buildings into which they were received.

The buildings were spacious and magnificent in external appearance; far more so, indeed, than any military buildings in Great Britain; and several of them were, apparently, better suited for Hospitals than any Military Hospitals at home.

This merely external appearance was, however, fatally deceptive. Underneath these great structures were sewers of the worst possible construction, loaded with filth, mere cesspools, in fact, through which the wind blew sewer air up the pipes of numerous open privies into the Corridors and wards where the sick were lying.

The wards had no means of ventilation, the walls required constant lime-washing, and the number of sick crowded into the Hospitals, during the winter of 1854-55, was disproportionately large, especially when the bad Sanitary state of the buildings is taken into consideration. The population of the Hospitals was increased not only without any Sanitary precautions having been taken, but while the Sanitary conditions were becoming daily worse, for the sewers were getting more and more dangerous and the walls more and more saturated with organic matter.

Some slight improvements were made in the beginning of March 1855. But it was not till the 17th March that effectual measures were initiated for removing the causes of disease in the buildings, viz., by the Sanitary Commission. By the month of June the improvements were nearly completed, the proportion of sick had fallen off, and the hospitals had become healthy.

This is the whole history of the frightful Scutari calamity. Even from the very beginning of the occupation of these buildings in October 1854, and before the sufferings of the winter had begun, the mortality was very high, although the number of sick was small, indicating the unhealthy state of the buildings even then. Nothing was done to improve them. But fresh ship-loads of sick were passed into them. The mortality of course continued to rise. Still nothing was done. Then came the great Crimean catastrophe, and ship after ship arrived with sick in so exhausted a condition, that the foul air of these Hospitals was almost certain death to them; and accordingly they died, in the month of February 1855, at 415 per cent. per annum. So that, in twelve months, at such a rate, the whole sick population of the Hospitals would have perished four times. In February two out of every five cases treated died in the Hospitals of the Bosphorus, and at Koulali one out of every two. Well may this incredible mortality teach us a terrible lesson!

The reduction in the mortality, after the Sanitary works were begun, is most striking, and it falls eventually to less than a sixth part of what it was when the Barrack and General Hospitals were occupied together in October 1854, and to a nineteenth part of what it was in February 1855. Our General Hospitals have been so deplorably mismanaged in all our wars that the question has been raised as to whether it would not be better to do without them altogether. The experience of Scutari proves that General Hospitals may become pest-houses from neglect, or may be made as healthy as any other buildings.

These are the facts of Scutari Hospitals during the first year of our occupation. Nothing in the Sanitary recommendations we have been analysing, unless it be some suggestions made when it was too late, would have led us to suppose that there was anything seriously wrong in the Hospitals or that their defects had any share in the destruction of the British sick, who have given a name to these buildings in history.

LORD WILLIAM PAULET. ADDENDA ON THE SUBJECT OF THE NEED OF SANITARY REFORMS AT SCUTARI.

"Brigadier-General Lord WILLIAM PAULET to Lord PANMURE.

"*Scutari, 25 April*, 1855.

"My Lord,—I have had the honour to receive your Lordship's despatch, dated the 11th instant, and numbered as per margin, by which I am gratified to learn that you approve of the measures which I am adopting with a view to obtain an increased amount of Hospital accommodation.

"With reference to the desire expressed by you to be furnished with more detailed information upon this subject, I beg to observe, in the first instance, that as the members composing the Sanitary

April 25, 1855.
Letter from
Lord William
Paulet.
Statistical and
Sanitary
Remarks on
the Hospitals
of the
Bosphorus.

Commission, and other superior and competent authorities, had signified to me their intention of transmitting to you a minute report upon the condition of these Hospitals and their inmates, I abstained from making further comment, under the conviction that the subject would thus have greater weight than if it emanated from myself.

"I have much pleasure, my Lord, in reporting that everything under my command is progressing as favourably as I could wish. Sickness has very much diminished, and so has the mortality. In January last the number of deaths was 1,480, in February 1,254, and in March 424, every month showing a steady decrease over the preceding one. The average mortality at present is 5½ per diem.

"I have exerted myself in every way to add to the comfort and requirements of these Hospitals, and am enabled to state that every patient has now above 1,200 cubic feet of space; thus exceeding by 200 that recommended by the Sanitary Commission; while six feet is allotted to each bed from centre to centre. There is besides vacant accommodation for 2,000 beds.

"In addition to the wooden Hospital about to be erected by Dr. Parkes, in conjunction with Mr. Brunton, the engineer, Her Majesty's Ambassador has offered to place at my disposal, if necessary, the house at Therapia belonging to the Russian Embassy.

"I have made further provision at Kululi by converting its fine riding-school into a convalescent Hospital which is capable of locating 180 men. It lies contiguous to the Bosphorus, and has proved very healthy. I have, moreover, applied to the same purpose, the buildings formerly used as stables which, having now been completed make spacious and airy wards.

"It is gratifying to me to inform you that the temporary wooden sheds constructed within this barrack are in course of occupation, and are reported by the senior Medical Officers as answering, in an eminent degree, the purposes of convalescence, from the ample space and free ventilation which they afford.

"I am constructing a temporary barrack on the common, between this and the General Hospital, for locating the depot, and when completed, it will add materially to the Hospital accommodation.

"I would also add that the Medical Officers are deserving the greatest praise for the zealous manner in which they discharge their duties. The Orderly attendance is also satisfactory.

"I may confidently assert, as regards the general condition of these Hospitals, that they surpass in cleanliness and comfort any I have seen in England and elsewhere; and this opinion is corroborated by the various and enlightened individuals, both English and foreign who have visited them.

"I have continual applications from the private practitioners, artificers, ladies, and nurses, for extra expenses, such as field-allowance, forage for horses, servants' allowance, &c., all of which, except their rations, I do not consider myself at liberty to sanction; and I beg to suggest that these expenses should be covered by the annual salaries of the individuals, which might be increased in proportion to the merits and abilities of each.

"I have used my utmost endeavours to carry out the suggestions made by the Sanitary Commission, most of which are already in course of operation.

"As regards this building, every window of which is open to the public thoroughfares, it is the depot of the Army in the Crimea, and contains the stores, prisons, depot stores of each division, the armoury, the offices, and Miss Nightingale's extensive establishment, all of which require necessarily the admission of a proportionate number of workmen, and all these render it more fit for a barrack than an Hospital.

"I have caused the Turkish hulk line-of-battle ship to be cleared, which I propose to retain in the event of a pressure, as a store, it being of no expense to Her Majesty's Government.

"The 'Bombay' convalescent transport-ship has also been cleared and given over to Rear-Admiral Grey.

"I have accommodation for 2,000 horses, to be stabled in buildings partly repaired and partly constructed for the purpose.

"I have had constructed stabling and barracks at Galata Sarae, in Pera, near the British Embassy, to serve as a depot for the Royal Artillery.

"I need hardly observe, my Lord, that besides this being the depot for the Army in the Crimea, all stores passing and repassing here, and all officers and troops having to report themselves to me, and in most cases to be transshipped, my time is therefore fully occupied.

"Hoping these arrangements will meet with your approbation, and that this report is sufficient in detail,

"I have, &c.,

(Signed)   "W. PAULET.

"*Brigadier-General commanding Troops.*"

"Dr. A CUMMING to Dr. SMITH.

"*Scutari, 7 April,* 1855.

"Sir,—With reference to your letter of 23rd ultimo, respecting the Palace Hospital, I beg leave to say to you, that nothing which has come to my knowledge leads me to think that the site is unhealthy, and since its occupation the returns show that disease has not been more prevalent there than elsewhere.

"Fever has been more or less rife everywhere, and every station, including Abydos and Gallipoli, and, as I am informed, Constantinople also, have suffered from it; and from this circumstance Medical Officers, confining their observations to their own locality, have, not very logically, pronounced it unhealthy.

"The states you receive are not altogether safe guides in this matter, because the greatest mortality generally occurs immediately, or two or three days after the arrival of sick, and it may happen that one Hospital gets more bad cases than another.

April 7.
Dr. Cumming to
Dr. Smith.
Salubrity of
Site of Palace
Hospital.

80

"The Hospital in question has had a large number of sick officers, who have arrived from the Crimea, and who occupy the kiosk, but only one death has taken place amongst them, and he was a recent arrival from the camp, and who, during convalescence, had a relapse and died. In my opinion, all the Hospitals here might, with equal justice, be pronounced unhealthy as the Palace. The ground it stands on is a shallow valley, and in rear of the buildings there are rather extensive gardens and vineyards, the whole apparently well drained by a small rivulet. In rainy weather, during the winter season, water no doubt lodges, from some of the ditches having been neglected, but at present the site is perfectly dry, and will, I conceive, remain so during the summer.

"A few of the Medical Officers doing duty there have, as well as those doing duty at the other Hospitals, had attack of fever, although not to an extent to excite the least apprehension, but some of them had got alarmed, and wished to be immediately removed; a proceeding not very encouraging to the patients, and which I resisted: all are now well.

"The Turks, I believe, are considered not bad judges of sites, and had this been an unhealthy one, it is not very likely that the Sultan would ever have made it his residence.

"I have just returned from making an inspection of this Hospital (which is, by-the-by, in excellent order). The gardens are in full bloom, the vineyards are being put in order, and the little meadow in front, which has probably obtained for it such a bad name, is covered with wild flowers, and full of ants; an indication, I am inclined to think of the natural dryness of the soil.

"I have, &c.,
(Signed)   "A. CUMMING,
"*Inspector-General of Hospitals.*"

"Dr. A. CUMMING to Dr. SMITH.
"*Scutari, 15 April,* 1855.

"Sir,—I beg leave to offer the following observations on your letter, dated 23rd March last, noticing certain points connected with the localities and sanitary condition of the Hospitals at Scutari and its neighbourhood.

"1st. There is no ward at the General Hospital occupied as an Apothecary's Store; but as a central position appears to have been considered desirable for a Surgery, one has been so appropriated, as I am informed, ever since the Hospital has been in our possession.

"As soon as a suitable room can be obtained for a Purveyor's Office the present one will be given up.

"2nd. Anything defective in the drainage at the General Hospital is being remedied; some suggestions respecting the drains were made by Drs. Sutherland and Gavin, along with a civil engineer, some time ago.

"3rd. In my opinion much unnecessary importance has been attached to the burial-ground; it is fully 100 yards from the Hospital,

April 15. Dr. Cumming to Dr. Smith. Reply to Dr. Smith's Letter of Sanitary Observations (of which an Abstract is given at p. xxvi, Preface to Section I.)

and situated near the edge of the cliff overlooking the Sea of Marmora. The graves are well covered, and are not shallow, and peat charcoal has been fairly used to guard against deleterious influences; the use of lime for this purpose is questioned.

"4th. I am at a loss to conceive what vermin can harbour under the flooring of the wards, some of which are of stone; fleas, I apprehend, do not, but, like bugs, reside near their feeding places. Turkish carpentering is so bad, and gaping beams so general, that it would require many months to remove this cause of complaint.

"5th. Previous, probably, to its being repaired.

"6th. The huts are now occupied by upwards of 200 convalescents, which diminishes by so many the numbers in the wards; this arrangement has been found very advantageous, and I should regret its being given up.

"7th. See my letter, 7th April.

"8th. No ill consequences can be detected as having arisen from this, but as other accommodation has become available at Kululi, the rooms over the stable have been partially dispensed with, and will probably soon be entirely given up.

"9th. The unsatisfactory state of the privies has been noticed by all, but no means have yet been found altogether to amend it. It is entirely, or nearly so, attributable to the careless dirty habits of the patients themselves; suggestions on this point were made by the Civil Engineer who accompanied the Sanitary Commissioners.

"I have omitted to mention that a new graveyard has been opened to the eastward, and at a greater distance from the Hospital. Both were visited by Drs. Gavin and Sutherland.

"I have, &c.,

(Signed) "A. CUMMING,

"Inspector-General of Hospitals."

"Dr. A CUMMING to Dr. SMITH, London.

"Scutari, 16 April, 1855.

"Sir,—In acknowledging your letter of the 30th instant, respecting the prevalence of fever in these Hospitals, I have to acquaint you that every precaution has been taken against any morbific influences which may be supposed to exist, and due attention has been given to ventilation, lime-washing, and the use of deodorants.

"At present the Hospitals are by no means crowded; and, as respects this Hospital, much less so than the numbers on the states indicate, in consequence of about 200 convalescents being removed from the wards and corridors, and placed for some time previous to final discharge in the sheds in the Barrack-square.

"I may remark that although the site of these sheds is objectionable, they have the advantage of being roomy, are well-ventilated, and afford sufficient accommodation to enable me to separate the dormito-

April 16. Dr. Cumming to Dr. Smith. Sanitary Condition of Hospitals.

ries from the dining-rooms. They possess also a large reading or day room, and when we can get rid of the depot, they will, I think, be found useful during the summer. As to encampment, there is unfortunately no tentage.

"Materials for hutting are now being placed on the common near the General Hospital, and I was informed by Captain Macdonald a few days ago, that they would be ready for occupation in a fortnight.

"I have, &c.,

(Signed)　"A. CUMMING,

"*Inspector-General of Hospitals.*"

MONTHLY REPORT of Dr. CUMMING to Dr. SMITH,
dated 28 *April*, 1855.

April 28.
Dr. Cumming
to Dr. Smith.
Monthly
Report
for March.

"The changes in the number of patients under treatment in these Hospitals during the month of March, as compared with those of the previous month, will be seen by the following numerical statement:

		Remained.	Admitted.	Discharged	Died.	Remaining.
February ..	Scutari ...	4,165	1,895	2,139	1,027	2,895
	Kululi	434	795	65	302	861
		4,599	2,690	2,204	1,329	3,756
March	Scutari ...	2,895	2,385	2,475	421	2,384
	Kululi	861	450	362	134	815
		3,756	2,835	2,837	555	3,199

"Thus the numerical state of the Hospitals for March is much more favourable than during the previous month: during February, we had under treatment in Hospital 7,289, and during March 5,591; of the former number, 3,533 ceased to appear in the Hospital Books, of which 1,329 were deaths; whereas, during March, a nearly equal number of men ceased to be inmates of the Hospital, viz., 3,392; but of this number only 555 died, a difference in the number of deaths in the two months of 774.

"This great improvement is attributable to numerous concurrent causes; in the first place, the condition of the men admitted into Hospital from the Crimea has undergone a great improvement in comparison with that of the men who arrived in previous months. The cases admitted from the Crimea during March were either slighter in character than previously, or were men already convalescent from fever.

"The admissions into Hospital for diseases contracted at the station have not only been fewer in number, but very much less severe in type.

"The milder weather which set in early in March was followed by an improvement in the cases under treatment. The mortality at the commencement of the month, although diminished, as compared with that of the previous month, was still high. The beneficial effects of a change from severe to a milder temperature is not apparent (in returns) for some little time after the change had taken place, for obvious reasons, although the influence of the milder temperature begins to be felt by the patients and perceived by the medical men. Yet the effects of the previous severe weather remain for a certain time afterwards. The consequences of the change in the weather are only developed at certain periods subsequent to the time at which the change takes place. The same observation applies to other causes of severe disease which existed during the winter.

"The mortality in weekly periods, during March, was as follows:—

From 3 to 9 March – – – –	Scutari – – – –	120	
	Kululi – – – –	58	
	TOTAL	178	
From 9 to 16 March – – – –	Scutari – – – –	100	
	Kululi – – – –	21	
	TOTAL	121	
From 16 to 23 March – – – –	Scutari – – – –	77	
	Kululi – – – –	28	
	TOTAL	105	
From 23 to 30 March – – – –	Scutari – – – –	52	
	Kululi – – – –	15	
	TOTAL	67	

"Hence, although the more potent causes of severe disease and death which had been in force during the winter, had already passed away at the commencement of March, yet the mortality remained very considerable to a later date; the decrease in the deaths, however, during March, as shown by the above weekly numbers, is very considerable, and a comparison of the mortality in the last week of March with that of the corresponding period in the previous month, viz., 67 to 257, is very remarkable.

"The deaths from the 23 to 28 February.

Scutari	....	....	....	....	....	201
Kululi	....	....	....	....	....	56
		Total	....	....	....	257

"The decrease in the mortality above adverted to, cannot be accounted for by a diminution in the number of patients in the Hospitals during the periods under consideration. This will be seen by a statement of the number of patients under treatment during the weeks of March, as follows:—

		Remained.	Admitted.	TOTAL.
From 3 to 9 March	Scutari ...	3,472	430	3,902
	Kululi	836	135	971
TOTAL		4,308	565	4,873
From 9 to 16 March	Scutari ...	3,296	212	3,508
	Kululi	875	64	939
TOTAL		4,171	276	4,447
From 16 to 23 March ...	Scutari ...	3,092	327	3,419
	Kululi	867	182	1,049
TOTAL		3,959	509	4,468
From 23 to 30 March ...	Scutari ...	2,580	608	3,188
	Kululi	979	16	995
TOTAL		3,559	624	4,183

"Hence the diminution of cases under treatment has not been great, and the number of fresh patients—the admissions—which tend to increase the mortality to a much greater degree than the number of cases remaining in Hospital, from time to time, have been remarkably uniform during the periods under consideration, except during the second week, when the admissions sank as low as 276. The number of patients admitted during the last week of the month to the 30th inclusive, was greater than any previous week.

"The improvement in the sick may, perhaps, be attributed in some degree to the improved condition, sanitary and otherwise, of our Hospitals. The milder weather, among its other beneficial influences, permitted more free ventilation.

"Diseases of the bowels, including Dysentery, were fatal to 226 cases, while in February the number of deaths from the same class of diseases 681. Fever of all types was fatal during March in 164 cases. These occurred in the various Hospitals as follows:—

"Mortality from Fever during March.

"In the General Hospital 37
     "   Barrack   do. 70
     "   Palace   do. 11
     "   Stable   do. 6

„	Turkish Hulk	...	...	...	...	3
„	Bombay Ship	...	...	...	...	2

Total, Scutari 129
Kululi Hospital 35

Total, Scutari and Kululi 164

"The diseases which have come under our notice in the greatest numbers during the month have been: Fevers, continued, remittent, and intermittent, displaying a well-marked tendency to relapse; rheumatic affections, chiefly chronic, and, in a few instances, subacute; Scurvy in some cases pure, but in the majority existing as a complication, more or less serious, of other diseases, and frost-bite.

"The fevers contracted at this station were frequent during February, both among patients under treatment in Hospital, among the Hospital attendants and Medical Officers; but although many cases of Fever have arisen at this station during March, the type of this disease, as already mentioned, has been much less severe, and the disease manifested much less tendency to run into the low typhoid form, which was so fatal during the previous month.

"The most important and serious class of disease during February was that of the bowels, Dysentery and Diarrhoea. These diseases, although attracting much less attention during March, were still very serious and numerous. The Dysentery being of a most severe form, complicated in many instances with Scurvy, a complication of disease, than which nothing can be more intractable or more fatal in result. In the great majority of *post mortem* examinations, the large intestine presented all the anatomical evidences of old, extensive, and severe Dysentery mingled with scorbutic appearances.

"The ulceration, old and rugged, extended from the rectum, through the colon, to a variable extent, in many instances to the locum, and in a few instances passed into the adjacent portion of the small intestine; in numerous cases the entire mucous membrane of the large bowel was involved, and in a few specimens the diseased action had penetrated through the other coats to the peritoneum.

"The number of men discharged from Hospital has been very considerable, viz., 2,838. Of these, 972 were deemed unfit for further service, at least for some time, in this country, or those who needed a change to the climate of England for a restoration to health. These men left this station in the following manner:—

Name of Ship.	Sick.	Wounded.	TOTAL.
"Adelaide," steamer	129	44	173
"Indiana" „	223	45	268
"Tynemouth" „	198	15	213
"Chapman," steam transport	122	12	134
"Julia" „	166	18	184
Total	838	134	972

"The state of the Hospital at the end of the month, in regard of the most important diseases remaining, and which will therefore appear in the following month, was extremely satisfactory.

"This will be seen by a comparison of the number of these diseases remaining under treatment at the end of February and March respectively.

		End of February.	End of March.	Decrease.
Febris CC.	Scutari ...	709	652	57
	Kululi	213	191	22
TOTAL		922	843	79
Dysentery and Diarrhoea	Scutari ...	882	643	239
	Kululi	262	217	45
TOTAL		1,144	860	284
Frost-bite	Scutari ...	216	164	52
	Kululi	120*	100	20
TOTAL		336	264	72
Vulnus Sclop	Scutari ...	153	64	89
	Kululi	6	3	3
TOTAL		159	67	92

"In concluding this report, it will perhaps be satisfactory to compare the return with that from Smyrna during the same period.

"The Hospital there was opened for the reception of sick on the 15th February, and to 31st March 993 cases were under treatment; of these 371 were discharged, and 127 died.

	Treated.	Died.	Per Cent.
SMYRNA:			
Fevers	209	28	13·30
Dysentery and Diarrhoea	279	62	22·22
Scorbutus	127	12	9·46
Gelatio	150	18	12·
SCUTARI:			
Fevers	1,607	129	7·55
Dysentery and Diarrhoea	1,447	160	11·05
Scorbutus	165	12	7·27
Gelatio	313	45	14·37
KULULI:			
Fevers	351	35	9·97
Dysentery and Diarrhoea	388	66	17·01
Scorbutus	96	1	1·04
Gelatio	144	20	13·88

"The return from Smyrna, however, embraced a longer period, by 13 days, than that from Scutari; but, on the other hand, the vessels which took the sick there from the Crimea touched here on the way. I deemed it advisable to disembark and admit into these Hospitals a great many of the worst cases, from 40 to 50 having been landed from some of the vessels, so that the comparison is made with every advantage in favour of that establishment; and as regards the Hospitals here, it must be added that fresh additions were made to them by frequent arrivals from Balaclava during the period, amongst whom were many in an extreme state of exhaustion, and who died soon after admission.

"(Signed)   A. CUMMING,
"*Inspector-General of Hospitals.*"

REMARKS ON THE PRECEDING CORRESPONDENCE

These singular documents are well worthy of attention, and require a little treatise to themselves.

They are admirably calculated to draw out the most striking features of the Scutari case, when seen by the light which the sanitary operations going on at the same time throw upon them.

These sanitary investigations established—

1. That the site of the Barrack and General Hospitals was good; that of Kululi not good; that of the Palace Hospital defective from the wetness of the ground. This last fact was admitted by the Inspector-General in the Cumming Maxwell Report, but is here denied.

Sanitary Defects discovered.

88

2. That the vicinity of the Hospitals was far from clean, with the exception of that of the General Hospital at Scutari.

3. That the water supply was defective, but measures were being taken to improve it.

4. That the drainage was most defective, the drains and sewers being loaded with filth,—none of the sewers trapped,—no ventilating openings, except the tubes of the privies, which formed, in fact, the means of ventilating the sewers, the wind driving the sewer air into the corridors and wards.

5. That the ventilation was defective.

6. That, although the Hospital accommodation at the time of the visit of the Sanitary Commissioners could not be considered as inadequate, yet there was still overcrowding, owing to the corridors being filled up with one, or, as in the Barrack Hospital, even with two rows of beds, and to the beds being too close and the cubic space allotted too small. This might have been prevented by a better distribution of the space.

7. That the walls and ceilings were not clean.

8. That the Burial-ground close to the General Hospital was overcharged.

Whatever recommendations had been made, little or nothing had been done to remedy these evils.

The Sanitary Commission—

Sanitary Remedies applied.

1. Drained the site of the Palace Hospital, and closed the worst wards in Kululi;

2. Organized a daily cleansing of the outskirts of the Hospitals;

3. Cleansed and deodorized with peat charcoal the latrines and sewers, and constructed flushing tanks to flush them.

4. Ventilated the Hospitals with plates of perforated zinc and wire gauze, and with foul air shafts in the ceilings;

5. Reduced the number of beds in the corridors to one row, fixed the distance between the beds at six feet from centre to centre, and allotted not less than 1,000 cubic feet of space to each bed;

6. Directed the constant use of lime-washing;

7. Regulated the burials and the burial-ground.

Scutari Hospitals, before and after the arrival of the Sanitary Commission, presented the same difference which existed between the Gaols of the last century, nests of Typhus Fever, and Colonel Jebb's Prisons of 1857, the most healthy buildings in existence.

To inexperienced eyes Scutari buildings were magnificent. To ours, in their first state, they were truly whited sepulchres,—pest-houses.

By the Principal Medical Officer of the East it has been stated, that no difference in our mortality took place in consequence of the sanitary improvements in Scutari, and that the decrease which was actually observed was solely due to the improved character of the cases from the Crimea, as manifested by the decrease of mortality on board the sick transports. That this assertion is founded on error of observation, and ignorance of the case, is proved by the following returns, compiled from official sources.

TABLE No. I

	Total Sick Remained and Admitted.	Died.	Per 1,000.	Under-statement of mortality in hospitals of Bosphorus.
SCUTARI.				
October 1 to November 4, 1854 . .	4,283	250	58	
To December 2	5,249	267	50	
SCUTARI AND KULULI.				
To December 30	6,471	393	60	
To January 31, 1855	8,297	1,235	147	
To February 28	7,289	1,329	182	
KULULI.				
February	1,229	302	245	
SCUTARI AND KULULI.				
Twenty-one days, ending March 17 . .	5,522	514	93	
„ April 7 . .	5,060	240	47	
„ „ 28 . .	4,063	127	31	
„ May 19 . .	3,428	71	20	
„ June 9 . .	2,557	49	18	
„ „ 30 . .	2,984	29	9	
KULULI.				
Twenty-one days, ending March 17 . .	1,127	133	118	
„ June 30 . .	610	4	6½	

The above is an illustration of a curious method of calculating the rate of mortality, which will be afterwards described. This method counts the cases remaining every month, or twelve times a year, and adds to them the cases admitted. So that, in addition to the cases really treated, it obtains also fictitious cases, simply by counting the same man a certain number of times, that is, by counting the patients remaining twelve times annually, and adding them to the new patients admitted.

It is evident that, by counting the cases *remaining* at the beginning of every month, week, or oftener, the cases may be multiplied, and the apparent rate of mortality reduced to any conceivable extent.

The above table is, therefore, not given as any approximation to the actual mortality, but as founded on Official Returns, and an under-statement of the real rate of mortality. It is an illustration of the method sometimes practised, which gives an unfairly favourable estimate. For our purpose it is useful, as giving a view of the number of patients brought together under the Sanitary influences of the Hospitals at about the same time.

From it may be gathered the terrible sanitary fact, that an increase of sick, by only one-third, more than doubled the mortality per cent.

But, as time went on, and the sanitary evils of the Hospitals became intensified for the next sick population, by means of the unfortunate sick who went before, although the number of sick actually diminished by one-eighth, viz., in February, the mortality continued to increase by more than one-fifth.

In Kululi, the worst of all the Hospitals, during February, one out of every two cases treated died, and in Scutari and Kululi together two out of every five, in the same month, according to the true method of computing the mortality, *vide* p. xxviii.

It is to be observed, that after each arrival of sick a frightful increase of mortality occurred immediately, or two or three days afterwards, and chiefly, as far as could be ascertained, among the admissions, who stand such sanitary conditions less well than those inured to them. By Sir John Hall's own showing, these admissions were cases of an improved character in February.

For mark the decrease in the number of deaths on board the sick transports, shewing that the improvement stated did take place in the character of the cases coming from the Crimea, while no corresponding improvement took place, as stated, in the mortality at Scutari, but the reverse.

TABLE II.

Period.	Sick embarked, arriving at Scutari during the period.	Died on Passage.	Deaths per 1,000 embarked.	Deaths per 1,000 on cases treated in Hospitals, Scutari.
1854. 1855.				
Sept. 15—Jan. 31. .	13,093	976	74·5	198*
January, 1855	2,902	262	90	321
February	2,178	41	19	427
Feb. 25—March 17	1,067	5	4·7	315
March 18—April 7	860	4	4·6	144

II.
Mortality on board Sick Transports and at Scutari compared.

* October 1, 1854—January 31, 1855.

And mark the two conditions to which Sir John Hall appeals
as the causes of the reduced mortality at Scutari. Both of these
we had in February, viz.:—diminution of numbers—improvement in the character of cases: yet, with both, the mortality
rose.

For the Hospitals had been brought into that terrible state
that the mortality could not but *increase* even upon these
improved cases. A considerable reduction in the mortality of
cases treated did take place in the first half of March upon that
in February, but it still remained about what it had been in
January, and more than half as much again of what it had been
during the four months, October, November, December and
January,—although the mortality on board the Transports, taking the same periods, had fallen to one-fifteenth of what it had
been. It was not till after the Sanitary works had been carried
out at Scutari, that the comparative safety of our men was
secured.

Then, and not till then, the diminution of the number of sick
by nearly one-half, reduced the mortality at all the Hospitals to
one-tenth; at Kululi, where the objectionable wards had been
emptied, to one-eighteenth.*

This statement will not surprise any one at all conversant
with such matters in Civil life, where such facts and such causation have been long since admitted; but they are still denied
in the Army.

In corroboration of the above, a statement, made by the
Principal Medical Officer, himself, of the Army in the East, the
published despatches, may be quoted:—

March 2.
Dr. Hall to
Lord Raglan.

"Dr. HALL to LORD RAGLAN.

"March 2, 1855.

". . . Out of 442 patients treated in the General Hospital at
Balaclava, between February 18 and 24, only three casualties have
occurred, which I think may fairly be termed a low rate of mortality,
considering the class of patients that are generally sent in there for
treatment, men brought down from camp, and found too ill to embark,
when they arrive at Balaclava."

The above mortality is 12 per month, or 27 per 1,000 per
month. If these men had been sent to Scutari in February,

---

* This last estimate is taken from Table No. 1, where, as has been stated, the
mortality is very much underrated.

there would have died not 12 but 189—the deaths to cases treated at Scutari, in February, being 427 per 1,000, instead of 27 per 1,000 and from February 25 to March 17, 315 per 1,000.

And according to Dr. Hall's statement, these cases treated at Balaclava were kept there, because they were in a worse state than those who were sent down to Scutari.

Compare with this the facts mentioned in the Scutari Inspector-General's letters, upon which we are now commenting, viz., that "fevers contracted at this station (Scutari) were frequent during February, both among patients under treatment in Hospital, among the Hospital attendants and Medical Officers." And it will be seen how much disease was actually generated within the fatal Hospital walls of Scutari, not only during February, but even during March, when "many cases of fever arose at this station," although it "manifested much less tendency to run into the low typhoid form, which was so fatal during the previous month."

This is most important, for "typhoid fever" is well known to be pre-eminently due to foul air, arising from overcrowding and want of drainage; and, till the sanitary works at Scutari were executed, it appears, by Dr. Cumming's own showing, to have prevailed there.

Dr. Hall, himself, appears to have been fully aware of this. For, in a letter addressed to Dr. Smith, February 23, 1855, he states that he anticipates much more benefit by treating the sick at the Castle Hospital, Balaclava, than by sending them down to Scutari. "At Scutari," he says, "the buildings are large, crowded, and difficult to keep well-ventilated. Fever has consequently made its appearance and proved fatal to many, both officers and men." It does not appear to have occurred to either Inspector-General that all this was preventible.

The Scutari Inspector-General, further, mentions the "frequent arrivals from Balaclava during this period," viz., March, "amongst whom were many in an extreme state of exhaustion, and who died soon after admission." Also, that he had "to disembark and admit a great many of the worst cases" (on their way to Smyrna) at Scutari—proving that, even then, although Dr. Hall retained "men found too ill to embark," "at Balaclava," yet either the voyage and the state of the Transports induced an increase of disease, or the state of Scutari Hospitals, always acting most fatally on fresh admissions, produced a rapid mortality, or both. Of Scorbutic dysentery, according to Dr. Cumming, there were "numerous" cases, "fatal in result," even through March. This may be another proof of the state of our Hospitals, as Dr. Hall tells us that the character of the cases from the Crimea was so much improved. But it may be that the effects of their winter diet would long be "fatal in result."

An estimate of the Mortality in the Hospitals on the Bosphorus, as exact as can be now made, is here annexed:

TABLE No. III

ANALYSIS of WEEKLY STATES of SICK and WOUNDED, from October 1, 1854, to June 30, 1855, in the Hospitals of the Bosphorus.

Date.	No. of Days.	Sick Population of the Hospitals (mean of weekly numbers remaining.	Cases Treated (mean of Admissions and discharges, including Deaths.)	Deaths.	Mortality. Rate per cent. per annum on Sick Population	Per cent. on Cases Treated.
1854. SCUTARI.						
Oct. 1—Oct. 14	14	1,993	590	113	148	19·2
Oct. 15—Nov. 11	28	2,229	2,043	173	101	8·5
Nov. 12—Dec. 9	28	3,258	1,944	301	121	15·5
SCUTARI & KULULI.						
Dec. 10 to Jan. 6, 1855	28	3,701	3,194	572	202	17·9
1855.						
Jan. 7—Jan. 31	25	4,520	3,072	986	319	32·1
Feb. 1—Feb. 28	28	4,178	3,112	1,329	415	42·7
KULULI.						
Feb. 1—Feb. 28	28	648	581	302	608	52·0
SCUTARI & KULULI.						
Feb. 25—Mar. 17	21	3,779	1,621	510	235	31·5
Mar. 18—Apr. 7	21	3,306	1,650	237	125	14·4
Apr. 8—Apr. 28	21	2,803	1,190	127	79	10·7
Apr. 29—May 19	21	2,018	1,350	70	60	5·2
May 20—June 9	21	1,504	996	48	56	4·8
June 10—June 30	21	1,442	1,266	28	34	2·2
Compare (i.e., omitting the worst time, viz., February.)						
1854. 1855.						
Oct. 1—Jan. 31	123	3,140	10,843	2,145	203	19·8
1855. 1855.						
Feb. 25—June 30	126	2,501	8,073	1,020	118	12·6

Correct Statement of Mortality in Hospitals of Bosphorus.

In order to estimate how excessive was the rate of Mortality suffered under the conditions of the first winter, and how low it

Comparison with rate of Mortality in London Hospitals.

fell under the sanitary improvements of the summer, we must compare it with that of our London General Hospitals. But the comparison is one entirely in favour of Military Hospitals, because, whereas, in these, every man unfit for duty is admitted, whether his case be slight or severe, in the London General Hospitals every case is severe.

Yet, we find, upon consulting the Registrar General's Returns, Vol. xiii, No. 8, p. 57, that in 1851, in the 11 General Hospitals of London, the Mortality per cent. on cases treated 7.6, the annual rate per cent. on sick population was 82. Even in the Fever Hospital, which might be thought to bear some comparison with the War Hospitals invaded by Epidemic Fever, the Mortality per cent. on cases treated was only 11, the annual rate of Mortality per cent. on sick population 110·5.* In the London General Hospitals, above mentioned, the highest rate of Mortality was at University College, being per cent. on cases treated 10·5; per cent. per annum on sick population 134·8. The lowest rate of Mortality was at St. Thomas's, being per cent. on cases treated 5·5; per cent. per annum on sick population, 53.

With rate of Mortality in London Military and Naval Hospitals.

Now let us take the Military and Naval Hospitals in and near London, and we find the Deaths to 100 cases only 2·4; the Deaths to sick population annually per cent. only 39—shewing that, as above stated, the sick population in a Military Hospital at home is a very different one, in the character of severity of its cases, from that in a Civil Hospital, which will be seen in a still more striking light, when we consider that London at the Army ages is nearly twice as healthy as the Army in London, and suffers little more than half its Mortality

The case therefore stands thus:—

Mortality.

		RATE PER CENT PER ANN. ON SICK POPULATION.	PER CENT. ON CASES TREATED.
11 London General Hospitals†		82	7·6
Fever Hospital		110·5	11·3
Military and Naval Hospitals in London		39	2.4
Scutari and Kulali General Hospitals . .	during 4 months	203	19·8
	„ 4 weeks	319	32·1
	„ 4 weeks	415	42·7
Kulali. . . .	„ 4 weeks	608	52
Scutari and Kulali, summer, 1855		34	2·2

* And this is nearly as great as the mortality from Yellow Fever in the Tropics between the beginning and the end of the epidemic.

† The mortality of the London General Hospitals is very much higher

In the London General Hospitals, therefore, 8 out of every 100 cases admitted die. In the Scutari General Hospitals, for several months, 33 out of every 100 cases admitted died. And at Kulali, during one month, above 50 out of every 100 cases admitted died.

In June 1855, again, when the Sanitary improvements were nearly completed, the Scutari rate of mortality fell to less than that of the London Military Hospitals, being 34 per cent. annually on sick population, and 2⅜ per cent. on cases treated.

A singular Statistical problem is thus stated by the Commandant, for the official information of Her Majesty's Government, p. xi:— "Sickness has very much diminished and so has the Mortality. In January last the number of deaths was 1,480, in February, 1,254, and in March, 424, every month showing a steady decrease over the preceding one. The average mortality, at present, is 5⅓ per diem." This problem is much like the celebrated riddle, "Given the height of the mast, to tell the captain's name." *Not* given the numbers in Hospital, to tell whether there is a "steady decrease" in its mortality. The real fact, alas! stood thus,—there was an appalling *increase* of mortality, up to the end of February, reaching nearly 43 per cent., in that month, of cases treated, from 32 per cent., which it was in January. The numbers in Hospital had diminished. Up to March 17 the mortality, although diminishing from what it was in February, which would, indeed, had it continued, have swept away the whole Hospital population in three months, yet continued half as much again of what it was from October 1, 1854, to January 31, 1855.

A "mortality of 5⅓ per diem" does not sound alarming, certainly, but it is 1,877 per *annum*. The fact, however, is useless without the strength—1,877 Deaths on a strength of 8,000 sick, which there was at one time, being a very different thing from 1,877 Deaths upon 3,000 sick, which there was at another time.

So incomplete was the information received by the Secretary of State for War.

Various returns will be given elsewhere (derived from official sources) of the mortality in Hospital. None of these will be

Marginal notes:
Curious Method of calculating rate of Mortality.

Discrepancy of Returns.

than it ought to be—the sanitary conditions of the London Hospitals very, very much lower than they ought to be. The selection of severe cases cannot altogether explain this very high mortality. In drawing any comparison, however, between the mortality in Civil and Military Hospitals, it must be remembered that the ages of cases admitted into the former differ from the ages in the latter, and that the class of constitutions admitted into Civil Hospitals is much worse than the class admitted into Military Hospitals. Civil Hospitals ought, therefore, to yield a higher rate of mortality.

96

found to agree. It is, indeed, impossible that accuracy of returns can be secured under our present system or no system.

In these months of January, February, March, now under consideration, the variations in the returns of mortality are as follows:—*

	Commandant at Scutari	Medical Returns.	Burial Returns.	Adjutant-General's Returns.
				Infantry alone.
January	1,480	1,235	1,473	1,193
February . .	1,254	1,329	1,151	1,261
March	424	555	418	587
TOTAL . .	3,158	3,119	3,042	3,041

Statement in Commandant's Letter about "Ladies and Nurses."

NOTE.—I may add two remarks, in parenthesis:—

(1) I am singularly at a loss to understand what is meant by the following paragraph, in the Commandant's letter, p. xii:—

"I have continual applications from the . . . . ladies and nurses for extra expenses, such as field allowance, forage for horses, servants' allowance, &c.; all of which, except their rations, I do not consider myself at liberty to sanction."

No such application was ever made to the Commandant by any of the "ladies and nurses" under my charge; and with regard to "extra expenses," both for patients and nurses, these were all privately undertaken. The sum of £9,537 12s. 8 1/2d. was thus expended from private funds, of which Her Majesty's Government repaid £2,601 14s. 2 1/2d. The salaries and wages of the ladies and nurses, their travelling expenses, outfits, and Regulation Dress were the only other items paid by the Government. For those expenses of the Nursing Staff, defrayed by me in the East, not a halfpenny was ever advanced to me, with the exception of one credit of £1,000 and another of £1,500, granted me, upon my first going out, by Her Majesty's Government; the money afterwards was always advanced by me. The rations were issued by the Government, but at Scutari nearly all the "extras," including generally tea, butter, wine, &c., both for patients and nurses, which were issued by us,

* The Deaths at Smyrna Hospital were 127, being from February 15 to March 31. This solves the difficulty of the excess of the Medical over the Commandant's Returns, supposing the Principal Medical Officer's Returns to contain these Deaths, during the above period, which, however, he expressly states they do not. But it increases the difficulty of explaining the excess of the Commandant's and Burial Returns over the Medical, during January; and it makes the similarity of the Totals quite inexplicable, excepting upon the supposition of lost ground having been made up by different Authorities in different months.

were provided by private funds. The annexed schedule will shew what was supplied to us by the Purveyor in the Barrack Hospital from November 1854, to December 1855, a period of fourteen months, which comprises all the time during which we issued "Diets" to the patients. The schedule includes all the Purveyor's issues to us, whether for these diets for patients or for rations for the nurses.

The Government was throughout most liberal in sanctioning these efforts of private enterprise; and nothing but thanks is due to them for their support.

It is only in refutation of an unintelligible assertion that this statement ever would have been offered.*

(2). The sentence about "Miss Nightingale's extensive establishment," as tending to fill up the "Barrack" Hospital, and, with others, "requiring necessarily the admission of a proportionate number of workmen," "rendering the building more fit for a Barrack than a Hospital," is obscure.

"Miss Nightingale's extensive establishment," consisting of 40 women, was housed in the Barrack Hospital, in the same space which, in corresponding quarters, was occupied by three Medical Officers and their servants, and in about the same space as was occupied by the Commandant. This was done in order to make no pressure for room on an already over-crowded Hospital. It could not have been done with justice to the women's health, had not Miss Nightingale taken a house in Scutari at private expense, to which every nurse attacked with fever was removed. The number was subsequently thinned by a part being moved into quarters in the General Hospital.

A CASE IN ILLUSTRATION

The tardy and irrelevant, and, so to say, out-of-date working of the Director-General's Department may be well illustrated by the following letter:—

DR. DUMBRECK to A. CUMMING, ESQ.

Army and Ordnance Medical Department,
SIR,   18th May, 1855.
Referring to the evidence of Miss Elizabeth Wheeler, page 329 of "The Report on the State of the Hospitals of the British Army," I am desired by the Director-General to request your attention to the sys-

* No mention is here made of the enormous distribution of private stores, independent of the above sums.

tem at one time apparently obtaining in the hospital under the immediate surveillance of Deputy Inspector-General of Hospitals Dr.
M'Griger, which permitted nurses to exercise their judgment and dis-
cretion in the selection of cases for the treatment of which stimulants
might be applicable. This is a state of things calling for severe repre-
hension, and for your direct and stringent interference, should a recurrence of it be attempted in the hospitals under your superintendence.

I have, &c.

A. Cumming, Esq. (Signed) D. DUMBRECK,
 &c., &c.   for Director General.

Inspector-General Cumming, to whom this letter was
addressed, was Head of the Commission by which the "evidence" in question had been taken. And, in consequence of this
evidence, from which it appeared that the orders of a Medical
Officer had been disobeyed, and his treatment misrepresented,
the Commission had very properly judged it necessary that the
"Sister" implicated should resign, which she did, with the
entire concurrence of the Superintendent-General. Five
months after she had left the Hospitals, the above letter was
written. It was never communicated to the Superintendent-
General at all. If it was no part of the duty of the Director-
General to put a stop to such a contradiction of every maxim of
medicine and of common sense as that of a "Nurse" giving
"stimulants" to patients without the orders of the Medical
Officer, why was the letter written at all? And if it were his
duty to interfere, why was it not done through the only person
who could check any "recurrence being attempted," viz., the
Superintendent of Nurses?

RETURN of Provisions, &c. issued to Miss Nightingale, Barrack Hospital, from November, 1854, to December, 1855, inclusive.

	1854.		1855.												TOTAL.
	Nov.	Dec.	Jan.	Feb.	Mar.	April.	May.	June.	July.	Aug.	Sept.	Oct.	Nov.	Dec.	
Meat, lbs.	1045	1575	2835	2915	3005	2455	1120	779	591	419	485½	483	417	638	18762½
Bread, lbs.	1100	1356	1182	736	976	1072	932	684	654	550	576	586	560	680	11644
Porter, pints	816	864	710	632	632	634	564	164	632	472	286	217	212	923	7558
Ale, pints	48	...	...	...	...	...	...	...	...	144	286	217	212	923	1830
Milk, pints	..	...	...	...	...	...	...	28	72	152	...	4	...	...	256
Fowls, No.	...	...	...	...	...	96	84	1	1	19	18	9	12	9	249
*Eggs, No.	1020	1584	624	...	336	2160	1416	1092	708	744	600	648	408	252	11592
Sugar, lbs.	112	24	...	...	697	840	670	405	360	335	345	361	266	270	4685
Potatoes, lbs.	325	20	...	...	310	...	326	380	424	527	476	450	528	...	3766
Vegetables, lbs.	...	...	1100	1400	1222	571	600	490	422	300	448	230	139	276	7198
Arrow root, lbs.	42	...	112	474	310	420	112	218	252	305	308	336	392	448	3729
Sago, lbs.	...	24	...	50	75	...	6	...	...	...	25	...	...	...	180
Barley, lbs.	...	105	345	475	448	112	137	75	100	95	25	14	36	20	1987
Rice, lbs.	188	473	934	906	1120	1232	437	75	100	125	50	41	56	40	5777
Oatmeal, lbs.	6	...	12	12	24	...	...	...	...	...	...	10	...	...	64
Coffee, lbs.	36	33	56	52	42	48	48	12	24	6	6	2	...	11	376
Tea, lbs.	8	...	...	...	1	...	...	...	...	...	...	...	...	...	9
Brandy, bottles	54	24	24	...	...	...	...	...	...	...	...	...	...	...	102
Marsala, bottles	...	...	...	...	12	32	...	...	...	...	...	...	...	...	44
Preserved Potatoes, lbs.	...	...	...	...	...	...	56	...	...	...	...	...	...	...	56
Essence of Beef, ¼ lbs.	...	10	80	...	...	184	11	...	48	...	24	...	...	...	357
Vinegar, bottles	...	...	...	1	...	4	13	6	6	...	...	...	...	...	30
Oil, pints	7	12	24	...	...	...	...	...	...	...	...	8	22	64	137
Sweetmeats, cases	...	...	...	2	...	...	...	...	...	...	...	...	...	...	2
Olive Oil, bottles	...	...	...	...	...	...	...	...	1	...	...	...	...	...	1
Soda Water, bottles	...	...	...	...	...	6	...	...	6	...	...	...	...	...	12
Soap, lbs.	55	...	...	...	50	80	87	100	87	25	51	77	75	86	773
Soda, lbs.	...	...	...	...	...	10	...	...	...	...	...	...	2	...	12
Candles, lbs.	60	84	132	84	...	...	...	...	72	82	80	80	100	100	874
Lamp Cotton, balls	...	...	...	...	...	...	...	...	...	2	...	...	1	...	3
Salt, lbs.	53	25	12	10	12	12	12	12	10	...	...	2	...	15	175
Oranges, No.	...	...	...	...	...	2176	2232	2160	1608	36	...	...	...	...	8212
Lemons, No.	...	...	...	...	...	...	48	2448	1320	216	84	48	100	24	4288
Ice, lbs.	...	...	...	...	...	...	255	...	...	...	...	...	...	...	255
Preserved Meat, lbs.	...	...	...	...	...	3	...	...	...	...	...	...	...	...	3
Soft Soap, lbs.	...	...	...	...	...	...	...	...	6	...	...	...	...	...	6
Butter, lbs.	...	...	...	...	...	...	...	...	...	10	44	58	92	82	286
Flour, lbs.	...	...	...	...	...	...	...	...	25	71	35	50	40	80	301
Cheese, lbs.	...	...	...	...	...	...	...	...	...	28	21	14	20	17	100
Pepper, lbs.	...	...	...	...	...	2	...	...	...	...	2	...	4	...	8
Mustard, lbs.	...	...	...	...	...	...	...	...	2	2	...	2	...	...	6
Capers, bottles	...	...	...	...	...	...	...	1	...	...	...	...	...	...	1
Pickles, bottles	...	...	...	...	...	...	...	3	...	4	7	5	...	...	19
Syrup de Cerises, bottles	...	...	...	...	...	...	...	1	2	...	...	...	...	...	3
Corks, No.	...	...	...	...	...	...	...	100	...	100	300	...	...	...	500
Gingerette, bottles	...	...	...	...	...	...	...	2	6	6	6	1	1	4	26
Spirits of Wine, bottles	...	...	...	...	...	...	...	...	1	...	...	1	...	...	2
Bath Bricks, No.	...	...	...	...	...	...	...	...	2	...	...	1	1	3	7
Rum, bottles	...	...	...	...	...	...	...	...	1	...	...	...	...	...	1
Vinegar, pints	...	...	...	...	4¼	...	...	...	...	...	10	...	...	...	14¼
Starch, lbs.	...	...	...	...	...	...	...	...	...	15	25	...	...	10	50
Apples, lbs.	...	...	...	...	...	...	...	...	...	...	...	12	36	60	108
Raisins, lbs.	...	...	...	...	...	...	...	...	...	...	...	14	10	33	57
Sauce, bottles	...	...	...	...	...	...	...	...	...	...	...	4	...	...	4
Macaroni, lbs.	...	...	...	...	...	...	...	...	...	...	...	...	6	20	26
Blue, lbs.	...	...	...	...	...	...	...	...	...	...	...	...	2	...	2
Sherry, bottles	...	...	...	...	...	...	...	...	...	...	...	...	6	...	6
Citron, lbs.	...	...	...	...	...	...	...	...	...	...	...	...	...	1	1
Spices, lbs.	...	...	...	...	...	...	...	...	...	...	...	...	...	1	1
Quinces, lbs.	...	...	...	...	...	...	...	...	...	...	...	...	...	6	6
Port Wine, bottles	37	...	...	...	...	...	...	...	...	...	...	...	...	...	37
Cows' feet, No.	32	...	...	...	...	...	...	...	...	...	...	...	...	...	32
Charcoal, lbs.	150	...	...	...	...	...	...	...	...	...	...	...	...	...	150
Lamp wicks, No.	...	...	...	...	...	...	...	...	...	...	...	288	...	...	288
Stout, bottles	...	...	...	...	...	...	...	...	...	16	...	...	...	...	16
Grapes, lbs.	...	...	...	...	...	...	...	...	...	...	20	...	...	...	20
Bacon, lbs.	...	...	...	...	...	...	...	...	...	16	...	...	...	...	16

* The greater part of these eggs, being worthless, was re-supplied to the Extra Diet Kitchens by private means. It appears from the Cumming-Maxwell Report, page 41, which of the articles issued by the Purveyor were not good.

PREFACE

SECTION X.

PART I. AUTHORITIES FOR THE STATISTICS USED IN THE SECTION, WITH AN ENQUIRY AS TO THEIR SUFFICIENCY.

Sources of the Statistics in Section X.

THE whole of the figures in the ensuing Section have been taken from official and authentic sources.

Those, from p. 247 to p. 251, have been taken from Sir A. Tulloch's invaluable "Statistical Report on the Sickness, Mortality, and Invaliding among the Troops in the United Kingdom, 1853," p. 3 to p. 75.

The strengths given, at p. 247, are the aggregate strengths for the 10 years, 1837-1846, and the whole of the data refer to the same period, which is the last given in the Report.

The Civil Mortality, p. 247, is taken upon the Deaths in seven years, 1838—44, in twenty-four large towns, Registrar-General's 8th and 9th Reports, quoted by Sir A. Tulloch, in the same Report, p. 81.

It is gratifying to learn that, during the nine years, 1845-53, the troops serving at home have experienced a slight reduction in the excessive mortality from which they suffer. Although so slight an improvement, it shows that the time is at hand when much greater sanitary advance will be made, and corresponding results enjoyed.

The improvement stands thus:—

Comparison of Rates of Mortality in Army serving at home, 1837—46 and 1845—53.

Annual Mortality per 1,000 of Mean Strength.

	Household Cavalry.	Dragoon Guards and Dragoons.	Foot Guards.	Infantry of Line.
1837—46 (ten years)	11·1	13·5	20·4	17·8
1845—53 (nine ")	10·5	13·2	19·2	16·7

The Table of Pensioners, p. 255, was furnished by Dr. Balfour, the able coadjutor of Sir A. Tulloch, and the materials for the Table at p. 259 by the Adjutant-General's Office.

The Statistics of the Metropolitan Police Force (p. 252), have been taken from M'Culloch's Statistics of the British Empire.

Those of the City Police were furnished by Mr. Borlase Childs, Surgeon to that Force.

Those of the Comparison of the Army serving at home with the Civil Population (pp. 253, 254) were afforded by the Registrar-General, as well as the Corrected Rate of Mortality for the Army at home (Note, p. 253).

A full Table will now be given, also furnished by the General Register Office, correcting the mortality for each arm of the Service at home.

Corrected Mortality for each Arm of the Service at Home.

The explanation of the difference which will be seen between this Table and that given in Sir A. Tulloch's Report, above mentioned, p. 31, is as follows:—

In instituting a comparison between the mortality of different arms of the service, at different ages, it is necessary to take into account the *number* of men in each arm at those ages, and for very obvious reasons:

Each period of 5 years (or any other period) in human life has an average mortality belonging to it, and the *number* of men in the Army at any such period must obviously influence the sum total of life for the period.

The mortality over (say) 5 such periods is made up of the mortality of each period, the whole being added together.

If there be a preponderance in any Arm of numbers at the ages at which the mortality is high, the *whole* mortality will be high.

If there be a preponderance of numbers of low mortality ages, the aggregate mortality will be low.

The problem is, in fact, a fractional one of this kind:—

$\dfrac{Mortality}{Numbers.}$ We must reduce all the fractions of this class to a *common denominator*, before we can either add, subtract, divide or compare them.

TABLE of the Mortality of the British Army, if the rates had been the same as those in—1. The Household Cavalry; 2. Dragoon Guards and Dragoons; 3. Infantry of the Line; 4. Foot Guards—serving at home.

Ages.	Effectives of the British Army. Numbers living in 1851.	Deaths, if the Mortality had been the same as in the				
		Household Cavalry.	Dragoon Guards and Dragoons.	Infantry of the Line.	Foot Guards.	Total of the British Army at home, calculated on the corresponding numbers at the same ages.
Under 20.	11,911	90	99	157	133	146
20—25.	50,387	588	626	896	1,087	858
25—30.	38,242	394	547	758	806	702
30—35.	22,099	293	326	438	431	406
35—40.	10,005	84	153	211	224	193
40 and upwards . .	3,633	49	67	85	95	76
Total	136,277	1,498	1,818	2,545	2,776	2,381

	Rate of Mortality per 1,000.				
	Household Cavalry.	Dragoon Guards and Dragoons.	Infantry of the Line.	Foot Guards.	Total of the British Army at home, calculated on the corresponding numbers at the same ages.
Total	11.0	13.3	18.7	20.4	17.5
Under 20.	7.5	8.3	13.1	11.2	12.2
20—25.	11.7	12.4	17.8	21.6	17.0
25—30.	10.3	14.3	19.8	21.1	18.3
30—35.	13.3	14.8	19.8	19.5	18.4
35—40.	8.4	15.3	21.0	22.4	19.3
40 and upwards.	13.4	18.3	23.4	26.2	21.0

The annual deaths among the 136,277 effectives of the British Army, if the mortality were the same as in the Household Cavalry, would be 1,498; in the Dragoon Guards, 1,818; in the Infantry of the Line, 2,545; in the Foot Guards, 2,776; in the men of all arms in the British Service at home, calculated on the same proportion of ages, it is 2,381.

The annual rate of mortality to 1,000 of the Household Cavalry is 11·0; of the Dragoon Guards, 13·3; of the Infantry of the Line, 18·7; of the Foot Guards, 20·4; and of the men of all arms in the British Service at home, calculated in the same way, it is 17·5.

If the 136,277 soldiers had been subject to the rate of mortality which prevails in the healthiest districts of England, the annual deaths would have been 1,051; in one of the unhealthiest cities (Manchester) 1,688; and in all England, 1,248.

Note.—The numbers of the men living in the British Army, in 1851, are obtained from the Census Report of 1851, Vol. I (Occupations), p. cccxlvi.

A full Table will now be given, showing the mortality of the whole Army, both at home and abroad, during fifteen years, from 1839 to 1853, and calculating the annual mortality upon these data, for both Officers and Men, with the annual mortality in healthy districts in England, annexed for the sake of comparison.

Table of Mortality of the Army at Home and Abroad, 1839—1853.

It will be seen that the soldier suffers a mortality of 33 per 1,000; the Englishman in healthy districts of 7·7 per 1,000;— that is to say, that one Englishman under these circumstances dies where die rather more than four soldiers.

It thus appears that, during a period of 15 years, terminating before the Crimean Expedition, 58,000 of Her Majesty's troops have perished. Comparing these Deaths with those occurring among the healthy part of Her civil subjects, we see that more than three-fourths, or 44,550, would have been saved, had they remained among that civil population, from which most, if not all, of them have come. It may be truly said that by far the larger portion of these 44,550 have been lost from ignorance and want of sanitary foresight. But fatalism is not confined to the Mahomotan races—it may still be found, and very largely, among the Christians.

58,000 than have perished in 15 years.

These are figures on the page—but, to us, these figures are men.

The following Table, a deduction from the last, will make the excess of Mortality existing in the Army over that in Civil Life still more evident.

TABLE shewing the Average Strength, Deaths, and rate of Mortality in each year form 1839 to 1853, of the Officers, Non-Commissioned Officers and Men serving in the Army, exclusive of Artillery, Royal Engineers, West India and Colonial Corps.

Years.	Average Effective Strength.			Deaths.			Annual Mortality to 1,000 living.			Annual Mortality to 1,000 living of Men of the Soldiers' Ages in Healthy Districts, taken on an average of 5 years.
	Officers, Non-Commissioned Officers and Men.	Officers.	Non-Commissioned Officers and Men.	Officers, Non-Commissioned Officers and Men.	Officers.	Non-Commissioned Officers and Men.	Officers, Non-Commissioned Officers and Men.	Officers.	Non-Commissioned Officers and Men.	
1839	104,275	5,363	98,912	3,017	103	2,914	28·9	19·2	29·5	7·7
1840	112,922	5,383	107,539	3,385	85	3,300	30·0	15·8	30·7	7·7
1841	116,523	5,389	111,134	4,278	111	4,167	36·7	20·6	37·5	7·7
1842	120,576	5,390	115,186	5,190	138	5,052	43·0	25·6	43·9	7·7
1843	124,023	5,480	118,543	5,371	101	5,270	43·3	18·4	44·5	7·7
1844	124,826	5,492	119,334	3,944	77	3,867	31·6	14·0	32·4	7·7
1845	123,550	5,479	118,071	4,691	104	4,587	38·0	19·0	38·8	7·7
1846	126,232	5,588	120,644	5,243	118	5,125	41·5	21·1	42·5	7·7
1847	132,811	5,566	127,245	4,317	85	4,232	32·5	15·3	33·3	7·7
1848	133,433	5,512	127,921	3,308	95	3,213	24·8	17·2	25·1	7·7
1849	129,226	5,553	123,673	4,146	94	4,052	32·1	16·9	32·8	7·7
1850	124,657	5,546	119,111	3,189	70	3,119	25·6	12·6	26·2	7·7
1851	122,282	5,452	116,830	2,785	56	2,729	22·8	10·3	23·4	7·7
1852	124,083	5,460	118,623	3,194	74	3,120	25·7	13·6	26·3	7·7
1853	124,711	5,440	119,271	3,454	62	3,392	27·7	11·4	28·4	7·7
Total and Average 1839–53.	1,844,130	82,093	1,762,037	59,512	1,373	58,139	32·3	16·7	33·0	7·7

The facts for this Table have been taken from a Return furnished by the Adjutant-General, July 6, 1857.

NUMBER of DEATHS of NON-COMMISSIONED OFFICERS and MEN, showing also the Number of Deaths that would have occurred if the Mortality were 7·7 *per* 1,000, such as it was among Englishmen of the Soldier's Age in Healthy districts, in the years 1849–53, which fairly represent the average mortality.

YEARS	*Deaths* that *would have occurred* in Healthy Districts among Males of the Soldier's Ages.*	Actual Deaths of Non-commissioned Officers and Men.	Excess of Deaths among Non-commissioned Officers and Men.
1839	763	2,914	2,151
1840	829	3,300	2,471
1841	857	4,167	3,310
1842	888	5,052	4,164
1843	914	5,270	4,356
1844	920	3,867	2,947
1845	911	4,587	3,676
1846	930	5,125	4,195
1847	981	4,232	3,251
1848	987	3,213	2,226
1849	954	4,052	3,098
1850	919	3,119	2,200
1851	901	2,729	1,828
1852	915	3,120	2,205
1853	920	3,392	2,472
Total . .	13,589	58,139	44,550

The Table may be read thus: in the year 1839 the number of Deaths among non-commissioned officers and men was 2,914 out of the strength (98,912, see preceding Table)—whereas the deaths among the same number of men of the same ages in the healthy districts of England would have been only 763; consequently the excess of deaths in the army amounted to 2,151.

After so frightful a table it is necessary to remind ourselves that matters have been much worse, viz., in the Army abroad.

If we compare the rates of Mortality of the Army at the various stations abroad, prior and subsequent to 1837, as Sir A. Tulloch gives us the means of doing, the proof of how much has been done, and how much still remains to be done, will be even more convincing.

* The exact mortality in the healthy districts is :0077112, the logarithm of which (3·8871801) has been used in making this calculation.

		RATIO OF DEATHS* PER 1,000 OF MEAN STRENGTH.	AGGREGATE STRENGTH.
Gibraltar.......	1818—1836	21·4	60,269
	1837—1856	11·7	66,412
Malta	1817—1836	16·3	40,826
	1837—1856	16·5†	47,961
Ionion Islands...	1817—1836	25·2	70,293
	1837—1856	16·4	55,723
Bermudas......	1817—1836	28·8	11,721
	1837—1856	32·3‡	22,398
Canada........	1817—1836	16·1	64,280
	1837—1856	14·1	133,925
Nova Scotia.....	1817—1836	14·7	46,442
	1837—1856	11·9	46,006
Newfoundland...	1825—1836	37·7	3,951
	1837—1856	9·3	6,908
Bengal Presidency	1817—1836	75·5	145,199
	1838—1856	69·5	227,306
Madras Presidency	1817—1836	76	142,939
	1838—1856	38·5	100,545
Bombay Presidency	1817—1836	62·7	66,208
	1838—1856	58·7	96,516

* These Deaths do not include those occurring out of Hospital, either suddenly from disease, or from accident. Nor are the killed in action included.

† The Deaths from Cholera were, prior to 1837, ·8 per 1,000.
          after   „   4·8   „

‡ This was the consequence of Fevers, the Mortality from which was
        11 per 1,000 of Mean Strength, before 1837.
      20·7   „   after, 1837.

			RATIO OF DEATHS PER 1,000 OF MEAN STRENGTH.	AGGREGATE STRENGTH.
Van Diemen's Land . .		1839—1856	7·8	17,600
New Zealand.		1844—1856	9·1	15,128
West Indies	White	1817—1836	78·5	86,661
		1837—1853	60	51,115
	Black	1817—1836	40	40,934
		1837—1853	28·4	19,967
Jamaica	White	1817—1836	121·3	51,567
		1837—1855	58·5	22,100
	Black	1817—1836	30	5,729
		1838—1855	35·3*	13,645
Ceylon . . .	White	1817—1836	69·8	42,978
		1837—1856	36·8	29,908
	Black . .	1837—1856	21·1	35,305
Cape of Good Hope. . . .	White	1818—1836	13·7	22,714
		1838—1856	12	73,508
	Black		10·9	4,136
		1838—1856	13·9†	10,066
Mauritius		1818—1836	27·4	30,515
		1838—1855	22·4	29,178
St. Helena. .		1818,19,29,21,36,37	25·4	5,908
		1837—1856	10·6	8,258

It will be seen from these statements that our home troops have actually suffered more in their own country than the troops do now, who are serving at some of our foreign and Colonial Stations, such as Cape of Good Hope, St. Helena, New Zealand, Van Diemen's Land, Newfoundland, Nova Scotia, Canada, and Gibraltar. Why should this be?

It will also be seen how frightful is the mortality, even now, of the troops in some of Her Majesty's possessions, as the West and East Indies, &c.

Only one-third of the Statistical case has, however, here been given. The other two-thirds, viz., the Recruiting and the Invaliding, remain still to be considered.

Statistics of Recruiting and of Invaliding necessary to make the case complete.

* The Deaths from Cholera were, *after* 1837, 11·7 per 1,000 of Mean Strength; prior to 1837, none.

† The Deaths from Diseases of the Lungs increased from 3·9 per 1,000, before 1837, to 6·7 per 1,000, after 1837.

108

Difficulty of
ascertaining
the relative
Mortality of
the Army and
of Civil Life
with any
precision.

The exact relative mortality of the Army to the mortality among the same ages in civil life is far more difficult to ascertain than would at first sight appear. Among the Civil population the elements of the problem are sufficiently constant, but it is not so in the Army. The first difference between the Civil population and the Army comes into play at the period of recruiting.

There is a process of selection out of the Civil population, whereby about a third of all men of the army ages who present themselves is rejected, as unfit for military service, very often from disease which will eventually shorten life; but the precise number rejected cannot be ascertained exactly.

There is besides a previous process of selection, so to speak, from the circumstance that a certain proportion of the Civil population is unable from sickness to present itself for recruitment, and this part remains to furnish deaths which raise the mortality of the Civil population.

Next, the Army is subject to reduction, and there is every probability that the strongest and most healthy men are retained at such times, and the weakest sent back into the civil population.

Additions to the Army also infuse into it younger and better lives than those already there, a circumstance which likewise interferes with the accuracy of the comparison.

Another disturbing element is invaliding, by which men in bad health are discharged altogether from the Army, and a large number invalided die within the first year, while many others die shortly afterwards from diseases contracted in the service. The ratio of mortality among men serving cannot, therefore, be taken as a ground of comparison with the mortality of the same classes in Civil life. If we had the means, which is certainly not the case at present, of calculating the value of all the elements affecting the life of the soldier, we should find the absolute mortality in the Army greatly higher than the statistics represent, and the comparison with the mortality in Civil life much more unfavourable to the Army.

It would be most desirable in the constitution of the statistical department, which is now contemplated, to provide the means of accurate comparison between the Army and Civil life, which do not now exist.

None of the numbers here given include the killed in action.

Mortality in the Army of the East, in Hospital, during 2¼ Years, from April 1, 1854, to June 30, 1856.

Period.	Years of Life or Aggregate Strength	Average Strength of the Army.	Deaths.	Annual Mortality per Cent.
April 1, 1854, to June 30, 1856 (2¼ years)	79,273	34,526	18,058	22·78

NOTE.—The years of life and the average strength of the Army have been derived from the weekly return of the strength, from April 1855 to May 1856 (inclusive) and for the previous period, April 1854 to March 1855 inclusive, from the return of the Deaths during each month, and from a return of the rate of Mortality during the same periods.

The following Table gives the Classes of Disease from which this mortality arose.

Class of Diseases.	Number of Deaths from specified causes.	Of the Total Deaths the Proportion per cent. from each class.	Of the Total Deaths (exclusive of Violent Deaths) the Proportion per cent. from each class.	Deaths Annually to 100 living.
1. Zymotic	14,507	81·9	94·3	18·7
2. Constitutional	204	1·1	1·3	·3
3. Local	668	3·8	4·3	·9
4. Developmental	19	·1	·1	. .
5. Violent	2,314	13·1	. .	3·0

110

Numbers
remaining
of 10,000
recruits at
each successive
year, serving
at home.

TABLE I.

TABLE showing, of 10,000 Recruits, at the Age 20, the numbers remaining at each successive year of Age, up to 40, and also the Numbers annually eliminated by Invaliding or by Death.—It has been constructed from the facts supplied, by the Army Reports and by the Tables of Dr. Balfour, or Invaliding. The principle of construction is the same as that employed at the General Register Office, in constructing Life Tables. It is assumed that the soldiers enter the Service at the age of twenty years.

Age.	English Soldiers.				Completed Years of Service.
	Living.	Dying and Invalided.	Dying.	Invalided.	
20	10,000	350	169	181	0
21	9,650	325	168	157	1
22	9,325	305	166	139	2
23	9,020	289	164	125	3
24	8,731	278	162	116	4
25	8,453	270	160	110	5
26	8,183	265	159	106	6
27	7,918	264	158	106	7
28	7,654	263	157	106	8
29	7,391	266	155	111	9
30	7,125	271	153	118	10
31	6,854	275	150	125	11
32	6,579	282	147	135	12
33	6,297	288	145	143	13
34	6,009	296	144	152	14
35	5,713	302	144	158	15
36	5,411	307	143	164	16
37	5,104	313	141	172	17
38	4,791	315	138	177	18
39	4,476	318	135	183	19
40	4,158				20

TABLE II.

STRENGTH and Invaliding in the Army serving at Home during the Years 1839–1853. (See Dr. Balfour's Table No. III, p. xviii..)

Years' Service.	Strength.				
	Household Cavalry.	Cavalry, Line.	Foot Guards.	Infantry, Line.	All Arms.
All periods of service ..	18,114	87,129	73,720	308,409	487,372
YEARS.					
0—7	8,332	48,541	36,761	195,628	289,262
7—14	4,988	21,721	20,731	70,549	117,989
14— 21 Infantry	..	..	12,707	39,097	51,804
14—24 Cavalry	4,188	15,453	..	..	19,641
21 and upwards Infantry ..	..	..	3,521	3,135	6,656
24 and upwards Cavalry ..	606	1,414	..	..	2,020

Invalided.

All periods of service ..	589	2,836	2,282	9,859	15,566
YEARS.					
0—7	52	713	526	3,105	4,396
7—14	68	510	335	1,486	2,399
14— 21 Infantry	..	..	254	2,174	2,428
14—24 Cavalry	147	568	..	..	715
21 and upwards Infantry ..	..	..	1,167	3,094	4,261
24 and upwards Cavalry ..	322	1,045	..	..	1,367

PROPORTION OF TROOPS INVALIDED TO 1,000 SERVING AT EACH PERIOD OF SERVICE, AT HOME.

All periods of service .. 31.93

0— 7 .. .. .. 15.19
7—14 .. .. .. 20.34
14—21 } 43.98
24 }
21 and upwards } .. 648.46
24 " }

112

Accumulated
Loss by Death
and Invaliding.

TABLE III.

PROPORTION OF TROOPS, serving at Home, who Died or were Invalided, out of 1,000 serving in the Household Cavalry, Cavalry, and Infantry in three septennial periods of Service.

Ages.	Years of Service.	Deaths at Home	Invalided at Home	Invalided and Deaths
		to 1,000 Serving.		
20—27	0—7	17·41	15·19	32·60
27—34	7—14	18·31	20·34	38·65
34—41	14—21 or 24	19·15	43·98	63·13

The Table may be read thus:—To 1,000 Troops who have served under 7 Years, of the Ages 20 and under 27, 17·41 DIE, 15·19 are INVALIDED, and 32·60 DIE OR ARE INVALIDED ANNUALLY.

NOTE.—Table I was constructed from the facts in Tables II and III.

Comparison
of the Loss
of Veterans
to the Army
as it is now
and as it
might be.

TABLE IV.

TABLE showing the Number of Effectives (distinguishing Young Soldiers from Veterans) remaining (1) in the Army as its is: (2) in the Army in an Improved State—if the number of Annual Recruits were 10,000, and the Army served only at Home in a time of Peace.

	Years of Service.	Ages.	To 10,000 Annual Recruits		Excess of Strength in the Army in an Improved State.
			Army in its present Sanitary State.	Army in an Improved State.	
			Upon the above hypothesis.		
Effectives	0—20	20—40	141,764	166,910	25,146
Young Soldiers	0—10	20—30	84,888	92,305	7,417
Veterans.....	10—20	30—40	56,876	74,605	17,729

NOTES ON THE NECESSITY OF SPECIAL SANITARY FUNCTIONAIRES IN CONNECTION WITH MILITARY HOSPITALS, AND WITH THE ARMY IN GENERAL, BOTH ABROAD AND AT HOME.

Is the *sanitary* or the *sanatory* element of most importance to the health of an Army? Let recent experience shew:—We have seen in the Crimean Army 12,025 men in Hospital, while 11,367 only were effective for duty. If men are not kept in health, an Army may be rendered ineffective by disease, though every sick man may be cured.

Sanitary measures include:—

1. The choice of localities, or (in those which for military reasons must be occupied), the removal of the causes of disease. To this branch belongs especially the selection and construction, the repair and adaptation of buildings, and the sanitary charge and management of towns.

2. The choice of Diet, with regard to climate,

fatigue,

exposure,

and the counteracting of the influence of Diets, unavoidably defective.

3. The choice of clothing with regard to climate, &c.

Various Acts of Parliament having lately passed in England, and Sanitary Commissions having been appointed, as well as sanitary powers given to Boards of Guardians and local Boards of Health, now governing the whole area of England, it cannot but be admitted that Sanitary Science is accepted by the country and by the Government, as necessary to the well-being of the inhabitants—and practical action derived from it is established in law and in fact. *(Necessity of Sanitary Supervision.)*

Therefore to establish a community of 500 to 1,000 Englishmen, densely congregated together, without a sanitary element of government, would not only be wrong in itself, but contrary to the principle distinctly established in this country: It is therefore proposed that a sanitary Officer be added to the Officers of every General Hospital. *(There should be a Sanitary Officer in every General Hospital.)*

He should have distinct powers to demand, in carrying out his objects, the assistance of the Engineer Officer, the Medical Officer, and the Steward. In case of conflicting opinions, the Governor should decide upon each case of sanitary requirement, after hearing the full explanation of these Officers. *(Powers and Responsibility of this Officer.)*

In cases of importance, the opinions of each Officer would be recorded. Under this plan, immediate action is obtained, an amount of independence as great as possible secured to the

Sanitary Officer, and the honour and character of each Departmental Officer secured by record, where desirable.

It is notorious that neither the knowledge nor the means necessary to effect sanitary improvements, at Scutari, existed before the arrival of the Sanitary Commission. The non-cleansing of the Hospital and its appurtenances, the neglect of the ill-constructed and non-acting drains of the place, and the accumulating an indefinite number of sick, as well as of Medical Officers, Orderlies, and Nurses, and soldiers in depot, within a narrow area, in the interior of the Hospital, placed its inhabitants in circumstances far more adverse to cure and to health than are afforded by even the most crowded and unwholesome alleys of the worst towns. No appliances for ventilation were resorted to, and, had they been so, they would have brought in a foetid (although cold) atmosphere, from the state of the yards and external drains.

It may safely be affirmed that even a magnificent stone Hospital, under the above-mentioned circumstances, leaves the soldier in a sanitary condition far inferior to that of the commonest hut. The French Surgeons, long accustomed to Hut Hospitals, in Algeria, distinctly affirmed that they preferred the separate huts in the Seraglio Gardens, at Constantinople, to the splendid Hospital on the heights of the "Campo di Pera;" and they were right. In this building, as at Scutari, the corridors, however wide and commodious, with their staircases and the wards opening into the corridors, acted as a series of tunnels towards the establishment of an uniform Hospital atmosphere, less salubrious than the external air.

The evils of Scutari have been fully described. The measures taken by the Sanitary Commission were as follow:

1. As to over-crowding.

They removed one row of beds from the Corridors of the Barrack Hospital; they fixed the distance of the beds at not less than six feet from head to head; they allowed not less than 1,000 cubic feet of space for each bed.

2. As to ventilation.

They introduced everywhere in the Hospitals plates of perforated zinc or wire gauze; and ventilating shafts for the escape of foul air in the ceiling of each ward.

3. As to drainage.

They drained the site of Haida Pacha, called the Palace Hospital; they closed fifty open privies under the wards at Kululi, removed 200 cavalry horses in one of the basements there, and closed the wards and quarters over them.

They closed the Stable Hospital at Scutari, and the two Convalescent Ships in the Golden Horn at Constantinople.

They constructed a large flushing tank at the head of every drain, which was flushed several times a day in order to sweep out the contents of the sewers into the sea.

The latrines, sewers, and drains, were cleansed and deodorized with peat charcoal. The sewers were trapped and ventilated, so as to prevent the wind blowing up through them into the Hospitals.

The outskirts of the Hospitals were daily cleansed.

4. As to cleanliness.

They ordered constant lime-washing for the walls and ceilings of all the Wards and Corridors, in order to cleanse and disinfect their saturated surfaces.

All this ought to have been done and finished before the Hospitals were occupied. It matters not whether or not these evils had been reported on. It is evident that the present system does not ensure the putting such buildings as those of the Scutari Hospitals into fit order for the admission of sick, before such sick are admitted. This is what is necessary, if the many lives are to be spared, which were sacrificed here. All these sanitary measures ought to have been taken from the first. The disgrace to our service is, not so much that they were not more speedily executed, as that they should ever have been required.

But then, as now, no adequate estimate of their importance had ever been formed, nor does it now exist. Much is thought of the importance of keeping a position against the enemy—little of that of keeping it against disease. Even now, sanitary measures are still called "humbug," although we have lost half an army by disease.

It is quite evident that, at the present time, considering the great advance during the last ten years of Sanitary Science and practical sanitary improvements in England (enforced by law, under appeals to the tribunals), no Army Medical Officer, having been on service during that period, can have acquired a competent knowledge of the subject. His sphere of observation, contined to a single regiment, or even to a detachment, is far too limited to give him a practical command of the subject.

The Sanitary Officer in a General Hospital should not be an Army Medical Officer.

It is therefore evident that, for the immediate purpose, no Medical Officer should be allowed to undertake the charge of a Sanitary Department in a Hospital, unless he has gone through the practical study of the science in civil life in England.

In order, then, to prove that the sanitary element is necessary to an army on active service, we have, first, the circumstances which

Necessity of having a Sanitary Officer attached to the army.

116

led to the appointment of the Sanitary Commission of the Army in the East; secondly, a large portion of the details which form its evidence. And in general, antecedent to the events of the War, we have at home a mass of facts such as those at the Serpent's Nest, at York, at Newcastle and Gateshead, and in Soho, London, which justify the proceedings of Sanitary Commissions and Boards, and of Cholera Investigations, &c., during the last ten years, in Great Britain. The military mode, probably, of representing this sanitary element would be a sanitary Officer, of superior attainments, placed not merely in every General Hospital, but in every Quarter-Master General's office, at Head Quarters.

He should have the power of reporting home and be independent and responsible for the execution of all necessary operations.

This Sanitary Officer ought not only to have power to record his observations and make his reports to the Commander of the Forces, like any other Officer, as well as to Generals of Brigades and Divisions, Commandants, or Town Majors, Naval Officers commanding ports used for military purposes, but the independent power of reporting home. In the meantime he would also have the power of demanding the means for enforcing such executive operations as would not interfere with the military tactics, or the military safety of the troops.

(Dr. Jackson's Statement, in 1799.)

That the above is neither drawn from partial observation nor from hasty conclusion will at once appear by the following quotation. Dr. Robert Jackson, in 1799, after recording the "state of things" which he considers "injurious to the character of the officer and the welfare of the soldier," prophesies (in the following words) that it "will continue until physicians have the place in Councils of Military Commanders that is due to science. The health history of the late wars in Europe is demonstrative in proof of the important fact that military life has been sacrificed in an enormous proportion to ignorance, i. e., to the unwillingness of Commanders to be advised on subjects which they could not themselves be supposed to know."

After half a century of progress in the division of labour, and what may be called the recognition of Sanitary Science in the last ten years, and after its progressive development up to this hour, the "Physician" of Dr. Jackson must be taken in the double sense of Sanitary philosopher and Medical Officer, a position occupied, indeed, by himself alone.

This Officer also should not be an Army Medical Officer.

Enough has been said, it is hoped, to show that this Officer also should not be an Army Medical Officer: the office of the Sanitary Officer and of the Medical Officer cannot be filled be the same person, however much it may be necessary for the latter to have Sanitary acquirements.

We are speaking of the Superior Sanitary Officer, attached to the Quarter-Master General's Department; the Medical Officer or Assistant would be the local adviser and enforcer of Sanitary measures, under the Sanitary officer: for the representatives of the Sanitary Officer, in different stations, would probably be, most conveniently, Medical Officers, specially instructed.

The want of sanitary care in the harbour of Balaclava, generally, is well known, and how late it was before any attempt was made for the formation of quays, or for raking the surface of the water, as it may be called, and towing the results to sea. Even after much had been done in the way of improvement, some of the dead carcasses were, nevertheless, allowed to collect, when driven by the eddy, immediately under the Castle Hospital heights. Dead horses were buried in the Sick Wharf at Balaclava; and the salt water filtering through, this nuisance became intolerable every evening after sunset in May, 1855, and most conducive to bowel complaints.

Instances showing the necessity of such a functionary. Balaclava.

In short, the following may be taken as a fair account of the condition of Balaclava, a town of from 500 to 600 inhabitants, in the spring of 1855, six months after we had occupied it, and at the time of the arrival of the Sanitary Commission.

Its condition in the Spring of 1855.

The east side of the harbour was, from end to end, a mass of putrefying animal and vegetable matter; dead animals were floating in the harbour; the village was filthy—there were no slaughter-houses and few latrines. The whole town was smelling of sulphuretted hydrogen. The horrible condition of the graveyard at the head of the harbour will be elsewhere spoken of.

The question is not, here, had recommendations been made to remove these evils?

This was the state the town was in—of this there is no question. The Commandant and Admiral were, it is true, using their best exertions, but the case appeared almost hopeless. It is far easier to prevent than to remedy such a state of things. The necessity of an Officer of Health, or his equivalent, was made apparent. Sanitary measures ought to have been taken immediately on the occupation of the town, and a sanitary police at once organized. From May till September, 1855, there were outbreaks of cholera and fever both in the shipping and the town. Admiral Boxer himself died of cholera early in June.

A few words will here be said on the course taken by the Sanitary Commission, in order to illustrate the steps necessary in such a case.

Improvements effected after the arrival of the Sanitary Commission.

118

The graveyard, and all filth that could not be burnt, were covered with lime, charcoal, and earth. Latrines were erected; a cleansing staff was organized; a Russian barge, which had been blown out of the harbour of Sevastopol, was employed at Balaclava in carrying such refuse out to sea as could not be burnt on shore; a slaughtering place was provided; houses were lime-washed inside and out; the shoal water at the head of the harbour filled up; the decaying matter along the east side of the harbour deodorized, and covered in with temporary quays. Drains were made; one of the sources of water supply was covered over. Three Naval Surgeons daily made an inspection of the ships; cleansed, lime-washed, fumigated, ventilated, or removed the ships out of harbour. Dead animals were towed to sea. The worst houses were pulled down. These works advanced slowly, from the deficiency of labour; but, by the end of July, they were so far advanced that the Commandant could carry them on alone—and Balaclava became, what it might have been from the beginning, as healthy a little seaport as can be seen.

The Camp. A very few words will suffice, in like manner, to describe the sanitary condition of the Camp.

Instances of the advantageous operation of Sanitary functionaries. Comparatively little had here to be done by the Sanitary Commission, and that chiefly in the construction of huts. Many were unventilated, many were partially buried, or had earth heaped up against them. There was fever in consequence. Ridge ventilation was introduced, the earth cut away, the sites drained, the huts lime-washed outside.

The camps of the Guards before Sevastopol, and of the Highland Brigade beyond Kamara, became sanitary models. Little fault can be found with the arrangements of the second winter. The large drains along the roads had a most beneficial effect.

Case of the 79th Regiment in Huts North-east of Balaclava. The following is an instance which shows the usefulness of a Sanitary Commission, when its powers can obtain any promptness of remedial action. About April, 1855, a great number of the 79th Regiment, part of Sir Colin Campbell's Brigade, were ill with fever, having been hutted on the heights to the north-east of Balaclava. The Sanitary Commissioners, having inspected the ground in consequence of Sir C. Campbell's representation, called his attention to the topographical defects of the spot. The huts were indeed placed on the sloping base of a steep acclivity, and stood upon clay and shale, one-fourth of each hut being "inserted" into the cutting of the hill. The result was, that the whole of the rain and moisture from the heights (the case being similar to that of Gateshead) was deposited beneath the huts, and even what would have in time oozed through towards the lower ground, was attracted by the heat of the men's bodies lying in the huts, the floors of which were not more than two inches above the surface. Sir C. Campbell was told that the cause must be local, and that the fever was generated by warm damp, in proof of which, when he ordered a board to be taken up, the General's can pierced through the oozy ground beneath, and was drawn up in a stinking state. In consequence of this, the sick were taken out and placed under canvass on the hill-side higher up, and recovered. The men were also removed higher up, and the fever immediately abated.

The 79th embarked for Kertch, but on May 25, 1855, the 31st arrived from Corfu and were quartered in the empty huts. They were almost immediately attacked with Cholera, of which thirty-four died. The 31st were marched to the front, but they carried the Cholera with them, and seventeen more deaths occurred. The huts remained empty from June till November, when four companies of the Royal Artillery were landed and marched to these heights. Three were quartered in these huts, and one in the immediate vicinity. Seven men died of Cholera in the huts, none in the company not in the huts. Upon all being moved out, and the same huts removed, and re-erected for the reception on higher ground immediately above, only one more case of Cholera died. *Mortality of the 31st and of four Companies of the Artillery in these huts.*

One of the first charges naturally given to a Sanitary Officer, would be that of the water supply, as to its quantity and quality. In all times, camps have been chosen with great regard to the supply of water, and always must be so; and the selection of the best springs, and economy in the use of them, will obviously conduce to the maintaining a position. During the occupation of the Crimea, no wells were at first sunk, except by the Naval Brigade. A great want of economy was observed in the use of water, by the horses being allowed to drink in the pools which had been formed, instead of the water being baled or raised with hand-pumps into casks. One portion of the British Cavalry was, however, supplied by a stream conducted into wooden troughs, viz., the Light Cavalry Brigade. The water down several ravines of limestone was allowed to trickle away and form marshy swamps, when it might have been arrested by short and low dams, and a little side walling, as used universally all over the East. The Sanitary Commission, it is known, reported upon this subject; and also, as required, gave in some opinions on the spot. *The Supply of Water.*

The fears which the progress of the hot weather, towards the middle of May, 1855, naturally created, were, however, cut short by the advance of the Allied Force, on the arrival of the Sardinians, which gave us possession of a considerable part of the Tchernaya. The fears at home on the same subject, arising out of the obvious reduction of water in a limestone country in the summer, may be judged of by the fact that not only a distilling vessel was sent out, but an expedition was talked of, with the object of pumping water out of the Tchernaya to the plateau, where the chief part of the army was encamped. This, however, was not carried out; the water-supply being, in fact, sufficient for an Army of ten times the strength; but large portions of the cavalry and other horses were habitually watered at the river during the rest of the year.

Medical men have not in general given any special study to Sanitary Science.

It may appear as if the question of the Medical Officers having an amount of sanitary knowledge, ready for immediate application, had been passed over. But when it is considered what is the multitude of sanitary facts brought to light in every town in England, and what the expensive action resulting from them, and also that every little town in England has several medical men, and yet no discovery or abatement of nuisances took place before the inquiries referred to; it is no discredit to the Army Medical Officers to suppose them not to be informed of the malign influences of causes, more or less difficult to detect, in a country which they have never seen before, and in a place where they are almost momentary sojourners.

Farther than this, Medical education as well Civil as Military, which includes the study of the organs of the human body in their normal state, that of their attributes or powers, that of these organs in their abnormal or diseased state, that of the art of healing, does not include the preservation of the human body from noxious influences, any more than it does from mechanical violence; in other words, the removing the human body from the causes of disease, or *vice versa* removing the causes. In general terms, these causes are removed by draining and ventilation, and the supply of wholesome aliment. This latter, which is called Sanitary Science, forms no part of the education of the medical man, nor is his observation exercised thereon in after life. The individual or the nation has been willing to pay for a restorative process, feeling the inconvenience of want of health, announced by pain or local inability. But the individual or nation has not hitherto been willing to pay for "preventive" action, securing the person from evils which, though he does not feel, the forewarnings of Science can indicate with certainty. From this false security the nation has been already awakened. It is only reasonable to require that the Army should be so also.

These are the arguments which, maturely considered, should lead, it is presumed, to the establishment of a Sanitary element, in addition to the Curative element long attached to the British Forces.

Whether the preceding conclusions should be limited to Armies in the field, and Hospitals at the base of operations; whether or not there is any similar want of sanitary improvement and sanitary supervision, in our military arrangements at home and in time of peace, may appear from considering the simple question:—

Is there excess in the mortality of Military over Civil Life? To estimate this we must compare similar ages.

Excessive Mortality among Soldiers, as compared with Civilians in large towns.

Annual Ratio of Deaths per 1,000 living.

AGES.	CIVIL.	GUARDS.	LINE.
20—25	9·6	21·6	17·8
25—30	10·4	21·1	19·8
30—35	11·4	19·5	19·8
35—40	16·1	22·4	21
40—45	16·7	26·2	23·4
45—50	24·5	26·2	23·4

The above Table refers to Troops serving in the United Kingdom.

It appears, therefore, that, in the Army, from the age of 20 to 35, the Mortality is nearly double that which it is in Civil Life.

The Civil Mortality takes the population of 24 large towns.*

The respective Strengths of the Guards and Infantry of the Line, taken according to the age of the men, are:

	GUARDS.	LINE.
Under 20	4,215	33,463
20—25	13,396	57,291
25—30	9,250	27,861
30—35	6,106	22,323
35—40	4,518	14,401

* The annual rate of mortality, among men living in the healthy districts of England, from 20—40, is 8 per 1,000; in London rather more than 11 per 1,000. Any rate above this is excessive, unnatural, preventible. The annual rate of mortality in the metropolitan police (1839—45) was 8 in 1,000; in English gaols the mortality of the prisoners was at the rate of 16 in 1,000, double the rate in the police force, but considerably less than the rate which has prevailed in the Guards and the Line at home. Such is the result of the want of Sanitary arrangement in our Army—See M'Culloch's Stat. of the British Empire, Vol. II, p. 565 and p. 581.

122

	Above 40	2,635	2,861
		40,120	158,200

Under 20, the respective Mortalities of the Guards and Line are 11.1 and 13.1. One-fifth of this age are Drummer Boys, between 14 and 18; the rest Recruits, between 18 and 20.*

Above 40, the reduction of the mortality in Military Life to a rate more nearly approaching that of Civil Life must be imputed to the discharge of sickly men.

Excessive Amount of Sickness in the Guards. The average period of sickness to each man in the Guards serving in the United Kingdom is, annually, 15½ days; the ratio per 1,000 constantly sick 42.9.

In Civil Life the average periods of sickness to each member of Friendly Societies is 8¼ days annually, or little more than half of what occurs among Soldiers. This refers to cities; but, in smaller towns, it is only 6¾ days annually in Civil Life.

It is said, that no comparison can be made between Military and Civil Life, because a soldier goes into Hospital for any cause which makes him ineffective, but which would not, in Civil Life, have incapacitated the person for daily labour, or found any record in Statistics; but, on the other hand, this instant recourse to medical treatment and means of cure ought to make the duration of disease less in the Soldier than it is in Civil Life. But this is not the result.

Taking 43 per 1,000 to be the average daily sick in the Guards, the number of days' sickness among 1,000 soldiers in each year would be 15,695, which, divided by the admissions into Hospital, being 862, give 18 days' duration of each attack. In the Line the average ratio of admissions into Hospital is 1,044 per 1,000 of mean strength; the proportion constantly

---

* The average annual ratio of Deaths per 1,000 of mean strength, including all ages, is,

GUARDS.	LINE.
20·4	17·8

The Guards are considered the finest obtainable troops in Her Majesty's Service, and yet the mortality among them, on home stations, when compared with that of country populations at home, and with the mortality of the Army in the Crimea, before the evacuation, shows an excess of 12 per 1,000 per annum. If the whole Army of, say, 100,000 men consisted of Guards, the loss of life from preventible disease would be equal to 1,200 men, or an entrie Battalion per annum, or twice our whole loss in action at Inkermann.

sick in the Line serving in the United Kingdom is 48 per 1,000; the average duration of each attack of sickness 17 days.*

Subject to so high a rate of inefficiency as this, the Army, it would seem, and not the worst part of our worst towns, must be now our illustration of the destruction caused by bad sanitary conditions. Instead of talking about the "healthy state," it must be called the *unhealthy* state of Her Majesty's troops; and, if it be remembered that the mortality during the last 22 weeks of our service in the Crimea was as low among the men as 12½ per 1,000, *i. e.*, nearly as low as it is in Civil Life in London, the above numbers may indeed make us ashamed.

We hear with horror of the loss of 400 men on board the "Birkenhead," by carelessness at sea; but what should we feel, if we were told that 1,100 men are annually doomed to death in our Army at home by causes which might be prevented?—as a much larger number have been doomed by causes which are now prevented. See our experience in the West Indies, where men fed for seven days in the week on salt meat, at one shilling per pound, in barracks on the low ground, died; where now men fed for two days in the week on salt meat, and for five days on fresh, at five pence per pound, live; having been moved to the high ground.

The men in the "Birkenhead" went down with a cheer. So will our men fight for us to the last with a cheer.—The more reason why all the means of health which Sanitary Science has put at our command, all the means of morality which Educational Science has given us, should be given them.

The Statistics of Invaliding show some improvement in the last twenty years, but are still excessively high. *Statistics of Invaliding.*

The invaliding in the Guards which was, from 1830 to 1836, 36·4 per 1,000, fell from 1837 to 1846, to 27·8 per 1,000: the chief reduction being in the invaliding of those under 14 years' service speaks much for the improvement of health. In 1846, this was still however 12·7 per 1,000; a very high rate, as disabilities at that period are likely to be real, while after 21 years' service they are only nominal. Because, by the Regulations of the Army, a discharge could not be obtained, even after the completion of 21 years' service, without pleading some disability.

In 1846, the ratio of invaliding per 1,000 of strength above 21 years' service was 10·6; but a high ratio at this period indicates only how large a number have lived to see so many years' service.

* May not this (hitherto) unaccountable excess of sickness have been the origin of the word "malingering"—the Medical Officer not having been able to account otherwise for the sickness!

124

Rate of
Mortality in
the Line and
the guards, in
the ten years
1837—46.

The Mortality in the Line from 1837 to 1846 was in the ratio of 17·8 per 1,000; being 4·3 higher than in the Cavalry.

This includes all the Line serving in the United Kingdom, except those Regiments recently arrived from foreign service, which would have raised the mortality higher by 6 per 1,000.

Considering that Soldiers are all "picked lives"—considering that so little of this mortality has "arisen from service out of the United Kingdom, it is indeed remarkable to find the loss greater than in Civil Life, in the proportion of 17·9 to 11·9, being exactly one-half more."

The Mortality per 1,000 is therefore

CIVIL LIFE IN TOWNS*	LINE.	GUARDS.
11·9	17·8	20·4

	BY FEVERS.	CONSUMPTION.
Civil in Towns	1·2	6·3 per 1,000
Guards.	2·4	13·8 "
Line	2·5	10·2 "

Why is there a greater amount of Mortality from Lung Disease alone in the Guards than from all Diseases put together in Civil Life?

The cause is made sufficiently plain by looking at their Barrack accommodation and their mode of life.

When the Line is put under the same conditions, the Line loses in the same or a still greater proportion; whereas, when the Guards, whose loss in England is 20·4 per 1,000, are sent to Canada, their loss is only 14·5 per 1,000, being less than that of the Line, which is there 16·5 per 1,000.

In the Tower, the Annual Deaths from Fever, of the Guards, for the period under review, was

4·1 per 1,000,

in St. George's Barracks

1·2 per 1,000 only.

This does not include those deaths which took place from the after consequences of fever, which are often disease of the lungs.

The proportion of deaths to cases of typhus is

* This is the unhealthy towns. It should be 8¾ only per 1,000.

Guards 1 to 3½,
Line   1 to 4,

which is fully as high as in West Indian Fevers.

Well may we say what was said of another Service: "The records show that the mortality may be raised to any extent; and that the Heads of the Department have the men's lives so absolutely in their hands that a given number may be put to death at will, without employing any other agency than bad food and bad air. To establish this fact, we shall state two or three experiments upon a large scale," (of which the Crimean expedition may be called the most remarkable,) "with others to show that the mortality may be brought down to an inconsiderable fraction."

We will take the Statistics of the Metropolitan Police Force, which is somewhat similar in the nature of its duty to the Guards.

Comparison with the rates of Mortality and Sickness in the Metropolitan Police.

ANNUAL MORTALITY PER 1,000

1831—38	9·4
1839—45	7·7

DAYS OF SICKNESS TO EACH MAN.

1831—38	10
1839—45	7·7

The average age at which the men enter is 28½.

The average duration of service 3 years.

The average number constantly sick 28 per 1,000, or nearly three years' sickness to each death.

They are "select" lives. Each man has to walk about 25 miles per day. During two months out of three, each Police Constable is on night duty, for nine hours each night.

The following table presents a comparison, in various more minute points, between the Guards and the City Police of 1856.

In the City Police of 1856.

	GUARDS.	CITY POLICE.
Average days of sickness to each man	15½	13 per 1,000
Average duration of attack of sickness	18	9 "
Admissions to hospital	862	1123 "
Constantly sick	43	36½ "
Mortality	20·4	7 "

Summary.

The whole case of the Mortality of the Army at home, as compared with that of the General Population, may be summed up in a very few words, with the aid of the following tables:—

126

Comparison of Mortality in Army with that of Civil Population.

No. 1.—Rate of Mortality per 1,000 per Annum (taking, among the Civil Population, the same ages as those of the Men of the Army).

Effective men of the Army at home   Total . . . . 17·5
                                        Guards . . . . . . 20·4
                                        Line. . . . . 18·7*

Population of England and Wales   Country. . . . . . 7·7
                                        General. . . . . . 9·2

Two of the unhealthiest Cities in England—
         Manchester and Liverpool   12·4

Relative Mortality of Army and Civil Population, at corresponding Ages.

No. 2.—Relative Mortality of the Army at home and of the English Male Population, at corresponding ages.

AGES.   DEATHS ANNUALLY TO 1,000 LIVING.
20—25 . . Englishmen . . . .   8·4
          English soldiers   17·0
25—30 . . Englishmen . . . .   9·2
          English soldiers   18·3
30—35 . . Englishmen . . . . 10·2
          English soldiers   18·4
35—40 . . Englishmen . . . . 11·6
          English soldiers   19·3

Mortality of Army ought-to be less than that of Civil Life: and is double.

That is to say, if the Army were as healthy as the population from which they are drawn, they would die at one-half the rate they die at now.

The Army are picked lives, and the inferior lives are thus thrown back among the mass of the population.

The health of the Army is continually kept up by an influx of fresh lives, while those which have been used up in the service are also thrown back into the general population, and give, as will presently be shown, a very high mortality.

Considerations essential in estimating relative Healthiness of one Arm to another.

* The apparent discrepancy between the Mortality of the Line, as stated here, and as given at pp. 247, 248, 251, will be explained by the following consideration:—

We cannot, on such a Table as that given at p. 247, judge of the relative healthiness of one Arm to another, unless the proportion of Ages to Total Strength be identical.

If the proportion of the Ages is not exactly the same in each Arm of the Service, then, although the mortality at each age may be safely compared, the Mortality for all Ages may be fallacious, if compared.

The rate of Mortality per 1,000 after correction, is—

HOUSEHOLD CAVALRY.	DRAGOON GUARDS AND DRAGOONS.	LINE.	FOOT GUARDS.	TOTAL OF THE BRITISH ARMY SERVING AT HOME.
11·0	13·8	18·7	20·4	17·5

The general population includes, besides those thus rejected by the Army itself (whether in recruiting or in invaliding), vagrants, paupers, intemperate persons, the dregs of the race, over whose habits we have little or no control. The food, clothing, lodging, employment, and all that concerns the sanitary state of the soldier, are absolutely under our control, and may be regulated to the smallest particular.

Yet, with all this, the mortality of the Army, from which the injured lives are *subtracted*, is double that of the whole population, to which the injured lives are added.

As allusion has been made to the very high rate of Mortality among the Invalided, which would considerably raise that among the Effectives, if taken into account, we add—

No. 3.—A Table showing the Number of Men placed on the Pension List, in the five years 1849-53, and the Number of these who have Died, within Twelve Months after being Pensioned.*

Mortality
among
Pensioners.

PLACED UPON PENSION LIST IN 5 YEARS 1849—53.		DIED WITHIN 12 MONTHS AFTER BEING PENSIONED.	ANNUAL RATIO OF DEATHS PER 1,000.
Household Cavalry . . .	194	29	149·48
Cavalry of the Line . . .	1,547	85	54·95
Foot Guards	934	115	123·13
Infantry of the Line . .	13,582	1,056	77·75
Colonial Corps	501	15	29·94
Horse Artillery	154	7	43·41
Foot Artillery	1,069	74	69·22
Sappers and Miners . .	197	16	81·22
. . . .			
. . . .	18,178	1,397	76·85

Conclusions
from Tables
of Mortality
of Prisoners.

* The conclusions upon this table are as follow:—

1. That the Army Statistics give no real idea of the Mortality.

There is this essential difference between the Registrar-General's and the Army Medical Returns,—

The first give the precise per-centage of Deaths to Population, within Army Ages; the second give no precise per-centage of Deaths to Army Population.

Soldiers die to the Army in two ways, viz., by death and by invaliding. The State loses them equally whether they die, or are invalided before their time of service is completed.

By the above table it appears that more than eighteen entire Regiments were lost to the Service in five years.

2. That the Army Mortality, as hitherto stated, cannot be accurately compared with that of Civil Life, at the same ages. To say that the Mortality in the Guards is double that of Civil Life is to make an under-statement of the truth. It is more nearly treble. For the Army Mortality merely shows the Deaths among those staying in

In order to estimate the difference which this would make, in calculating the rate of mortality among the effectives, we require to know what is the mean *strength* of the several Arms, from which the Pensioners come, during the five years.

Assume that the aggregate strength of the Foot Guards was as in 1842—6, viz., 22,948.

We must add for the strength of the Pensioners—

$$\frac{934 + (934 - 115)}{2} = 934 - 58 = 876$$

the Service long enough to die in it. It does not show the Deaths among those discharged to die elsewhere.

A low rate of mortality, therefore, may not imply not a high state of health, but a high rate of invaliding.

And Statistics thus arranged may give all the results which Sanitary measures would give.

For, if every man likely to die were invalided, the Army would appear immortal; for not a man in it would ever die.

The above table shows that, in five years, nearly $1\frac{1}{2}$ Regiments were swept away, within twelve months, after invaliding.

And most of these men who died were between 30—35 years of age, had had an average of ten years' service; for those invalided after completing their term are not those who show this high rate of mortality, as their disabilities are likely to be only nominal.

The difference between the different Arms shows that method by which the apparent Mortality in some is reduced, *e.g.*, that the Life Guards is stated at 11 per 1,000 (*v.* p. 253. Note), while their Invalids actually reach an Annual Mortality of nearly 150 per 1,000—that of the Invalids of the Horse Artillery being as low as $43\frac{1}{2}$ per 1,000.

3. The result of these considerations is that, as we do not possess reliable Statistics of the Army Mortality, we cannot accurately compare with those which we have the rate of Mortality in our Army with that of any other Armies.

Nor can we compare it with Civil Life.

Nor can we even compare Regiment with Regiment.

In order to enable us to do this, the Statistics of the Army must include,—

(1.) Accurate tables of invaliding, stating the disease and deaths for twelve months, or such other period, if practicable, as would include the termination of the cases up to what would have been the termination of the man's service. Deaths from other disease, not contracted in service, should not be included.

(2.) Accurate tables of the annual drafts of health lives, at know ages, into the Army.

(3.) The adoption of an accurate nomenclature and classification of disease and mortality.

4. The true Army Mortality would than be calculated as follows:—

Mortality in Army Hospitals, *plus* that from all disease or injuries of which men are invalided, *minus* that from diseases or injuries taking place after what would have been the expiration of the term of service—the percentage being taken on the active Force, *plus* the Invalids.

Thus making the aggregate strength for a year 23,824, out of which—

> 454 Effectives
> 115 Pensioners
> ———
> 569 died in the year.

Thus the mortality was at the rate of 24 in 1,000 annually, among the Effectives and Pensioners, whereas the mortality among the Effectives alone was—

$$\frac{454}{22,948} = 20 \text{ in } 1,000.$$

But, to make the comparison at all fair, between the mortality of the Foot Guards and that of the General Population, some allowance must be made for the selection at entry, which excludes the sick.

This may be put down as nearly equivalent to half the Deaths among the Pensioners. Thus the true Strength and Deaths will be about—

E.g., take a case:—

STRENGTH.	DEATHS.	INVALIDED.	DEATHS OF INVALIDED.*
10,000	100	1,000	100

This Mortality would, according to present Statistics, be represented at 10 per 1,000 upon 10,000, but, in reality, it would be 18.2 per 1,000 upon 11,000.

If it is impracticable to trace each case to the end of the man's term of service, take a year or some other convenient period, as the term for calculation.

5. Preventible invaliding is of just as much importance as preventible sickness or death.

Invaliding is, in fact, only another term for the man becoming dead to the Service.

By the above Table it appears that , estimating a soldier of ten years; service at only £100, the annual *premature* invaliding of 4,000 men is equal to imposing on the country a tax of £400,000 per annum.

No Army Statistics give real information to the country which do not give—

(*a*) Strength of its Army.

(*b*) Annual drafts from its population required to keep up the Army.

(*c*) Amount of sickness,
> > mortality,
> > invaliding.

(*d*) How much of this sickness
> > mortality,
> > invaliding,

is preventible.

* Within term of service.

130

	STRENGTH.	DEATHS.
Effectives	22,948	454
Pensioners	876	115
Excluded Sick of Dangerous Diseases	438	58
	24,262	627

The real annual Mortality per cent. of the Foot Guards, after correction, is 26 annual deaths to 1,000 living, whereas the mortality of the male population, at the same ages, is about 9 annual deaths to 1,000 living, or one where there would be three in the Guards.

No. 4.—Average Strength and Deaths in each year, from 1849—53, of the Non-commissioned Officers and Men serving in the Army.
CAVALRY, GUARDS, AND INFANTRY
(*exclusive* of West India and Colonial Corps, Artillery, and Royal Engineers).
Non-Commissioned Officers and Men.

YEARS.	EFFECTIVES. AVERAGE STRENGTH.	TOTAL DEATHS.	RATE OF MORTALITY PER 1,000
1849	123,673	4,052	
1850	119,111	3,119	
1851	116,830	2,729	
1852	118,623	3,120	
1853	119, 271	3,392	
	597,508	16,412	27·4

Now the number of men placed on the Pension List, in the five years 1849—53, and the number of these who died within twelve months after being pensioned, were, as has been seen,—

PLACED UPON PENSION LIST IN 5 YEARS 1849—53.		DIED WITHIN 12 MONTHS AFTER BEING PENSIONED.	ANNUAL RATIO OF DEATHS PER 1,000.
Household Cavalry ...	194	29	149·48
Cavalry of the Line...	1,547	85	54·95
Foot Guards	934	115	123·13
Infantry of the Line ..	13,582	1,056	77·75
	16,257	1,285	82·2*

$$* \frac{16,257 + (16,257 - 1,285)}{2} = 15,614.$$

Then $\frac{1,285 \times 1,000}{15,614}$ a mortality of = 82·2 per 1,000 per annum.

To find the Mortality of the Army, with the addition of the Pensioners, we must take—

	STRENGTH.	DEATHS.
Army.	597,508	16,412
Pensioners	15,614	1,285
	613,122	17,697

Then $\dfrac{17,697 \times 1,000 \text{ Mortality}}{613,122} = 28.8$ per 1,000 per annum.

The Pensioners, therefore, raise the Mortality of the Army from 27.4 to 28.8, or 1.4 per 1,000.

It is important to remember the difference between this calculation and that referring to the Foot Guards.

The effective strength, in Table No. 4, refers to the *whole* Army, in all climates, and the Deaths also include those abroad.

The Pensioners, also, are those of the whole Army, in all climates.

The Mortality among the Pensioners is therefore added to the Mortality of the *whole* Army at home *and abroad*, in order to ascertain the total Mortality of the Army. This must not, therefore, be compared with the Deaths in our Civil Population, as may fairly be done with reference to that among the Household Troops.

In the calculation referring to the Foot Guards the average strength has been obtained, by adding *their* Pensioners, and also the Mortality in the same way.

The total Mortality thus obtained may be fairly compared with the Mortality in Civil Life at home.

This ought to be done, also, with the other Household Troops.

But, to make it more fair, the number of men purchasing their discharges should be taken into account.

To sum up, we have, then, the Statistics of Mortality in the Army, but they are incomplete for the comparison with Civil Life, which may be made as far as the Household Troops are concerned.

We want, for complete Statistics,—

1. The number of men who have purchased their discharge for the same years for which the Returns are given.

2. For the same years the number of men invalided, and the Deaths among them during the first year of their discharge of pension.

3. The number of men who die of diseases for which they have been invalided, up to the completion of their period of service.

Comparison with the rates of Mortality and Sickness in the Duke of Wellington's Army, 1811—14.

In 1854, a few months only before the great disaster of the Crimea, these remarkable words were published:

"During the 3 years and 5 months ending May 25, 1814, the English Army had 22½ per cent. constantly sick, and the sickness from wounds did not amount to more than 1½ per cent. It is probable that if some of the subjects discussed in this paper, if the causes of disease and the means of their removal had been as well understood as the use of the amputating knife and the Materia Medica, the Duke of Wellington would have had 8,000 more men at his command, and the country would have had to pay and support less than 5,815 inefficient men constantly sick in Hospitals. In that case 36,999 years of sickness might have been saved."

The writer of these lines would apparently have found it difficult to believe that an Army was then leaving the shores of England which, even before that year was out, would be losing men at the rate of 60 per cent. per annum, would lose, in the short space of seven months, 39 per cent. of its whole number from disease alone, and that "the country would have to pay and support" more than half that Force as "inefficient men sick in Hospital." Apparently he found it impossible to believe that, with our present advance in sanitary knowledge, which he here complacently records, we should keep an Army in the field under the sanitary conditions of 500 years ago, that we should see again the same state of the Soldiery repeated which Shakspeare and Froissart describe as existing in the British Army before the battle of Agincourt, and before those of Cressy and Poitiers—see, too, the same courage and unflinching endurance, but the same sufferings, the same famine, greater mortality, and far greater disease. Apparently he would not have credited his senses, had he heard the Principal Medical Officer of such an Army doubting whether the ration of raw salt beef was not enough to preserve in health men undergoing the severest duty, day and night, in the trenches.* Requiescat in Pace. But let not the British Army "rest in peace" at home in the sanitary state of fifty years ago, when all around is making progress—let it not be a monument to the disgrace of our Regimental System, in which money is held to be worth more than men.

* It could have been "foretold, as a certain consequence, sooner or later, of their dietary, that the British troops would fall into the calamitous state of health which befell them last winter, in the Crimea."—DR. CHRISTISON.

If we were to look into the construction of Military Hospitals
and Barracks, this, if fully appreciated, would be almost sufficient, of itself, to account for the ill-health of our Army.

We have not one Barrack which can be compared, in point of
construction, to the Caserne Napoléon, at Paris, or to the Petit
Château, at Brussels.

Over-crowding is the fault in both of these. Yet they both give
800 cubic feet of space per man.

Our Regulations allow only 450—500 cubic feet per man; but
a Return will show that 300 feet even of cubic space is more
than is actually given in some Barracks in England, at this
moment.

The cubic space allowed per man at this very day, is as low
as—

CUBIC FEET.

At Chatham — Infantry	350—219
„ St. Mary's Casemates	375—243
Hull Citadel	315—273
Brompton	450—243
Gravesend	294
Portsmouth	550—219
Dover Castle	412—147
London — Wellington and St. George's	390
„ Tower	397
„ Portman Street	331
„ St. John's Wood	370
Woolwich — Artillery	583—369
„ Engineers	576—433
Windsor — Cavalry	475
„ Infantry	332
Parkhurst	520—333
Winchester	467—344

In eight instances only in England and Wales does the maximum of cubic space allowed in barracks reach 600 feet per man.

The Barrack rooms are still the day and sleeping rooms of our
soldiers, and are still without partitions, which is equally
destructive to health, morality, and discipline. A partition
might be given to each man to sleep in, constructed, with little
additional expense, of corrugated iron, about 5 feet 9 inches
high, and 6 inches from the floor, the space thus divided off
being 5 feet wide and 7 feet long, with curtain at the end, something after the fashion of Colonel Jebb's Asylum for Female

Convicts, at Fulham, where two tiers of cells are thus seen, with a hanging balcony for communication for the upper tier, in one large well-ventilated dormitory.

Till we do this, we shall never see our soldiers respect themselves; and till we see them with good, airy, well lighted and well warmed day-rooms, we shall never see them temperate, healthy, or long-lived.

Hospitals.   With regard to our Hospitals, it would be difficult to institute a comparison between those of Portsmouth, Chatham, and Brompton, and the Military French Hospitals of Val de Grace and that (not yet occupied) at Vincennes; they bear about the same relation to each other that the Gaols of the last century did to those of our day.

In the Hospital at Portsmouth, which is simply and expressly a building containing four Regimental Hospitals, the cubic space is about half what it should be, the means of ventilation are wholly inadequate, the length of wards is placed in the width instead of in the length of the building, so that they have only windows at each end; the staircases, which are of wood, are dirty; the wards are dirty; the lavatory, which is on the ground-floor, is ill-lighted; there are no conveniences for baths, the Hospital is ill-placed.

Yet the Director-General says, in his evidence before a House of Commons' Committee, that "it is a new and splendid Hospital."

"8792. With regard to the men coming to this country, had provisions been made here for the reception of them?—Full provision.

"8793. Have you heard any complaints of the state of the Hospital at Portsmouth?—None.

"8794. How were the men transported from the ship to the Hospital?—Those that were seriously ill were supported in cradles fitted up specially for the purpose, to be carried by four men; those who were not so ill were transported in omnibuses or spring waggons, and those who required neither conveyance, I presume marched to the barracks.

"8795. You have seen, have you not, various statements in the papers as to the bad treatment of those persons who arrived, and as to the neglect existing; have you made any inquiries upon that subject?—Yes.

"8796. Were they founded or unfounded?—They were denied by the medical officers.

"8797. Have you heard no complaint whatever as to the Hospital at Southsea?—None whatever. I do not think it is hardly possible to make a complaint against it; it is a new and splendid Hospital."

Our Regulations give from 700—800 cubic feet of space to each Patient, about half of what is given in Civil Hospitals, less than half what is given in the Military Hospitals of France.

Yet even this meagre space is reduced at Chatham; and I have seen there patients with only 350 cubic feet of space. Casemates are altogether inadmissible as wards for a Hospital; yet they are thus used at Chatham. In the Garrison Hospital, at Brompton, the wards, long and narrow, with ten beds in each, with only one window at one end and a door opposite at the other end, with one window over it, are so ill-contrived that, if the roof were taken off, proper ventilation would not be secured. The cubic space for each Patient is under 500 feet. The wards are intolerably close at night, both here and at Fort Pitt. In the wards of Fort Pitt, the Patients have 713—357 cubic feet each. But the minimum in the five casemate wards, is only 236 feet. In the Fever Female Ward each Patient has only 735 cubic feet.

Now the minimum granted by all Civil Medical authorities is from 1,200—2,000 cubic feet.

Our Regulations give 2 feet from bed to bed. In Fort Pitt it is only 1½ foot, in the Casemates less. Civil Medical authorities give 4—6 feet as the minimum distance between the beds.

The cubic space allowed per Patient in this year (1857), is—

	CUBIC FEET.
Tower of London.	575
Croydon	437
Woolwich	883—248
Plymouth	575—524
Portsmouth	513—213
Windsor	748—599
Winchester.	591—526

In nine instances only, in England and Wales, does the maximum of cubic space allowed in Hospitals reach 1000 feet per Patient.

There are probably no Barracks either by original construction, well-selected locality, or improvements, in a good sanitary state in these islands; probably even no Dormitory, in which the most simple processes of ventilation have been adopted and preserved. We have heard of troops in the West Indies moved to positions, deemed to be safe, in Yellow Fever. We have even seen a portion of a town population moved under tents in

136

England on an attack of Cholera. Some improvements have taken place in Hospital Architecture in England—greater still in France and Belgium. The improved normal rules have been laid down and acted upon for the vast number of Lunatic Asylums and Prisons which have been erected during the last ten years. Yet nevertheless the plan of the building of the new Royal Victoria Hospital, near Netley, the foundation stone of which was laid by the Queen herself in May, 1856, contains within itself most of the Sanitary defects which accurate observation and judicious criticism have condemned in existing structures of this kind.

Surely no trouble can be thought too great in collecting the reasonings of eminent men, and in examining the examples of buildings on sound principles, when we consider that this noble Building, which will contain 1,000 patients, is intended to become a monument of the War, and a testimony of the beneficence of the Queen and nation towards the British Army. But, if still further stimulus were wanting, it would be found in the awful exaggeration of the bad principles of this kind of building (admitting of so easy a misuse) which was seen at Scutari.*

Argument against the Construction of Scutari Hospitals.

* If it be objected against condemning the plan of Scutari buildings, as a bad system of Hospital construction, that the Sanitary arrangements adopted there brought the mortality, in the Hospitals, down to 2·2 percent (which was actually the case in June, 1855, instead of being 42·7 per cent., as it was in Feb., 1855) it may be answered, or rather asked, upon what condition? Upon that of not allowing above 800—1,000 Patients in a building such as the Barrack Hospital, upwards of 700 feet square and three flats in height. Had this building been differently distributed in its construction, it might easily have accommodated 3,000 Patients, with good recovering conditions. It is ruinous to build after this fashion. The question, both sanitary and economical, is to find that construction which will accommodate the greatest number of Patients upon a given area, with the greatest facilities for recovery.

However good construction and ventilation of any Corridors, if they are filled up with Patients, it is tantamount to having two Hospitals "back to back," it is tantamount to building up a street. In all our experience, whether of healthy or of sick men, such a construction generates disease.

If it objected that the condition of the men (sent down from the Crimea during the first winter) was such that they could not, by possibility, have lived, under any circumstances, I answer, as I have done before, that the Land Transport Corps sent us down men exactly the same condition, the second winter, and that, under different circumstances, they did recover—witness our low rate of mortality.

But, as has been said, it was at the expense of limiting a building upwards of 700 feet square to an extravagantly small number of Patients.

And again, has there been an Epidemic, no Sanitary precautions could have prevented it from spreading, in a building so constructed.

XI. NOTES ON THE INACCURACY OF HOSPITAL STATISTICS AND THE
NECESSITY OF A STATISTICAL DEPARTMENT.

The acknowledged importance of Statistical Science in England, proved by the elaborate system of the Registrar-General's Office, founded about twenty years since, seems to show the absolute necessity of a Statistical Department.

In the General Standing Hospitals, it would seem that the Officer charged with this duty should not be one charged with the treatment of the sick. Otherwise he would be reporting to himself, which is contrary to the action of the National Registration under the late statute.

If the Army Registration is to be analogous to the National Registration, which in all reason, it would seem should be the case, it appears to follow that the nomenclature of disease should be that used by the Registrar-General; the more so, as the latter is fixed so as to correspond with the technical words in French and in German, determined by the Statistical Congresses at Brussels and at Paris, held in the years 1853 and 1855.

Nomenclature identical with that of the Registrar-General cannot be obtained, unless that used by the Medical Officers in the Reports and Returns, and on the bed-ticket of each patient is made also to correspond.

Another reason for this change will appear from the consideration that the present terms, which are inadequate to their purpose, are no others than those used in Cullen's Nosology of 1785, with a few additions.

The Army Statistics have never been incorporated with the Civil Statistics of England, producing a very unjust inconvenience to the relatives of the dead, the more so as our soldiers are volunteers. This, however, would be a minor grievance, if the Army Statistics themselves could be relied upon. Of the soldiers who are no longer paraded with their regiments, one portion is returned killed, one portion missing, and the rest in Hospital or invalided. In the late war, the second class will be found, from special circumstances, unusually small. It is in the last two classes that large discrepancies arose. Those in Hospital must be considered to include those on the passage from the Crimea to the Bosphorus, and from the Bosphorus to England. The discrepancy, between the truth and the returns, was supposed to be greater than in the Peninsula War, and may be accounted for as follows. Great numbers of men were

Want in General Military Hospitals, of a Statical Department separately engaged in Registration.

The Nomenclature of Disease should, for uniformity's sake, be that used by the Civil Registrar-General.

The present Military Nomenclature of Disease is, moreover, quite inadequate and obsolete. General Inaccuracy of Army Statistics, even as regards the mere Registration of Deaths.

embarked, not only after Alma, but during the succeeding autumn and winter on board transports, and even on board the afterwards-appointed sick ships, without any nominal list. Of these it appears, by comparing the numbers of those who embarked with those who landed, that about 949 died and were thrown overboard on the passage. For the reason above stated, many of these were not reported nominally. As we have no security for the accuracy of the Military or Medical Officers in charge, sometimes invalids themselves, this figure (949) may or may not represent the actual number lost. In one instance, the Captain of a transport has asserted that seventy bodies were thrown overboard from his ship in one voyage, without their names, regiments, or ranks being entered into any report on board the ship.

On entering the gates of the Hospitals on the Bosphorus, many men were unable to give their names to the serjeant stationed to require them, and consequently were entered by a simple number; in other cases, the name of the regiment was added, which could not be ascertained except when the accoutrements were sufficiently complete. Of these men, unable to account for themselves, a large proportion died. Each was entered simply as "a man" in the death books; but, as the returns show that the excess of burials over deaths numerically reported (in the "Orderly Room") during the six months after the Battle of Alma, amounts, in the Hospitals of the Bosphorus, to 530, it follows that that number, which actually entered the Hospitals, died without the Death being reported, nominally or numerically. In some cases, the card remained after the occupant of the bed which it represented had been removed by death; the first real name thus representing its proper owner and his successor or successors, who followed him rapidly to the graveyard. But, till about February 1855 we had no bed-tickets at all; nor, till about that month, was a nominal Return of deaths made by Surgeons in charge of the Wards. The name of the man who died was, up to this time, simply scratched off the Diet Roll.

Another source of inaccuracy was that, although all who left the Hospitals of the Bosphorus for home, were recorded with nominal lists on embarkation, yet those who died during the voyage were not reported to their respective regiments. Many cases of this kind have occurred indisputably, as appears from correspondence, ultimately proving that the man never was again present either at his Depôt or with his Regiment on service, and was not discharged from Hospital at home.

This great amount of inaccuracy is the more surprising, because, in this War, there were no such causes as have occurred in almost every other, viz., desertion, fatal accidents occurring to troops dispersed over a populated country, or falling out during long marches, especially retreats.

Another obvious defect in the Statistics of Disease of our Army (which are not published, even at any subsequent period, when military reasons no longer exist for their concealment) is, that the Returns are only made up on one day of the week, of the men then in Hospital. Consequently a man, entering the Hospital on the following day and dying, or being discharged, previous to the subsequent Report, will not appear in the column of Total Sick, which shows those at the end of the week. In cholera and diseases which run their course in a few hours, the Returns may actually only show one-seventh of the cases. The other six-sevenths will, however, appear in the Death and Admission Returns for the week. But, in the *Regimental* Return, a man admitted and discharged to duty during the week would not appear.

Statistical Returns, whether of the Hospital or of the Army, can be, comparatively, of little use, till extended, with a sufficient nomenclature, over periods adequately distinguished, and over portions of the force, under different geographical or sanitary circumstances. For example, the total loss in the last war, over the period of two years, unless classified into monthly Returns, will not indicate the fact that we were losing men at the annual rate of 1,173 per 1,000, in January 1855, and in January 1856 at the rate of 21 per 1,000, which shows that, the weather being similar at both periods, the influences of climate were not to be looked to as the grand causes of disaster.*

For the purposes of accurate comparison, it is absolutely necessary to reduce all our facts to

Requisites for accurate comparison.

1. Unity of time.

2. Unity of strength, or numbers under observation.

Now the standard of comparison, as to mortality, all over the civilized world is the per-centage of deaths per *annum*; as to sickness, the per-centage of admissions into hospital, *in the same time*, together with the number of days' sickness *in the same time*.

And, without reference to the *same* standard, it is impossible for the most intelligent to judge.

* This is very much wanted for comparison. Every man, whatever his experience, wants an *unit* of comparison.

By dividing the *weekly* deaths by the force in the Crimea, as was done in the published Returns, the high mortality of the Crimea *appeared* to be exceedingly low. For people naturally took the mortality per cent. per *week* for the mortality per cent. per *annum*.

From the Extracts given below, which are taken from letters of the Principal Medical Officer to the Commander of the Forces, in the published Dispatches, the meaning of what is here suggested will at once be seen.

False impressions created by Medical Statistical Returns in the Crimea.

"(Enclosure)

"Dr. HALL to LORD RAGLAN.

"MY LORD,   *Before Sebastopol, March* 19, 1855.
"In transmitting the weekly state of sick of the Army to the 17th instant, I have the honour to state, that though the sickness still amounts to 14.31 per cent., the mortality does not exceed 0.51 per cent., which is a proof that the diseases are milder in character; and I think I may safely say the general health and appearance of the men is greatly improved; and had not the duty, by the unavoidable operations of the siege going on, been increased of late, I think the sick list would have been still more diminished, as the men's condition is in every other way so much improved, both in diet, dress, and accommodation.

"(Inclosure.)
"Dr. HALL to LORD RAGLAN.
"MY LORD,   *Before Sebastopol, April* 3, 1855.
"In transmitting the weekly state of sick to the 31st March, I have the honour to state, that I am sure it will be pleasing to your lordship to learn, that the general health of the Army continues steadily to improve; and although fevers and bowel complaints continue to prevail, they are both assuming a milder character, and the latter are of much less frequent occurrence.
"During the present week the admissions to strength have been in the ratio of 3.93 per cent., and the deaths to strength 0.38 per cent.
"Last week, the admissions to strength were 4.35 per cent., and the deaths 0.52 per cent.; which makes a decrease of 139 in the admissions, and 43 in the deaths during the week."

The facts which the Commander of the Forces and the War Department want to know, and ought to know, concerning the health of an Army in the field, are not, as is thus shown, supplied them.
What they want to know is—

1. How long the army will last at the then rate of mortality.

2. Whether the diseases are preventible from which the mortality arises.

3. What proportion of the army is inefficient from sickness.

The mere information that "the admissions to strength have been in the ratio of 3.93 per cent." during "the present *week*," and "the deaths to strength 0.38 per cent." is simply misleading to the authorities, unless indeed, which is hardly likely, they are thoroughly *au fait* of statistical inquiries.

0.52, 3.93 per cent. look nothing.

But multiply 3.9 by 52 = 2,028, in order to find the *annual* admissions per 1,000; and it will be seen that the whole force will go twice through hospital in a year, at that rate. And multiply 14.3 by 52 = 7,436 per 1,000 per annum; and the whole force will go seven times through hospital in a year.

This "sickness" of "14.31 per cent." must, however, include the admissions and the remaining in hospital. Some remarks will be offered, further on, upon this method of calculating the mortality. But is this a state of things to congratulate a Commander of the Forces upon, as being "pleasing" to him "to learn?"

Multiply 0.52 by 52 in the same way, and it will be found that the mortality is 270 per 1,000 per annum;—in other words, that more than one-fourth of the whole population of the army will perish in a year.

2. At a time when every one in the Crimea was expecting cholera, which actually did come, which is shortly after recorded by the Inspector-General himself, the Commander of the Forces is congratulated on the "steadily improving" state of the "health of the army."

During the ten weeks intervening between May 5 and July 14, 1855, 96 per cent. of all the deaths from disease were of the classes usually considered mitigable and zymotic. That is to say that, granting that the remaining four per cent. were not preventible, there might have been saved to the Commander of the Forces a large part of the 96 out of every hundred men he lost from disease.

Is not this important to him to know from his returns at a glance?

3. For a Commander in the Field, the number of deaths among his men is, after all, not so necessary for him to know as the rate of inefficiency from sickness in his army, granting that a large amount of that sickness may be mitigated or prevented.

In January 1855 more than half the Infantry of the Army before Sebastopol* was sick in hospital, and three-fourths of all that sickness zymotic, and so it continued from October 1854 till July 1855. Nay, even in that dreadful week which included the attack on the Redan, June 18th, 1855, even in that week nearly 65 per cent. of all the deaths in hospital were zymotic.

Of what vital importance is it not to a Commander and a Government to know this?

Now take the unit of 1,000 per annum, include the deaths in the General Hospitals at the base of operations, without which it is obvious that no correct result as to the mortality of an army can be obtained, and let us compare the mortality at different periods of our history in the Crimea.

PER 1,000 PER ANNUM.

January	1855 . .	1,173½
	1856 . .	21½
May.	1855 . .	203
	1856 . .	8
January 1 to May 31	1855 . .	628
	1856 . .	11½
Crimea, May 1856.		8
Line at home.		18·7
Guards at home.		20·4

Thus we were losing in the Crimea, in May 1856, less than half of what we lose in the Line at home, and two-fifths of what we lose in the Guards at home.

What Statistics are requisite for a Commander of the Forces.

It is obvious that what is wanted is for the Commander of the Forces and the Secretary of State for War to be made instantly and continuously acquainted, (both as to an Army at home and in the field,) with not only (1) the real proportion of mortality; (2) the real proportion of disease; but also (3) the *kind* of disease and mortality.

Therefore—

1. Present strength.
2. Sick in hospital at a given date,
3. Total admissions since last report,
4. Total deaths since last report,
5. Percentage of sick to present force,
6. Percentage of deaths to present force, *per annum*,
7. Percentage of admissions from zymotic disease to total admissions,

---

* *Vide* p. 17, where is given the Adjutant-General's Return of Sick (Present and Absent) for the Infantry Divisions before Sebastopol.

8. Percentage of zymotic cases in Hospital to total sick.
9. Percentage of deaths from zymotic disease to total deaths
    from disease,
10. Admissions and deaths from wounds,—

at short periods, both Departments should be furnished with a statement of these 10 points, in such a form as that they shall be able to appreciate them at a glance.

It may easily be ascertained what the weekly states of an Army in the field are now, as furnished to the Commander of the Forces by his Principal Medical Officer, and the daily states furnished by his Adjutant-General*.

The following is a specimen of what we remember to have seen furnished by the Principal Medical Officer:—

WEEKLY MEDICAL STATE.
1. Strength in field, as given by Adjutant-General, this morning.
2. Admissions.
3. Deaths.
4. Present Sick.
5. Admissions to strength.
6. Deaths to strength.
7. Sick to strength.
8. Decrease of mortality this week;

but nothing as to per-centage "per annum," or as to zymotic disease.

Again, with an Army in the field, to give the admissions and deaths for the Field Hospitals is to give no just idea of the mortality, unless it is also stated how many of those admissions were sent to and died in the General Hospitals at the base of operations.

In the case of the Crimea, till the spring of 1855, no account was rendered of these.

---

* The States, furnished by the Adjutant-General, include,—
    1. Present under arms;
    2. Sick { Present,
              Absent;
    3. Missing;
    and the numbers employed on varous duties.
For military purposes these States are, of course, adapted; and it is unquestionably not intended here to offer any impertinent suggestion on a purely military question. It is only mentioned now to show that the information required for the above purpose is not here, either, to be found, since these States show neither the Reinforcements nor the Deaths.

E. g. Published Return.
Crimea.
October 1, 1854—April 1, 1855.

AVERAGE STRENGTH.	ADMISSIONS.	DEATHS.
28,623	52,548	5,359

General Return.

Crimea and Scutari.
October 1, 1854—April 30, 1855.

AVERAGE STRENGTH.	ADMISSIONS.	DEATHS.
28,939	56,057	10,053

The admissions at Scutari are not given, because they were nearly all re-admissions from the Crimea.

When we see the loss *thus* given, the real extent of it strikes us. It stands thus:—

	STRENGTH.	DEATHS.
Infantry	23,775	9,015
Cavalry...............	1,915	280
Artillery and Engineers ..	3,249	568
Undistinguishable.......		190
	28,939	10,053

Sir Alexander Tulloch gives the mortality for those seven months, at a percentage for the seven months. It shall now be given per annum:—

Strength of the Army	28,939
Deaths in seven months ...	10,053
Mortality per annum......	60 per 100

Novel Methods of calculating Mortality.

It must now be stated that the statistical returns made at various times are very discordant.

It will be found, also, that some of the methods of calculation employed are quite novel, and in a form to mislead persons who have not closely studied these matters.

The following is an illustration:—

Given a Hospital of 1,000 beds, constantly occupied during one year, into which during the year 10,000 sick are admitted, and 10,000 discharged, viz. 1,260 dead, and the rest cured. Then if we divide the deaths in the year by the *average strength*, as is ordinarily done in determining the mortality of the whole Army, it will be found that the 1,260 deaths in a year out of a mean strength of 1,000 imply that the mortality was at the rate of 126 per *cent.* per *annum.* If this method be employed, it will show the comparative sanitary condition of the sick in two or more such Hospitals.

Again, as the number of deaths (1,260) took place among 10,000 cases, the mortality was at the rate of 12.6 deaths in every 100 cases.

In the case supposed, the new method would make the cases 62,000, out of which the 1,260 deaths occurred, and the mortality of these cases would be stated at 2 per cent.

The way in which this result is obtained is sufficiently simple. 1,000 cases would remain in the Hospital at the beginning of every week; the new method counts the cases remaining every week, or fifty-two times in a year, and adds to them the cases admitted, so that, in addition to the 10,000 cases really treated, it obtains 52,000 fictitious cases, simply by counting the patients remaining 52 times annually, and adding them to the new patients admitted.

If the number remaining at the beginning of every month were counted, 12,000 would be added to the 10,000 real cases treated.

It is evident that, by counting the cases *remaining* at the beginning of every day, or oftener, the *cases* may be multiplied to any conceivable extent.

Now it is hazardous to offer any conjecture as to the nature of some of the published Returns with which we have been furnished, or to found any calculation upon them, without knowing what they are meant to represent:—*e.g.*

January, 1855.

1.	2.	3.	4.
(No. of Sick in Hospital in the Crimea and at Scutari.* (Infantry before Sebastopol alone.)	Total Admissions into Hospital in the Crimea.	Total No. of Sick in Lord Raglan's Army.†	Total No. of Cases Treated at Scutari.
12,025	11,290	23,076	23,076

* This is a summary of the Adjutant-General's Weekly Returns, as given at p. 17.

† As given at p. 16.

It is easy to understand Nos. 1 and 2; but what is No. 3? Independently of the fact, elsewhere noted, of its showing the same sum as No. 4, it is difficult to know what it represents. Is it the "cases *admitted*," added to the "cases *remaining*?" And if so, are the latter added *weekly* or *monthly*, or at what successive periods?

But Hospital Statistics should include also a Registration of the causes of Death and a Record of the Treatment of Disease.

But Statistics of a Hospital ought to include not only the nominal list of dead, but the cause of death.

As to the records of the treatment of disease, which are a subordinate part of Statistics; in some of the London Civil Hospitals and in the Military ones of France and Sardinia, the Case-books are kept with such accuracy, that the diagnosis of the primary or secondary disease is recorded, with the treatment, and proximate cause of death—if death ensues. In the French Army, the Case-books being sent home, the competent authority abstracts the more interesting cases, from which a second selection is made, which is published once or twice a year, as the cases make up a convenient octavo volume, at the expense of Government. Each case is accompanied with the place, time, and circumstances, and the names of the superior and inferior Officers under whose treatment it has been.

Gross Inaccuracy of the very Registration of the Men's Diseases, in British Military Hospitals.

Hasty Diagnosis.

In the British Military Hospitals, the diagnosis is affixed to the card, by order, within twelve hours after admission. If the disease changes, the Surgeon must go through the form of discharging and re-admitting the man, in order to change the ticket, so that, were this rule strictly carried out, the Patient who contracts another disease in Hospital, would appear as two men, the first of whom had recovered

If the Surgeon wishes, for the sake of honesty and science, to change his diagnosis, which he has been obliged prematurely to decide upon, consideration of the above difficulty would probably induce him not to do so. In Civil Hospitals, this decision, exacted in Military Establishments within twelve hours, is frequently deferred for a period of several days or even weeks.

Way in which the Medical Returns were made at Scutari.

The way the Returns of the Army Medical Department were made at Scutari was as follows:—At first, no Nominal List was sent with the Patients. Afterwards, when such was regularly received at the Principal Medical Officer's Office, stating also the men's diseases, these were not communicated for the guidance of the treating Surgeon. The Patient was interrogated: "What is the matter with you?" "Oh, Sir, I have Diarrhoea," or "Fever," or "Dysentery." Some Assistant Surgeons put down what was thus said as the Diagnosis, and afterwards it was entered in the Returns as the Cause of Death, in the event of a fatal termination to the case.

Or the Patient said, "Oh, Sir, I have pains in my back and my legs." This was entered as Chronic Rheumatism. Thirty-three deaths from "Chronic Rheumatism" have been seen in one Quarterly Return from one Hospital. These cases, so returned as Chronic Rheumatism, were generally Scurvy, and frequently ended in death; but a great number of Medical Officers were so little in favour of the idea that Scurvy prevailed in the Army, that they would not acknowledge the cases as such—even when the *post mortem* appearances demonstrated the nature of the disease. The great number of cases which appear as Fevers, which were not Fevers, will also be remarked. Very few who came down from the Crimea to Scutari, during the first part of the first winter, came with Fever. It was contracted afterwards in Hospital, and was that called Hospital or Camp Fever, and by the French, Typhus. With us it was called Febris c. c., Common Continuous Fever (which means—what?)

It was not till the spring of 1855 that there appeared in the British Army, among the cases sent down from the Crimea to Scutari, what the French call "Fievre Typhoide." The French and Russian camps were decimated, in the spring of 1856, with the same Fever which the British had the preceding spring, and from some of the same causes, viz., an inadequate supply of fuel, food, and clothing, combined with want of sanitary precautions.

But, in the British Hospitals, if a man came in with feverish symptoms, it was very common to return him under F. c. c., though afterwards it might prove to be Pneumonia, &c., and therefore the numbers of Feb. c. c. must appear unduly increased.

In the first winter, a great number of those returned as Fever died not in the acute stage, but afterwards in the secondary stage of Consumption, or something else.

What was called Frost-bite was almost always the consequence of Diarrhoea or Dysentery; for, if the man were questioned, he said that he had contracted it in his tent or in bed in Hospital. There was rarely that degree of Frost which would justify its being called Frost-bite. It should more truly have been called Gangrene, the consequence of the depression caused by Scorbutic Dysentery. It was true that the men, when debilitated by bowel-complaint and sent on duty, sometimes fell asleep, for a few hours, in the trenches, and awoke frost-bitten; but this was the consequence not of the great degree of cold, but of the state of depression of the men's constitutions. Perhaps but one case could be mentioned of a perfectly healthy man really suffering from Frost-bite—he had lost one toe.

Sketch of the Diseases from which the Army suffered in the Crimea.

The diseases contracted in the Crimea, with their respective causes and period, might, roughly, be classified thus:—

TIME.	CAUSES.		DISEASES.
1854.			
November	Exposure		Diarrhoea
December	Bad food		Dysentery
	Deficient clothing	Scorbutic Type.	Rheumatism
1855.	Fatigue		Frost-bite
January	Damp		Scurvy
½ February			
	Bad drainage		Fever
	„ ventilation		typhoid
½ February	Overcrowding		continued
March	Nuisances	Malarial Type.	remittent
April	Organic effluvia		Diarrhoea
	Malaria		Dysentery
	Damp		Cholera

Inspection of the Medical Register.

After an inspection, the Inspecting Officer determines, by the evidence or rather the neatness of the books, whether the "Treating" Surgeon is a meritorious officer or not. So that often the most active and zealous in his profession is set down as undeserving, because some form has not been complied with; while another, who has filled up all his forms, though it may easily happen without knowledge or skill, is reckoned a most praiseworthy officer.

Absence of reliable Returns of Disease.

In one instance, at Scutari, an Assistant Surgeon was sent from one General Hospital, between eight and nine P.M., to receive upwards of 100 patients at another, whose Names, Regiments, Regimental Numbers, he had to take, and the diagnosis of whose diseases he had to make, and to send in to the Principal Medical Officer's Office, before nine the following morning! Of what value to the Medical Returns was this diagnosis supposed to be?

Five men were dead before morning, whose Names, Diseases, and Regiments must remain for ever unknown, except as subsequently traced back, so far as to strike them off the strength of the Regiments; and for this alleged neglect, the unfortunate Surgeon received what is called in official slang a "wigging."

One instance may be cited, among many, of the difficulty of obtaining reliable Returns. A Surgeon came down twice from the Crimea in charge of Patients. On one occasion the voyage lasted upwards of three weeks—twelve Orderlies were told off for the service of the Sick, of whom few lived to arrive at Scutari. The Sick were put on board, without lists or returns of any kind; when they arrived at Scutari, they had neither food nor medicines. The Surgeon went on shore and was unable to obtain what he required, owing to confusion and "want of transport" (sic. in the Bosphorus) until the case was represented. Finally, by the exertions of the Military Officer on board, the "case was represented" to the Commandant, who ordered an ample supply of everything. The larger portion of the first day on board, this Assistant Surgeon, who was thus in charge of 200—300 Sick was occupied in making a Nominal Roll of his Patients. In that same vessel, sick were put on board, on one side, at Balaclava, and thrown overboard, dead, on the other.

Of how much value, then, are our Medical Returns?

Nearly all of the men treated in the Hospitals of the Bosphorus had been inmates of one of the Hospitals, Regimental or General, in the Crimea. In no case did any history of the disease and treatment accompany the Patient. Later in the war, records were sent down, but these went to the Principal Medical Officer's office. *Neglect of all Pathological Record.*

In the case of post mortem investigations, the Examiner had no information given him of the Patient during life. Pathological investigations were therefore of comparatively little value to what they would have been, could diseases have been traced up to their source.

It must be discouraging and disappointing in the extreme to the zealous and scientific Surgeon to know that his accounts of cases, however interesting and useful, are doomed to remain unclassified and probably unexamined; while with the careless and the ignorant Surgeon, this well-known probability justifies slothfulness and conceals want of knowledge. *Neglect of all Pathological Record.*

The Case-books of the Regimental Surgeons and of those treating sick in Hospital are sent in periodically to the Principal Medical Officer, who forwards them to the Director-General, in whose archives they remain, without hope of examination, since examination without classification and publication would be useless.

Already the mass of valuable matter derived from the Peninsular War and the Expedition to Walcheren has been destroyed, as too bulky for the disposable room at the command of the Director-General; and it is but too probable that the recent records, including doubtless a far greater variety of Medical experience, now demanding fresh space in the Record Chamber, will share the fate of their predecessors.

It may be of little consequence whether a Naturalist, sent on board the frigate which conveyed the bodies of the King and Queen of Otaheite home from England, be or be not allowed by "Their Lordships" at the Admiralty to publish the Sulphurs of the Volcano, or the Flora of the Island; but when the Surgeon is doomed not only to see his Official Records shelved, but to suffer under an absolute decree that his own private memoranda, or even correspondence, shall not see the light, unless by leave and after censorship of the Director General, we may estimate the amount of discouragement to energy, and injury to the advance of science produced by abstracting from the Scientific Treasury of the Nation all that large field of observation which official advantages place at the command of the Army Surgeon.

Analogous to this system, by which the world is deprived of valuable results, is that by which the visible Material of self-recorded facts has been allowed to perish. Few or no preparations can have been made of bones and amputated limbs, since few or none have been sent home. How can it be expected, when the only encouragement is the probable interment of a preparation in the underground Museum at Fort Pitt, by order of the Director General, that Army Surgeons, in the midst of their labours, should select specimens and send them home, to be afterwards prepared and deposited, if thought worthy of Fort Pitt? This Museum is one of the first in the world; and it is not here meant that to enrich it ought not to be the legitimate object of ambition to the Army Surgeon—but that it ought to be placed in a *locale* worthy of it and accessible to Students.

From what is above stated, it becomes evident that, notwithstanding the treatment of gun-shot wounds is less known than any other branch of Surgery, after twelve months of actual campaign and two years of Hospital treatment, no classification will be obtained of the facts, recorded in the manner they have been, which can be of any public utility. Even were they published as they have been sent home, no Pathologist could collect from them arranged data from which he could draw valuable conclusions, for the use of those who may make future researches in this branch of Surgery.

For the completeness of a Military General Hospital, a separate Pathological element is required. Its officer, during the time of his investigations, in order that his Reports may be above suspicion, must be independent of those who treat the patients.

Necessity for a Pathological Department in Military General Hospitals.

His duty would be to demonstrate in the School, to tabulate such criticisms and illustrations as he might make upon the Statistics of Disease, and to act as Curator of the Museum, unless in the very large Hospitals, where this would be a separate office.

It may be thought necessary to give a short resume of what has been said of the method in use at Scutari, on the opening of the Crimea campaign, for receiving sick and registering their admissions and diseases—this having been, as it were, an improvised scheme of General Hospitals—as well as for recording the results, deaths and burials. I shall be obliged to use some repetition.

Resume of the Method in use at Scutari for receiving Sick, and registering their Admissions, Diseases, and Deaths.

Up to the middle of February 1855, the method said to exist was the following:—The Adjutant or his Serjeant stood at the landing-place or hospital gate and took the names of those who were able to speak, receiving a verbal report, from the Officer in charge, of the number who had died during the voyage. At first, there was no arrangement for registering the sick when they were received into Hospital; and the erasure of the man's name from the diet roll was long the only record of his death, excepting the Adjutant's head-roll of burials.

I believe that the Medical Officer in charge always endeavoured to make a nominal roll on the voyage from Balaklava to Scutari; more than one has stated that it took him half a day from his professional duties about the sick to do so. But, whatever this nominal roll was, it went into the Principal Medical Officer's office, and not into the wards; one copy was given, I have been told, to the Deputy Assistant Quartermaster-General on landing; but at what period this was first done I am not aware. It has been stated to me by several Medical Officers that, even as late as March 1855, the Inspecting Medical Officer of Transports, upon going on board, frequently found this list imperfect, owing to the illness of the Medical Officer in charge, or other unavoidable cause, and had to complete it then and there.

Till the middle of February, or late, we had no bed-tickets, and no regular death returns. It is well known that the sick were put on board at Balaclava without nominal or numerical lists up to February 1855. Upon their admission at Scutari, an Assistant-Surgeon was charged, sometimes late in the evening, to take the names, regiments, regimental number, &c., and to make the diagnosis of perhaps 100 patients before nine the next morning. One-twentieth have been known to die before they could give their names.

After the end of March all this confusion ceased. But it was not till the end of April that a census of the Hospitals was taken, and returns "squared" with the Adjutant-General in the Crimea.

Returns probably existed of which I knew nothing. I am speaking only, first, of what I saw; secondly, of what I was informed of by witnesses on the spot and at the time. The Director-General may have other witnesses and other returns.

Conclusion.
A Registrar is necessary.

The conclusion I draw from all this is, not that any one was to blame, for all were burdened with work beyond their strength, but that there was no system ready organized of registration for General Hospitals, and that a Registrar is an essentially necessary Officer for such an institution.

Excess of Burials over Reported Deaths.

In consequence of the great confusion of the Hospitals from the battle of the Alma till a late period of the winter of 1854-55, a number of men were buried from the Hospitals, exceeding in six months the deaths reported in the "orderly room" by 530; but the deaths reported in the orderly room exceed those reported in the Hospital books,

In November by........	12
" December "........	143
" January "........	125
	───
	280

while, as if to make up the lost ground, the medical returns, which had exceeded the orderly room returns

by 12 deaths in October, exceed again
by 253   "   "   February,
265

bringing the sum of deaths very nearly equal. The Adjutant having buried 280 men more than the total number reported by the Inspector-General as dead, the account had to be balanced at a subsequent period.

A census was taken of the Hospitals, April 30, 1855, by which it appeared that 517 non-commissioned officers and soldiers had been buried whose deaths were unrecorded. An official report was then sent up to the Adjutant-General in the Crimea, and they were struck off the strength of the army. The names and regiments of 28 others remained unknown.

I have carefully compared the statistics from the six different official sources and none of them agree. Statistics from six different Sources, all different.

It is possible that, in some of these cases, the numbers of deaths may be the numbers occurring in the several months,—in other cases, the numbers recorded in those months. At the same time, the great discrepancies in the several numbers shake confidence in their accuracy, and render it difficult to make use of them for statistical purposes.

From details inserted in the Appendix, it will be seen

1. That there are four different returns of the deaths on board the transports bringing Sick fro Balaclava to Scutari, and that the number reported is different in each separate return. Nay, there is scarcely a single ship for which the three returns agree, which report the ships separately.

2. The Adjutant's head-roll of burials, the most trustworthy record of deaths, exceeded in six months by upwards of 500 the number reported as having died in the Hospitals; and the Adjutant states that this list of burials does not include civilians.

3. The Director-General himself represents the very numbers in the "return of total sick *treated in Lord Raglan's army*"* as having been *treated at Scutari* alone in November, December 1854, and January 1855.

4. The returns of dead at Scutari from October 1 to December 31, 1854, vary as follows:

ADJUTANT'S RETURN OF BURIALS.	REPORTED DEATHS.	PRINCIPAL MEDICAL OFFICER'S RETURN.	CRIMEAN RETURN (INFANTRY ALONE.)
1,301	1,046	910	795†

* Appendix, Third Report Committee before Sebastopol, p. 470; Second Report, p. 705.

† The deaths of the Cavalry, Artillery, and Engineers, averaged together about one-ninth of those of the Infantry at Scutari, according to the Inspector-General's return for seven months, viz., October 1, 1854 to April 30, 1855. This would not have equalized the numbers, for 9) 795 (88, 795+88=883.

154

Smyrna Hospital did not then exist: and Koulali Hospital did not exist till December, and contained then, as a maximum, but 240 patients.

These sources of discrepancy are therefore eliminated.

The result of my examination of these statistics is simply this, that, however satisfactory they may be to the departments who have put them forth, and whichever of them may be correct, exhibiting as they do such palpable diversity, still, to any one not in the secret as to how things which apparently differ so widely are nevertheless identically the same, they convey no trustworthy idea as to the sickness and mortality of the army in the East, and that, for any practical purpose, they are as put forth to the public, who are most interested in the matter, not absolute truths, but only approximations. The calculations which I give, I believe, understate the mortality actually experienced.

Fatal Consequences of the hasty and imperfect Diagnosis, illustrated by the want of notice of the widely spread Scorbutic character of the Men's Diseases in the late War.

The superficial mode of entering Disease, according to the symptoms appearing during the first twelve hours after entrance into Hospital, led to the following result: that, notwithstanding subsequent symptoms displayed themselves and treatment was altered to meet them, the Scorbutic character of disease, although prevailing, it is said to the extent of 80 per cent., was never recorded. Consequently, so striking a characteristic of disease, spread over so large a number of Patients, never led to the investigation of the common causes of so general an effect, which it otherwise would have peremptorily commanded.

Had the search been made after the cause which produced 80 per cent. of the disease among our Troops, this being Scorbutic Dysentery and Diarrhoea, &c., no other conclusion could by any possibility have been arrived at than the following: that the disease was caused by salt provisions, cooked in mess-tins capable of containing so small a quantity of water that the salt remained undischarged in that large proportion which is got rid of by cooking as performed in the Navy; the addition to which ration was rum and biscuit. This was the food of the Soldier day after day, while exposed to cold and wet, and undergoing extreme labour. The compensations of diet usually afforded to the Sailor were nevertheless in store at Balaclava, viz.: rice and lime-juice; and soft bread might have been provided, partly by baking at Balaclava in the existing Russian ovens, and partly by importation from Constantinople, as was subsequently done. Vegetables might have been obtained, potatoes supplying the want of green vegetables during the dead of the winter.

It may fairly, then, be anticipated that, had the Scorbutic taint been reported to have existed to the extent to which it really did, it would have been seen that the death of the British Soldier should rather have been ascribed to his diet (which might have been modified or changed), than to the climate (which at all events was not worse than that of his own country), or even to the over-work in the trenches (which, however excessive, had he been supported by nourishing and well-cooked food, he could have better borne till reinforcements arrived to reduce it.)*

For an example of the vital importance of accurate Statistics of Disease to a Commander of the Forces and a War Department, the following may be taken:

We derive from Official Returns for January 1855, that there were in that month

Vital importance of accurate Statistics of Disease.

Total Admissions into Hospital (Primary)	11,290	Total Deaths in Hospital ..	3,168
Per 1,000 per ann. to strength ..	4,176	Per 1,000 per ann. to strength ..	1173·6

Of these, the Admissions and Deaths from Diseases of the Scorbutic type are returned as follows:

	ADMISSIONS	DEATHS
Scurvy	542	31
Scorbutic Dysentery	181	44
	723	75

Or, 75 deaths from Scorbutic disease in that month, when from two-thirds to three-fourths of all the Disease in the Army were due to the Scorbutic type. The larger part, if not all, of the Admissions and Deaths, recorded below, which are for the same

* This will be considered in greater detail in the Notes on Diet. Here it is enough to say that the food was at once uncooked and insufficient. Even had it all been eaten, which it was not, it would have contained only 23 oz. nutritive value, instead of 28 oz., the quantity necessary for health. The fact of the food being thus disproportioned to the labour, would have been in itself sufficient to account for a large part of the destruction of the British Army. The want of shelter and of warm clothing did the rest.

156

month of January, 1855, may be read "Scorbutic type" or "Bad food," which is the same thing.

		ADMISSIONS	DEATHS
	Acute Dysentery* ...	865	210
	Chronic "	143	578
	Scorbutic "	181	44
	Diarrhoea	4,191	1,199
	Acute Rheumatism ..	342	58
	Chronic "	84	9
	Frost-bite	1,413	124
	Scorbutus	542	31
		7,761	2,253

(Scorbutic Type bracket spans the rows.)

Yet instead of 7,761 admissions, and 2,553 deaths from Scorbutic disease, or bad food, are returned admissions 723, deaths 75.

In the case of Armies in the Field, where half an Army may melt away from such a cause, or be rendered inefficient, just when its services are most wanted, not by wounds but by disease—as was actually the fact with ours in the Crimea, in January 1855,—of what vital importance is it, then, in such a case, for the authorities to be furnished with such information as the above, leading, as it does, directly to the discovery of the true cause—the remedy for which, in our instance, was close at hand.†

Comparison with the amount of Zymotic Disease in a Civil Population.

But what shall we say when we see the proportion in which the Army in the East suffered from Zymotic disease, compared to that in which the Civil Population suffers at home? and the utter insignificance into which sink the Deaths from Wounds of an Army in the field, even when engaged in constant warfare, compared with the Deaths from Zymotic disease? The two Tables annexed give this information; and, when we consider that Zymotic death is as much a "Violent death" as that which has usually been called such, we may indeed say that the one has killed its "thousands," but the other its "tens of thousands!"

* Acute and Chronic Dysentery furnished a mortality of 78 per cent., and was by far the most fatal disease in this fatal category.

† The whole of General Sir W. Codrington's admirable Evidence, in the Report of the Crimean Commissioners, will corroborate the above, in its essential features.

TABLE No. 1.
Annual Rate of Mortality per cent., in the Army of the East and in the English Male Population of the Ages 15—45.

Class of Diseases.	Deaths Annually to 100 living.	
	In the Army in the East.	English Male Population, 15—45
1. Zymotic diseases.. ..	18·7	·2
2. Constitutional Diseases	·3	·4
3. Local Diseases	·9	·3
4. Violent Deaths	3·0	·1
All Causes	22·9	1·0

TABLE No. 2
Table showing the Estimated Average Monthly Strength of the Army; and the Deaths and Annual Rate of Mortality per 1,000 in each month, from April 1854 to March 1856 (inclusive), in the Hospitals of the Army in the East.

Comparison between Deaths from Wounds and Zymotic Deaths, in an Army in time of War.

	Estimated Average Monthly Strength of the Army.	Deaths.			Annual rate of Mortality per 1,000		
		Zymotic Diseases.	Wounds and Injuries.	All other Causes.	Zymotic Diseases.	Wounds and Injuries.	All other Causes.
1854. April ..	8,751	1	..	5	1·4	..	7·0
May ..	23,333	12	..	9	6·2	..	4·6
June ..	28,333	11	..	6	4·7	..	2·5
July ..	28,722	359	..	23	150·0	..	9·6
August ..	30,246	828	1	30	328·5	·4	11·9
September	30,290	788	81	70	312·2	32·1	27·7
October ..	30,643	503	132	128	197·0	51·7	50·1
November	29,736	844	287	106	340·6	115·8	42·8
December	32,779	1,725	114	131	631·5	41·7	48·0
1855. January ..	32,393	2,761	83	324	1022·8	30·7	120·0
February	30,919	2,120	42	361	822·8	16·3	140·1
March ..	30,107	1,205	32	172	480·8	12·8	68·6
April ..	32,252	477	48	57	177·5	17·9	21·2
May ..	35,473	508	49	37	171·8	16·6	12·5
June ..	38,863	802	209	31	247·6	64·5	9·6
July ..	42,647	382	134	33	107·5	37·7	9·3
August ..	44,614	483	164	25	129·9	44·1	6·7
September	47,751	189	276	20	47·5	69·4	5·0
October ..	46,852	128	53	18	32·8	13·6	4·6
November	37,853	178	33	32	56·4	10·5	10·1
December	43,217	91	18	28	25·3	5·0	7·8
1856. January ..	44,212	42	2	48	11·4	·5	13·0
February	43,485	24	..	19	6·6	..	5·2
March ..	46,140	15	..	35	3·9	..	9·1

The Deaths under the head of "Wounds and Injuries" comprise the following Causes:—Luxatio, Sub-Luxatio, Vulnus Sclopitorum, Vulnus Incisum, Contusio, Fractura, Ambustio, and Concussio-Cerebri.

158

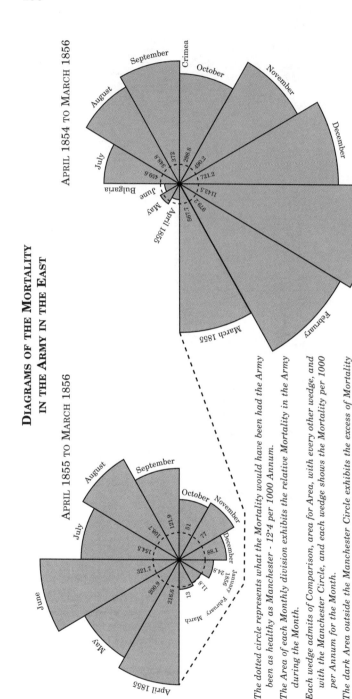

DIAGRAMS OF THE MORTALITY IN THE ARMY IN THE EAST

APRIL 1854 TO MARCH 1856

APRIL 1855 TO MARCH 1856

The dotted circle represents what the Mortality would have been had the Army been as healthy as Manchester - 12·4 per 1000 Annum.

The Area of each Monthly division exhibits the relative Mortality in the Army during the Month.

Each wedge admits of Comparison, area for Area, with every other wedge, and with the Manchester Circle, and each wedge shows the Mortality per 1000 per Annum for the Month.

The dark Area outside the Manchester Circle exhibits the excess of Mortality in the Army for the same ages over that of one of the most unhealthy Towns in England.

The figures show the Mortality per 1000 per Annum.

In eight Regiments, viz., the 46th, 95th, 63rd, 33rd, 23rd, 50th, 28th, and 44th, the mortality from disease alone, in seven months, was 73 per cent.; a fact unparallelled in English history, except in the short Burmese war of 1826. Walcheren, so often referred to, gives only the statistic of 10¼ per cent. from disease in seven months, and the Peninsula 12 per cent. in a year.

The 46th presents the apparent anomaly of losing more than its average strength.

That part of the Infantry, actually engaged in the siege throughout these seven months, lost 45 per cent. from disease alone, in these seven months.

The average of the whole force gives a mortality of 39 per cent., including the Highland Brigade, never employed in the trenches, but encamped near Balaclava, the average loss in which was only 24 per cent.; the Cavalry partially dismounted and therefore not performing picket duty, which therefore lost only 15 per cent.; four Regiments arriving after Christmas, which were sent immediately to the front, and lost 27 per cent.; and four Regiments arriving in January, and remaining three weeks without taking any part of the duty in the front, which lost only 7 per cent.

The Naval Brigade shews the astonishing difference in per centage of mortality from disease of 3½ per cent., instead of 73 per cent. for the eight Regiments above specified.

The mortality from disease among Military Officers, who suffered in action a loss greater in proportion than the men, was about 6 per cent. only, including the deaths from wounds at Scutari, which are not included among the men.

The account of one day of a soldier's life in the trenches during the winter of 1854–55 will remove any surprise which the above statistics may have created.

Mustered with great coat and blanket, half an hour before dusk, the soldier marched, through the mud, into the trenches, which, owing to the nature of the ground, were full of deep holes, out of which the boulders had been dug, filled with water, into which he could not but fall in the darkness: he took his seat with his back to the bank, in a cramped position, to allow of others passing before him along the bottom of the trench, only four feet wide. There he remained, if no alarm occurred, whatever the weather might be, till morning, when he was relieved and arrived again at his quarters.

In the early part of the winter, he was thus on duty in the trenches two nights out of three; later, one night out of two, but the average of duty was, till the termination of the winter,

Account of Soldiers' Day, when employed in the Trenches.

excessive. The 46th Regiment actually served in the trenches six nights out of seven, then ceasing to be able to furnish parties for trench-duties.

The soldier, on his return, had to collect fuel to roast his green coffee, without tools, although the chief part of the fuel consisted of roots. He next ground his coffee between a fragment of shell and a stone, and then boiled it for use. But the majority of the men were too much exhausted to go through this process. They breakfasted on their rum and biscuit, and then lay down on the muddy ground of the tent, without other covering, either above or below, but the great coat and blanket, brought wet from the trenches. In the afternoon, the soldier might be ordered to go from five to seven miles, on fatigue duty, to Balaclava, to fetch the rations of his regiment. On his return, he had again to gather fuel, to boil the salt rations in the mess cans, which did not hold water enough to abstract the salt. A portion only of the salt beef was, therefore, consumed, and it became the duty, every week, of the Quarter Master General's Department to bury what was thrown away, to the amount of hundreds of lbs. per regiment. The salt pork, issued two days out of the seven, containing less salt, was eaten often wholly or partially raw. Towards dusk, the soldier was either marched again to the trenches or retired to his tent, if not on sentry or picket duty.

He had on either a shirt, which he had worn for six weeks, with swarms of vermin on his person and hair, or was without linen altogether. His kit having been left on board, by order, when he landed at Old Fort, was in very few cases recovered, and that after a period of from six to ten weeks.

He wore, during the winter, a single pair of laced boots, which, being wet through, he was afraid to unlace, lest the heat of the tent should dry them, so that they could not be put on again. Thus, even when asked by the Regimental Surgeon, he denied that he felt numbness in his feet, lest he should be ordered to unlace his boots.

(The French soldier, with his shoes and gaiters, and the sailor with his shoes, obtained warmth to his feet.)

What was done with him when Sick.

A man who has reported himself fit for duty, over night, has not unfrequently been carried back sick by his comrades from trenches in the morning, and has died on his way or a few hours afterwards, so little inclination was there to shirk duty. This does not refer to cases of cholera, which are essentially sudden.

The soldier, if reported sick, was removed from his own tent to the Hospital tent, in most instances precisely similar, for very few Hospital marquees had been brought to the front. Here the men lay, often in the mud, generally with only salt provisions and biscuit, sometimes without medicine or medical comforts, and with so little room that the Medical Officer could hardly pass between the patients. The Medical Officer, unable thus often to procure medical comforts, medicine, or marquees, sent down his patient, as the most humane means of dealing with him, on a mule or cavalry horse, sometimes led and sometimes not, through the rain and storm, to Balaclava. Both deaths and frostbite occasionally occurred on the way, and falls were necessarily frequent. On arriving at Balaclava (the small General Hospital there, formed out of the school-house, containing only 300—400) the large majority of the sick and wounded were laid upon the beach for several hours, foul or fair, awaiting their turn of distribution into transports. (The "Sick Ships" were not organised before January 1855.)

During the voyage the sick man may have been on the decks, in a hammock, or in a bunk. He seldom received anything but water, or tea and biscuit, for the first twelve hours, at least until after the organization of the Sick Ships.

He was detained, previous to sailing from the Crimea, and after arriving in the Bosphorus, on board ship for a period greatly exceeding (as an average) the length of the voyage, which was from 36—60 hours.

On landing, he was carried, if unable to walk, up to the Hospitals, suffering a still further delay, sometimes of hours, the final order for his reception into a particular Hospital or ward not having been issued.

The universal impression in, nevertheless, that, among the men, there never was heard a murmur, and that, from first to last, they continued as eager "to get into Sevastopol" and "to go back to their comrades," as if they never had suffered.

Even when in Hospital, they were never heard to refer to past hardships, otherwise than as a simple matter of necessity "in war-time."*

Unfailing endurance of the Men under hardships.

* On those who saw the simple courage, the enduring patience, the good sense, the strength to suffer without words, of this handful of men defending the position, like the Greeks at Thermopylae, who drew their blankets over their heads and died without a word, like the Greeks of old, it has made an impression never to be forgotten. Their devotion to one another, when scorning to report themselves sick, for fear of throwing more labour on their comrades, has made a still deeper impression. There is scarcely any example in history to compare with it. More will be said of this hereafter. But surely the blood of such men calls to us from the ground, not for vengeance, but for mercy on their survivors!

162

After this short account of a soldier's day, in the first winter of the Campaign, the following statistics of the Sickness and Mortality of the Army, month by month, during the whole Campaign, will be in no way unaccountable. It will be observed that, in January 1855, the Annual Rate of Mortality per 1,000 was 1,174: a higher rate than that which prevailed during the month (September) when the mortality was highest in the year of the Great Plague, 1665.

Deaths and Admissions into Hospital in the British Army in the East:

1854.	Deaths in Hospital, including Crimea, Scutari, Transports.	Deaths to Force per 1,000 per Annum.	Admissions into Hospital (Primary) to Strength per 1,000 per Annum.
April	6	8·4	468
May	21	10·8	1,224
June	17	7·2	1,116
July	382	159·6	2,100
August	859	340·8	3,384
September	939	372	2,676
October	763	298·8	2,832
November	1,237	499·2	3,336
December	1,970	721·2	3,888
1855.			
January	3,168	1,173·6	4,176
February	2,523	* 979·2	2,760
March	1,409	561·6	2,316
April	582	223·2	1,716
May	594	202·8	1,944
June	1,042	318	3,396
July	549	152·4	2,832
August	672	181·2	2,760
September	485	121·2	2,004
October	199	49·2	1,380
November	243	† 52·8	1,176
December	137	32·4	1,332

* The health of the Army before Sevastopol was then improving. But this enormous per-centage was kept up by the bad state of the Scutari Hospitals, which was growing *worse*.

† If it be asked how it was that the Mortality in November 1855, being 53 per 1,000, should still be so high, it may be answered there were causes enough.

1. With regard to the Crimea, the whole Army was not hutted till the end of January, 1856: half, at least, was still unhutted in December 1855.

Deaths and Admissions—*continued*

1856.*	Deaths in Hospital, including Crimea, Scutari, Transports.	Deaths to Force per 1,000 per Annum.	Admissions into Hospital (Primary) to Strength per 1,000 per Annum.
January	92	21·6	1,116
February	43	9·6	924
March	50	10·6	972
April	41	8·4	840
May	29	7·2	720
June	6	2·4	432

The Naval Brigade, in which the mortality from disease shows so remarkable a difference as that above referred to, were placed under the following circumstances, largely differing from those of the troops. *(Contrast offered by the Navy.)*

They obtained far better shelter than the common bell-tent, by burrowing into the sides of the hill by keeping sheltered ground, by erecting loose stone walls, by covering themselves in with tarpaulin, slate, board, and portions of condemned sails, by making tubular chimneys of pierced canister, &c.

They formed boilers of the empty powder-cans, about two feet cube, with a large orifice on the top, which are used for the great guns. They were served with fuel, chiefly from the ships. Their water was near; indeed, their Commander sunk a well, with well-sinkers obtained from the army.

As a corps attached to the army, they obtained issues of certain necessaries, on application of their active Commanders,

And the whole of the excess of Mortality in November was produced by Cholera, arising from the men being crowded together in the old huts (unventilated), from the dampness of the ground, and from the ground being *used up*, which it soon becomes with a careless army.

2. With regard to Scutari, it was the month of the fatal outbreak of cholera, which began with the German Legion; these troops are not, however, of course, included.

110 out of the Total Deaths, 243, in November 1855 were produced by Cholera.

It might be important to bring out yet more strongly the difference between the cause of the Mortality in the winter of 1854–55, which was chiefly bad food and bad clothing, and that of the summer of 1855, which was neglect of Sanitary measures.

* The total Admissions into Hospital, during the last six months of the occupation, from January to June, 1856, were 21,659, and the Deaths 261, being at the rate of 24 deaths per 1,000 *Admissions* per annum. The Deaths to *Strength* in the Household Troops at home are 26 per 1,000, per annum, according to the calculation given in the Sanitary Section, including Invalids.

164

irrespective of the long-established forms for issues to the troops.

In the morning, coffee or cocoa was prepared for a sailor, as it would have been on board ship. In the evening, hot soup was served out to him, on his return from the trenches, made for him from salt meat with ample time to soak out the salt, by processes used on board ship, or from ox-heads, which, if not thrown away at the neighbouring Commissariat Divisional Slaughter-house, were at least not issued to the troops.

The sailor, having theoretically the same advantages as the soldier, as to extra issues, having his own warm clothing, and the purser's stores at hand, enjoyed a still greater benefit in the care with which his officers exacted that his wet clothes should be taken from him on his return from the trenches, and dried in a hut at a stove prepared for the purpose; that he should have a pair of dry blankets ready to receive him, and a change of shoes and stockings, till he went on duty again. Oranges were also served out, in pursuance of the custom of the Navy, which classifies acids as additional rations, and not as medical comforts, issuable on the Surgeon's order.

An exception to the above statement is to be made, however, with regard to that small portion of the Naval Brigade, separated and brigaded with the Light Division, which suffered in like manner, being under like circumstances.

Illustration of the imperfect Nomenclature of Disease.

The importance of using a more elaborate and specific nomenclature of disease is shown, from the consideration that the "Febris c. c." (Common Continuous Fever) of the British Military Hospital, a term including Typhus, Typhoid Fever, Relapsing Fever, and Febricula, indicates neither the origin of the disease nor the kind of treatment, inasmuch as it is made to include every kind of fever, together with drunkenness. We want a new heading, "Drunken Fever," to separate these casualties from fevers arising from other causes. All apoplexies, almost without exception, in our Army might be styled "Drunken Apoplexy." A formal posting of the drunken statistics might exercise a salutary influence. In the proposed nosology of Dr. Farr, we find the disease termed "Alcoholismus," which includes "Delirium Tremens." This last is made to appear in Army Statistics under "Diseases of the Brain." But the terms which are used e.g., in the Sardinian army, and copied from our own Civil Registrar-General's Office (with the addition of some diseases, incidental to camps), *do* indicate both the origin of the disease and the mode of cure, and the mode of prevention. General La Marmora was visited, in consequence of a request from home, by one of our Sanitary Commissioners, who was able to discover, from private returns, the absence of vegetable food, or the peculiarities of the encampment, as the remediable cause of the disease.

Another example of want of definition, still stronger than that of Febris c. c., which includes tipsy head-aches, is the heading "All other Diseases," which has been seen to occupy fifty per cent. of a given Register. This is "Hamlet," with half of the "part of Hamlet left out."

If classification means assigning a place to each object, this is not classification.

It is essentially necessary that we should have an Army Statistical Department.

Hitherto all that has been done for the Army in this way has been done by the able Colonel Sir Alexander Tulloch, at first as a labor of love.

From him should now be obtained,

1. A summary of the results of all his statistical enquiries into the mortality and diseases of the Army.
2. A comparison between the mortality of
   (*a.*) Officers,
   (*b.*) Privates and Non-commissioned Officers, at the several ages specified in his reports,
   (*c.*) Distinguishing Cavalry and Infantry,
   (*d.*) Distinguishing results in

   England and Wales,
   Scotland,
   Ireland,
   Foreign or Colonial Stations.
3. Taking each Station, as

   West Coast of Africa,
   West Indian Islands,
   East Indies,
   Mediterranean, &c.,

a statement of

(*a.*) What the mortality of the Army is collectively, at each of such Stations,

(*b.*) What the mortality of the Native population and of the Troops at corresponding ages, where this is known.

Necessity of a Statistical Department for the Army in general. Col. Tulloch's Materials.

Now, is it not a fact that the mortality of the British Soldier exceeds the mortality of the Civil population in many of those Stations abroad?

Looking at home, and comparing the mortality of the Soldier, year by year, in ordinary times and in epidemic years, with the mortality of the Civil population, is not the mortality of the Soldier excessive?

To what extent, we ought now to know, is the mortality of the Army excessive? How many in the 1,000 perish annually in excess of the mortality experienced amongst healthy classes of the community?

It has been attempted, in the preceding Section, to give an accurate though short and imperfect answer to this.

The mortality of the general population, as has there been shown, embraces the mortality of vagrants, of nearly 1,000,000 paupers (*vide* Poor Law Returns) and of all the weakest and worst people in the country, as well as the healthy and vigorous. If such classes as the former were excluded, would not the mortality of the residue be greatly below the general average?

Now, in the Army, is there not a double selection constantly at work having a direct tendency to reduce the per-centage of mortality?

The tests of health which the recruit has to undergo, before he can become a soldier, exclude all laboring under actual disease, such as consumption, and some of those predisposed to disease.

Again, if a soldier becomes consumptive, he is discharged or pensioned, in many cases, before he is cured or dead.

Now, what is the annual rate of morality per 1,000 among soldiers so discharged or pensioned, during the months after discharge,

0—3

3—6

6—9

9—12?

It is to be feared that this is very high, from the imperfect data given at p. 259, Sanitary Section. Now, if the strength of the invalided, one year after discharge from the army at home, and the deaths among them, were added to the strength and deaths of the Army from which they are drawn, would not the mortality be raised considerably higher, as has been shown for five years, 1849—53, in the same Sanitary Notes?

What kinds of diseases are, then, so fatal to the Guards, the Infantry, and the Cavalry at home?

If it is consumption, is not consumption the effect of bad ventilation chiefly? If it is fever, is not fever always preventible?

What are the causes to which the bad Sanitary state of the Army is attributable? and how should these causes be combated?

At home, the Line suffers twice as much from Consumption as men in Civil life, at the same ages. It suffers more than twice as much from Zymotic disease. Now, there is no *à priori* reason for this. The mere statement of it would excite inquiry into its causes and their remedies, if generally made known.

Annual Rate of Mortality, per 1,000 living from *All Causes, Zymotic Diseases, Chest and Tubercular Diseases*, and *other Causes*, amongst the *English Male Population* (1848—54), and amongst the *Infantry of the Line*, serving at Home, (1837—46).

Comparison of the Mortality of the Line with that of the Civil Population.

Causes of Death.	Annual Rate of Mortality per 1,000 living.	
	Males aged 15 to 45 in England and Wales during the seven years 1848—54.	Infantry of the Line, serving at Home, during the ten years 1837—46.
All Causes	9·7	16·7
Zymotic diseases	1·9	4·9
Chest and Tubercular Diseases	4·5	9·2
Other Causes	3·3	2·6

The Deaths in England and Wales (1848—54) are taken from the Registrar General's 19th Annual Report, p. 150; and the Deaths in the Infantry of the Line, from Colonel Tulloch's Report of 1853, p. 62.

Now, recurring to the latest date of Colonel Sir A. Tulloch's valuable Reports, which is, we believe, 1853, and the last date in which, referred to, is 1846,—recurring to the non-arrangement for their regular publication, we would ask, is there any *annual* medical and sanitary report whatever published, containing summaries and analyses of the reports of the Medical Officers of the Army?

If the causes of death among 2,600,000 people in London can be printed *weekly*, on the Tuesday following the week, and if the births and deaths for the whole of England and Wales can be printed *quarterly*, within a month of the end of every quarter, could not classified returns of the attacks of sickness, and of the mortality of the Army be published periodically, with equal punctuality?

Why cannot what is done with apparent ease for Civilians, be done for Soldiers, in whose case the

168

Does not the organization of the Army offer the greatest facilities known for statistical registration?

Could not the *mean strength* of each regiment be determined by monthly musters? Could not the *mean number* of *sick* from fever, consumption, and other causes be determined by the same method?

Were the *strength* thus determined compared with the *deaths* by the various causes, and with the *attacks of sickness*, a complete view would thus be obtained of the main results of the sanitary or fatal influences to which the regiment had been exposed.

If these results could be collected for *one* regiment, they could be collected for every regiment. This follows necessarily from the Army organization.

The practical utility of such information would be greatly increased by its embracing the whole Army, and above all, by its being collected and analysed immediately: the object being for the Secretary of State for the War Department to be able to see the movements of the health of the Army, as clearly as the movements of time on the face of a clock.

The great utility of partial returns, published many years after the events have happened, after the men to which they relate are dead or have been discharged, has been shewn by Sir A. Tulloch's Blue Books. Would not complete returns of the whole facts for every portion of the Army be still more useful than these partial returns?

Would not recent information, punctually supplied, be practically of greater use than the retarded, almost posthumous returns which have hitherto been published in England?

The difference in the efficiency of a healthy and an unhealthy Army has been practically illustrated in the most terrible manner by our late Crimean campaign; where more than half the Infantry was sick in Hospital at once, part of the remaining half was told off to attend upon them, and the remainder only was capable of trench and fatigue duty, and of keeping the position.

It is unquestionable,—and our experience of the way in which, in Civil life, mortality can be, and has been, reduced, need hardly be referred to,—it is unquestionable that the mortality and sickness of the Army in peace may be reduced to one-half, at most, of its present excessive amount. It is a thing beyond all doubt to be done. The degree to which this would affect our system of recruiting, our system of pensioning, the well-being of our men can scarcely be calculated.

One question remains; Are Vital Statistics made a branch of Medical education? Are the Medical Officers examined on this subject? To what extent have published works of Army medical Officers assisted Sir A. Tulloch in his Statistical researches?

Twenty years hence it will scarcely be credited that a time has been, so late as the year 1857, when there was nothing analogous to our Civil General Register Office in Military organization.

The main end of Statistics should not be to inform the Government as to how many men have died, but to enable immediate steps to be taken to prevent the extension of disease and mortality.

Main end of Statistics.

It is therefore of paramount importance to have special reporting for special occasions: *e.g.*, the Yellow Fever breaks out in consequence of the locality or overcrowding of a Barrack, or Dysentery in consequence of monotony of diet.

If the Government had known, week by week, that Scorbutus was ravaging the Army in the Crimea, the very first appearance of the disease in the weekly states with a reason why the disease had appeared at all, would have led the Government immediately to have sought for the requisite supplies to arrest it.

If the Medical Officer waits till the time of reporting comes round, all that is accomplished is that the Government know that they have lost a certain number of hundreds of men in a way which might have been prevented.

In France, in the event of an epidemic breaking out in any part of the Army, the facts are noted, day by day, to the "Conseil de Sante," at Paris, who notify them, day by day, to the Minister of War.

It is therefore to be concluded, from the above considerations, that

1. Whatever Statistical system be adopted should be uniform; and in every case where there is likely to be any doubt as to the precise meaning of a nosological term, it ought to be defined.

2. Whatever period is laid down for sending in the Statistical Reports, these periods should be departed from at the first appearance of any epidemic in the Army. And the progress of the disease, with its *causes*, the means adopted to arrest it, and the success of these means, should be reported, day by day, to the War Department, wherever practicable.

3. An Officer should be attached to the Army Medical Department, with suitable assistance, to enable him to make up the Army Statistics with due accuracy.*

4. There being already an authorized and official form of registration for the Mortality in Great Britain, it is in the highest degree important that the form used in the Army should be the same.

5. The Registration of Disease and Mortality would come under the Statistical Department of the Army Medical Department, for all medical and sanitary purposes; while the mortality might be very well transmitted to the Registrar General's Office, and published quarterly.†

6. The forms required for such a system of Army Medical Statistics as are here proposed, are

I. Weekly Regimental State,‡ shewing Strength:
   1. Zymotic Diseases under their various heads.
   2. Mortality from these.
   3. More prominent Diseases of other classes and mortality from these.
   4. All other Diseases.
   5. Total Admissions during the week.
   6. Total Deaths during the week.
   7. Per-centage of Admissions from Zymotic Disease to Total Admissions.
   8. Per-centage of Deaths from Zymotic Disease to Total Deaths from Disease.
   9. Admissions and Deaths from Wounds.
   [This Return to shew the *causes* of Zymotic Disease and Mortality in connection with 1 and 2.]

II. Return, as already proposed, to be made up by the Principal Medical Officer, and sent home, week by week, to the War Department, and also to the Commanding Officer.

---

* One Form, made up at home, should not be the same as the Registrar-General's Form.

† It appears to follow, from the proposal to transfer the Statistics of Death from the War Department to the Registrar-General's Department, that the same form of Registration should be used.

‡ The Regimental Medical Statistics should be kept on the same Form as that used by the Registrar-General of England.

APPENDIX I

SECTION XI

ACTUAL AND PROPOSED FORMS FOR MEDICAL STATISTICS
IN THE ARMY

It need hardly be stated that a correct set of Statistics is the basis of all Army hygiene.

Therefore, whatever forms are adopted should have reference not only to numerical data, but to causation.

1. Preventible disease, and especially the whole zymotic class, should be clearly distinguished from other types.

2. We should have an account of all zymotic cases, whence they arise, their nature and causation in

Climates,
Soils,
Defective drainage,
Marshes,
Position of Stations or Garrisons,
Diet,
Duties,
Water,
Barracks, tents, &c.
State of Hospitals,
    Ventilation of Barracks and Hospitals,
    Overcrowding,
    Temperature,
Intemperance.

Medical Statistics should always be drawn so as to indicate the Causation of Disease.

Every local or personal cause should therefore enter as an element into the returns, and by due classification of these afterwards, the Government would be kept fully informed, not only of the health of the Army, but of all the conditions influencing it at a particular time and place, as well as of the care with which the Medical and Commanding Officers look after the men.

The weekly State—the weekly State sent to the Commander of the Forces—the weekly State transmitted, as it ought to be regularly, to the Army Medical Department at home, should be so framed as to group together all zymotic and mitigable diseases, in order that, at a glance, the government at home should be able to tell, to what extent sanitary measures are requisite and to what extent they have been neglected. Any general summary of army disease and mortality should be drawn up on the same principles. All our existing weekly forms and summaries are practically useless, except for simple numerical purposes. Her Majesty's Ministers want to know, in fact, what they are to do to preserve the numerical efficiency of the force, rather than what the force has suffered from sickness and death.

Present form
of
Classification
of Diseases.

The classification annexed below, which is that at present in use, is of scarcely any value as pointing out the causes from which our mortality springs; almost as well might the word witchcraft be assigned as a cause.

Fevers
Eruptive Fevers
Diseases of the Lungs
    "   "   Liver
    "   "   Stomach and Bowels
Epidemic Cholera
Diseases of the Brain
Dropsies
Rheumatic Affections
Venereal   "
Abscesses and Ulcers
Wounds and Injuries
Corporal Punishment
Diseases of the Eyes
    "   "   Skin
All other Diseases.

Compare with this the following proposed Details for Regimental, Divisional, or Army Weekly Medical State, and for any general summary to be used for immediate practical purposes.

Week ending

        Strength: Officers,   Men.

Mitigable or preventible diseases

Fevers: Intermittent
    "   Remittent
    "   Yellow
    "   Continued
    "   Typhoid
    "   Typhus
    "   Plague
    "   Eruptive (Small Pox, Varioloid, Chicken Pox,
                     Miliaria, Scarlet Fever, Measles,
                     Quinsy, Diphtheria)
Erysipelas
Erythema
Pycemia
Hospital Gangrene
Cholera
Diarrhoea
Dysentery: Acute
      "   Chronic
      "   Scorbutic
      "   with Liver diseases
Scorbutus
Ophthalmia
Scrofula
Phthisis pulmonalis
Catarrh
Influenza
Intemperance
Rheumatism
Carbuncle
Farunculus
Syphilis
Gonorrhoea
Sun-stroke
Frost-bite
Foot lameness
Wounds and Injuries
Other Diseases of Brain
      "   "   of Chest
      "   "   of Abdomen
      "   "   of Eye
Diseases of Liver
    "   of Skin
Abscesses and Ulcers
Corporal Punishment

174

This form is merely given as a rough illustration of what is here meant. As an equally rough explanation of the suggestion, it may be stated that the name "Intermittent Fever," conveys the idea, as to its causation, of marshy ground in low temperatures; "Remittent," of marshy ground in high temperatures.

The names of some of the Fevers suggest defective drainage as a cause; but over-crowding, where all other conditions were good in a Crimean hut, would produce Continued Fever; a little more would produce Typhoid Fever; and a little more Typhus. The three Dysenteries have frequently dietetic causes. Phthisis is again mainly owing to over-crowding and bad ventilation.

Were the Sanitary element represented, as it ought to be, in the Army Medical Department, a form like this would immediately suggest causes, to be enquired into, as producing the kind of mortality indicated as predominant at the respective Stations. It is not often, it may be as well to say, that any one cause is to be found operating alone, in *separate* action, as might sometimes be seen in the Crimea.

Considerations for the Construction of a Sanitary Nomenclature of Disease.

The following considerations are suggested as those on which such a Sanitary nomenclature, as is here indicated, might be founded.

1. Nosological arrangements have generally been based on some scientific ground.—Fevers have been classed together; also Cachectic diseases, and constitutional diseases generally, as indicating some common origin or a common constitutional defect.

Again, Diseases of Cavities (head, chest, abdomen) have been classified together, mainly for pathological purposes.

2. Why should there not be an arrangement of diseases according to their *causes*, and with a special view to the removal of such causes, and the prevention of such disease? Why should the attention of the Medical man be always directed to what disease has caused, and not to what has caused the disease; to what it *has done*, and not to its prevention? A Sanitary nomenclature is thus of importance. It recognizes prevention. It recognizes preventible causation.

3. In the present state of Sanitary knowledge, it would be impossible to arrange all known diseases according to their causation; but many of the most important may be so grouped and experience will, in time, add greatly to the numbers.

For example, we have diseases of Malarial origin, such as intermittent and remittent fevers,—

Diseases from animal exhalations, such as plague, typhus, continued fevers,—

Diseases proceeding partly from the one, partly from the other class of causes, such as cholera, diarrhoea, dysentery,—

Diseases arising from bad food, such as scorbutus, and other blood diseases,—

Diseases, in which several causes co-operate, as for example, in phthisis, which arises from foul air, want of exercise bad food—in ophthalmia, where foul air alternates with dryness, light, dust, &c.

4. Speaking generally, the whole Zymotic class may be considered mitigable and several of its divisions of disease preventible.

It would be a great means of directing the attention of Medical Officers to the causation, if, in all cases of prevailing Zymotic disease, they were required to state distinctly the cause. If two or three consecutive cases of any such disease happened to appear in a regiment, the cause should be at once searched for, reported, and removed.

5. It would be unsafe at present to lay down *precisely* the diseases and their causes:—the one as being an invariable consequence of the other; because disease is the result of the operation of many causes, and perhaps the *determining* cause is one, which, by itself, and in the absence of others, would produce no effect. It may be the last straw which breaks the camel's back. It will be enough at present to indicate the importance of the matter.

The Diseases of the Crimean Army which caused the Deaths enumerated at pp. 320, 321, are given here, re-classed, according to the Registrar-General's nomenclature.

Classification of Diseases of Crimean Army, according to that of Dr. Farr.

General Return showing the Primary Admissions into the Hospitals of the Army in
the East, from the 10th April, 1854, to the 30th June, 1856; also the deaths from
Primary as well as Secondary Admissions, together with those occurring on
board Transports, conveying Sick and Wounded, during the same period.—
Arranged according to the Classification of Causes of Death proposed by Dr. Farr,
in the 16th Annual Report of the Registrar-General, pp. 82—96.

Class.	Causes of Death.	Admissions.	Deaths.
	All Causes	162,123	18,057
	Specified Causes	161,297	17,712
	DISEASES.		
I	Zymotic	112,651	14,507
II	Constitutional	828	204
III	Local	25,043	668
IV	Developmental	214	19
V	Violent	22,561	2,314
	(Orders)		
I	1. Miasmatic	108,577	14,503
	2. Enthetic	3,748	4
	3. Dietetic (included in Order 1) . .	—	—
	4. Parasitic	326	0
II	1. Diathetic	458	84
	2. Tubercular	370	120
III	Diseases of the—		
	1. Nervous System	4,051	117
	2. Organs of Circulation	263	41
	3. Respiratory Organs	2,607	384
	4. Digestive Organs	4,592	84
	5. Urinary Organs	239	6
	6. Organs of Generation	—	—
	7. Organs of Locomotion	129	1
	8. Integumentary System	13,162	35
IV	1—3. Not occurring in the Army . .		
	4. Diseases of Nutrition	214	19
V	1. Accident	2,484	532
	2. Battle	18,283	1,761
	3. Homicide	—	—
	4. Suicide	20	20
	5. Punishment and Execution	1,774	1
	Causes not specified	826	345

Class.	Causes of Death.	Admissions.	Deaths.
I	Order 1.		
	Small-pox	21	4
	Measles	5	2
	Scarlatina	3	0
	Quinsey	924	9
	Erysipelas	78	21
	Phlebitis	3	0
	Typhus (and continued) Fever	25,841	3,075
	Carbuncle	—*	—*
	Influenza	9,506	144
	Dysentery	8,278	2,259
	Diarrhoea	44,164	3,651
	Cholera	6,970	4,512
	Ague	2,406	60
	Remittent Fever	2,957	311
	Rheumatism (acute and chronic)	5,044	233
	Order 2.		
	Syphilis	3,748	4
	Hydrophobia.	—*	—*
	Order 3.		
	Privation	1*	1*
	Purpura and Scurvy (see above, under Dysentery)	2,096	178
	Alcoholism	—*	—*
	(includes only		
	Delirium Tremens	281	44
	other cases not returned.)		
	Order 4.		
	Scabies	257	0
	Worms	68	0
	Dracunculus.	1	0
II	Order 1.		
	Gout	—*	—*
	Dropsy	294	63
	Cancer et Tumores	62	1
	Mortification.	79	20
	Cachexia	23	0
	Order 2.		
	Scrofula	90	3
	Phthisis	279	116
	Hydrocephalus	1	1

* No admissions or deaths were returned under this head.

Class.	Causes of Death.	Admissions.	Deaths.
III	Order 1.		
	Cephalitis	11	7
	Apoplexy	87	70
	Paralysis	42	10
	Insanity (Dementia)	44	4
	Epilepsy	261	17
	Tetanus	10	8
	Cephalalgia	128	0
	Neuralgia	28	0
	Ophthalmitis.	3,307	0
	Otitis	133	1
	Order 2.		
	Pericarditis	24	4
	Aneurism	9	8
	Heart Disease	127	29
	Varix	58	0
	Palpitatio	45	0
	Order 3.		
	Epistaxis	10	0
	Laryngitis	—*	—*
	Bronchitis	1,688	199
	Pleurisy	264	23
	Pneumonia	590	161
	Asthma and Dyspnoea	55	1
	Other Lung Diseases	—	—
	Order 4.		
	Gastritis	29	8
	Enteritis	36	11
	Peritonitis	16	9
	Ascites	—*	—*
	Ulceration of Intestines	—*	—*
	Hernia	101	2
	Ileus et Constipatio.	1,862	5
	Intussusception	1	1
	Stricture of Intestines	—*	—*
	Fistula	129	3
	Dyspepsia	906	3
	Haemorrhois.	358	0
	Haematemesis	15	2
	Singultus	1	0
	Pancreas	—*	—*
	Hepatitis	251	17
	Jaundice	878	22
	Other Liver Diseases	—*	—*
	Spleen Disease	9	1

* No admissions or deaths were returned under this head.

Class.	Causes of Death.	Admissions.	Deaths.
	Order 5.		
	Nephritis (and Nephria)	26	2
	Ischuria	39	0
	Nephria (see above)	—	—
	Diabetes	8	1
	Stone	—*	—*
	Haematuria	1	0
	Cystitis	9	1
	Stricture of Urethra	139	2
	Hydrocele	15	0
	Varicocele	2	0
	Order 6. (Not applicable to the Army.)		
	Order 7.		
	Arthritis	87	0
	Ostitis and Periostitis	7	0
	Joint Disease	25	1
	Exostosia	2	0
	Necrosis, Caries, &c.	10	0
	Order 8.	8,323	23
	Phlegmon	4,090	11
	Ulcer	749	1
	Skin Diseases		
IV	Orders 1—8. (Not applicable to the Army.)		
	Order 4.		
	Atrophy and Debility	214	9
V	Order 1.		
	Gelatio (frostbite)	2,389	463
	Pernio (chilblain)	9	0
	Sunstroke	13	2
	Asphyxia	2	2
	Poisoning	6	0
	Other violent deaths.†	65	65
	Order 2. (It is not stated that all these wounds and injuries were incurred in fighting, but, there being no means of distinction, they have all been referred to this order.)		
	Luxatio	80	1
	Subluxatio	1,453	1

* No admissions or deaths were returned under this head.

† These are not properly returned, but appear under the collective head of "Accidental, Sudden, Ebrietas, and Cold, &c."

Class.	Causes of Death.	Admissions.	Deaths.
	Order 2. (*continued*)		
	Vulnus Sclopitorum	10,691	1,706
	" Incisum	1,270	18
	Contusio	4,006	21
	Fractura	380	14
	Ambustio	399	0
	Concussio Cerebri	4	0
	Order 3.		
	Homicide	—†	—†
	Order 4.		
	Suicide*	20	20
	Order 5.		
	Execution	1‡	1‡
	Punishment	1,773	0
	Causes not specified	826	345

Classification of Diseases of Infantry of Line serving at Home, according to that of Dr. Farr.

If this Classification of Causes of Death, as proposed by Dr. Farr, be adopted, then the classes of mortality from diseases most prevalent in the Infantry on Home Stations, as compared with the extent of the same types of disease in Civil life, at the same ages, may be shewn by the following Table.

The differences between this Table and that given at p. 327 will be explained by the two facts:—1. That the diseases are there classified according to the imperfect system of nomenclature in use. 2. That the deaths from accident and "unaccounted for" in the Infantry are there not given, which raise the mortality 1·1 per 1,000.

* Unsuccessful attempts at suicide were, apparently, not recorded.
† No admissions or deaths were returned under this head.
‡ This case was returned simply as hanging.

Note.—The names of certain Orders as well as those of certain specific Diseases are omitted, as not applicable to the Army.

DEATHS and ANNUAL RATE of MORTALITY per 1,000 from ALL CAUSES, ZYMOTIC DISEASES, CHEST and TUBERCULAR DISEASES, and ALL OTHER DISEASES amongst the ENGLISH MALE POPULATION, aged 15–45 (1848–54) and amongst the INFANTRY of the LINE serving at HOME (1837–46).

CAUSES OF DEATH.	DEATHS		ANNUAL RATE OF MORTALITY per 1,000 living	
	Of Males aged 15 to 45, in England & Wales during the 7 years 1848–54.	Of Infantry of the Line (serving at Home) during the 10 years 1837–46.	Of Males aged 15–45, in England & Wales during the 7 years 1848–54.	Of Infantry of the Line (serving at Home) during the 10 Years 1837–46.
All Causes	283,167	2,865	9·8	17·9
Zymotic Diseases	56,347	659	2·0	4·1
Chest and Tubercular Diseases	130,753	1,612	4·5	10·1
All other Diseases (including Violent Deaths)	96,067	594	3·3	3·7

Males, aged 15–45, living in England and Wales, in the middle of 1851	4,130,331
Aggregate Strength of Infantry of the Line (serving at Home) in 10 years 1837–46	160,103

Note.—The Deaths in England and Wales (1848—54) are taken from the 18th Annual Report of the Registrar-General, p. 150, and the Population (1851) from the Census Report, Occupations, Vol. 1, p. clix. The Deaths and aggregate strength of the Infantry of the Line (1837—46) are taken from Sir A. Tulloch's Report on the Health of the Army for 1853, p. 62 and p. 9. At p. 9, in addition to the 2,683 deaths from Disease (p. 62) are returned the particulars of 127 deaths by Violence, leaving, however, 55 deaths unaccounted for—2,683 + 127 + 55 make the above 2,865 deaths.

Bronchitis and Influenza have no place in the Army nomenclature. The "Chronic Catarrh" of the Army Returns is believed to be really "Phthisis" in the great majority of cases; "Acute Catarrh" comprehends, probably, both "Epidemic Catarrh" or Influenza, and Bronchitis. The 55 deaths from "Acute Catarrh" have been treated as Influenza and referred to Zymotic Diseases. The Deaths from Tubercular and Chest Diseases comprise Scrofula, 24 (including Apostema Lumbare, 10, Hydrarthrus, 1); Phthisis, 1,241; Haemoptysis, 36; Chronic Catarrh, 135; Hydrocephalus, 2; Asthma, 2; Dyspnoea, 7; Pleurisy, 10; Pneumonia, 155. The Zymotic Diseases are, as far as the nomenclature allows, the same as those enumerated in the Registrar-General's 16th Annual Report, pp. 83-5 of the Appendix.

182

APPENDIX II.

SECTION XI

Sources of the Statistics Used in the Section

Sources of the
Statistics.

Inaccuracies
and
Discrepancies.

I have carefully collated all the statistics from six different official sources.

The sick appear to have been sent from the front to Balaclava without any accurate account of their numbers—to have been put on board without any steps having been taken to keep a proper register. The number of deaths on board during the passage is reported different in each separate return. When the sick arrived at Scutari, there was, at first, no provision for registering them on landing, or when they were received into Hospital. And, even after death, the only trustworthy record of the fact was the Adjutant's Head Roll of Burials, which exceeded in six months by upwards of 500 the number reported in the Orderly Room as having died in the Hospitals. While, to complete the chain of defects, the return of total sick treated in Lord Raglan's Army including in it all who were sick both in the Crimea and at Scutari, is used by the Director-General himself as the number treated at Scutari.

The Returns of Dead at Scutari from Oct. 1 to Dec. 31, 1854, vary as follows:—

1. PRINCIPAL MEDICAL OFFICER'S.	2. REPORTED DEATHS.	3. BURIALS.	4. INSPECTOR-GENERAL'S INFANTRY ALONE.*
910	1,046	1,301	795

The sum of these three months has been taken, in order to cover any unavoidable discrepancies arising from Burials not taking place on the same day as the Deaths.† Yet the Return of Burials exceeds in three months that of Deaths reported in the Hospital Books by nearly 400.

Another reason for taking these three months was, in order to eliminate the unavoidable delays in reporting from Smyrna,

* *Plus* one-ninth, roughly speaking, for Calvary, Artillery, and Engineers, *vide* statement, p. xii, of the Mortality of these Arms at Scutari. These figures are quoted from Sir A. Tulloch.

† The burials generally took place within twenty-four hours of the deaths.

where the British Army Hospital did not exist till the middle of February, and from Koulali, which was opened December 2, 1854, but contained during that month a maximum only of 240 patients.

The result of my examination of these Statistics is simply this—that, however satisfactory they may be to the Departments who have put them forth, and however correct they may be, although exhibiting such palpable diversity,— still, to any one not in the secret as to how things which apparently differ so widely are nevertheless identically the same, they convey no trustworthy idea as to the sickness and mortality of the Army in the East—and that, for any practical purpose, they are, as put forth to the public, who are most interested in the matter, but approximations to the truth.

The results can only be regarded as approximations.

I will here put in four sets of returns.

RETURN NO. I.
Deaths on board Sick Transports, between the Crimea and Scutari.

Name of Ship.*	Deaths according to		
	Cumming-Maxwell Return.	House of Commons Return.	Adjutant's Return.
Kangaroo	—	22	—
Dunbar	22	10	30
Cambria	—	21	—
Vulcan	18	10	25
Andes	15	4	—
Colombo	30	30	57
Arthur the Great	24	50	30
Orient	32 or 33	26	45
Caduceus	114	104	—
Courier	16	33	16
Cornwall	6	6	8
Negotiator	6	6	—
Lady McNaughten	3	3	3
Australia	8	3	12
Cambria	None	—	—
Echunga	7	6	1
Palmerston	11	7	5
&c. &c. &c.			

In the Adjutant-General's Return from the Crimea, it will be seen that the total number of "deaths in the Infantry, from October 1, 1854, to May 1, 1855," "on board ship or elsewhere" (meaning not on the Bosphorus or in the Crimea) is 715.

* The above comparison is made, taking the first seventeen ships in order as their names stand in the return.

Returns from the Medical Officer of each Corps serving in the Crimea, and from the Inspector-General of Hospitals at Scutari, show that, during the same period, the number of deaths in Cavalry, artillery, and Royal Engineers, was, compared with those in the Infantry, thus,*

	CRIMEA.	SCUTARI.
Infantry	4,963	4,052
Cavalry }		
Artillery }	378	470
Engineers }		

in other words, the deaths of the Cavalry, Artillery, and Engineers were one-thirteenth of those of the Infantry in the Crimea, and rather more than one-ninth of those at Scutari. Now the mortality on board ship, including all arms of the service, is, according to

Cumming-Maxwell Report. Sept. 15, 1854, to Feb. 11, 1855.	House of Commons Report. Same period.	Scutari Adjutant's Report. Same period.	Crimean Adjutant-General's report. Oct. 1, 1854, to† May 1, 1855.
923	915	888	715 $+\frac{1}{13}$ or $+\frac{1}{9}$

RETURN No. II.
From Returns of Adjutant's Office at Scutari.—Recapitulation.

MONTHS.	No of Burials in each Month.	No. of Deaths reported in each Month.	Excess of Burials over Deaths in each Month.	Remarks.
Sept. 1854	165	78	87	
Oct. "	266	219	47	517 of the 545 have
Nov. "	368	291	77	been struck off the
Dec. "	667	536	131	strength of the General
Jan. 1855	1,473	1,360	113	Depot, the other 28 were
Feb. "	1,151	1,076	75	men brought ashore either
March "	418	416	2	dead or insensible, with no
April "	165	152	13	marks to ascertain their
May "	76	76	—	names of regiments.
	4,749	4,204	545	

* 190 Deaths took place in the General Hospital at Balaclava, in the record of which no distinction is made as to the Arm of the Service to which the dead belonged.

† The Deaths from September 15 to October 1 are reported as about 272, from February 11 to May 1 about 27.

RETURN NO. III.

APPENDIX TO REPORT FROM THE SEBASTOPOL COMMITTEE, 2ND REPORT, P. 705.

RETURN SHOWING THE TOTAL NUMBER OF SICK AND WOUNDED TREATED IN HOSPITAL AT *Scutari*:

MONTHS.	TOTAL TREATED.
During November 1854.	16,846
" December 1854.	19,479
" January 1855.	23,076

A. SMITH, M.D., *Director-General.*
13, *St. James's-place, 28th March,* 1855.

APPENDIX to REPORT from the SEBASTOPOL COMMITTEE, p. 470

No. 1.—RETURN showing the TOTAL NUMBER of MEN of *Lord Raglan's Army* SICK During each MONTH, from the Landing in Turkey.

MONTHS.	Total Sick or Wounded of all Arms during each Month.	
1854, April	503	
May	1,835	
June	3,498	
July	6,937	
August	11,936	
September	11,698	
October	11,988	
November	16,846	Compare numbers
December	19,479	for same months at
1855, January	23,076	Scutari, above.
To 17 Feb ... Crimea ...	9,284	
To 25 " ... Scutari ...	6,725	
To 17 " ... Abydos ...	385	
To 25 " ... Gallipoli ...	70	
To 20 " ... Smyrna ...	500	
Total to latest dates in Feb.	16,964	

Army and Ordnance Medical Department,
14 *March,* 1855.

A. SMITH, *Director-General.*

186

RETURN NO. IV.
DEATHS AT SCUTARI AND KOULALI HOSPITALS.
October 1, 1854, to April 30, 1855.

	1. Com- mandant at Scutari	2.* Medical Returns.	3. Head Roll Burials.	4. Reported Deaths.	5. Depot Returns.	6. Inspector- General (Infantry.)†
October	—	250	266	219	213	144
November	—	267	368	291	244	228
December	—	393	667	536	493	423
January	1,480	1,235	1,473	1,360	1,079	1,193
February	1,254	1,329	1,151	1,076	1,254	1,261
March	424	555	418	416	324	587
April	—	200	165	152	213	216
						4,053 ‡Rem. 470
	—	4,229	4,508	4,050	3,820	4,522
	At Scutari and Koulali.		At Scutari.			

The above are the returns from six different official sources. The discrepancies in them will no doubt be explained to us at some future time. Smyrna is not included. The Smyrna Hospital was opened to sick February 15, and from that day till March 31, 127 deaths occurred, by the Inspector-General's Return. Returns 1 and 2 purport expressly to be for Scutari and Koulali—Returns 3, 4, 5 to be for Scutari alone. Return 6 *may* include Smyrna. Otherwise, being for the "Infantry" alone, it

* For the first four months of Return 2, read:—

  October 1 to November 4 250
  November 5 to December 2 267
  December 3 to December 30 393
  December 31 to January 31 1,235

Another Principal Medical Officer's Return shows from—

  October 1 to November 4 258

being a trifling difference between the two Principal Medical Officers, but one easily explainable. According to the latter, the Return of deaths is—

  October, 231.   November, 279.

This Return, however, could not be taken, because there were no means of ascertaining the mortality, separately, of December 1 and 2.

The "Medical Return" (2) for April is only up to April 28, yet exceeds by 35 the Head Roll of Burials, which is till April 30.

All other figures are copied absolutely as they were found in different Returns.

† As given by Sir A. Tulloch.

‡ Being Cavalry, Artillery, and Royal Engineers.

would prove that a part is greater than the whole. For the deaths in the month of March of Infantry alone are greater than those recorded by the other Returns in March for all Arms of the Service. However, the Smyrna supposition does not account for the difference to those unacquainted with these matters—as Return 6 is something less than Return 2 (the Medical Return) for February, although something more for March.

Some light may be thrown upon the discrepancies in the Medical Returns, when it is mentioned that, up to a period variously stated as sooner or later than February, 1855, the Medical Returns of Deaths were made up from the Purveyor's Diet Rolls, upon which the name of the dead man appeared as scratched out, and from verbal or imperfect Reports made by the Medical Officers in charge; that no bed-tickets existed up to this somewhat obscure period; and that it appears uncertain at what period the Medical Officers were required to fill up regular Returns of deaths. I am led to believe this from evidence collected on the spot.

Returns 1 and 2 purport, as has been said, to be for both Scutari and Koulali; nevertheless the numbers are sometimes greater, sometimes less than Returns 3, 4, 5, which purport to be for Scutari alone. Returns 1 and 5 show the same for February, 1855, although purporting to include different places.

The Amount of the Soldier's Duties as a Cause of the Mortality in the Crimea.

The severe Duties of the Soldier in the Crimea.

The awful mortality, recorded in those pages, will appear less extraordinary when it is seen what the duties of these men were.

The 95th Regiment, belonging to the Second Division; the 50th, 28th, 44th, belonging to the Third; the 46th and 63rd, belonging to the Fourth; the 23rd and 33rd, belonging to the Light Division;—these ill-fated Regiments all lost 73 out of every 100 men, from disease alone, in seven months. They could not, however, have been other than thus swept away—for the excessive labour which, in addition to their privations, they underwent will be seen from the following Extracts:—

Extracts.

"This will be seen better by referring to a summary of the Returns* for some of the months, say January, which gives the following result:—

Rank and File.	Brigade of Guards.	2nd Division.	3rd Division.	4th Division.	Light Division.	Total.
Effective and present under arms	948	2,469	2,668	2,332	2,770	11,367
Detailed for duty of various kinds daily	403	827	1,170	1,431	1,490	5,321

"The results for December and February were much the same as in January; indeed, it was not till the termination of the winter, when the sick began to return to duty, when considerable drafts and other reinforcements arrived, and when a new division of the ground between the British and French armies was made, that any material relaxation took place.

"One obvious cause of this extreme pressure may be traced to the circumstance, that at this time the number of sick in Hospital and at Scutari, considerably exceeded the force fit for duty, as may be seen by the following summary for the month of January:—

* Returns showing the Rank and File in each of the Infantry Divisions of the Army before Sevastopol.

	Brigade of Guards.	2nd Division.	3rd Division.	4th Division.	Light Division.	Total.
Sick—Present	403	534	1,023	1,004	1,194	4,158
Sick—Absent	1,068	1,708	1,373	1,802	1,921	7,367
Total Sick ..	1,466	2,242	2,396	2,805	3,115	12,025

"So that the 11,367 effectives shown on the preceding page, had to perform not only their own duty but that of the 12,025 who were sick and this, too, under the most adverse circumstances. So large a number of sick also involved the necessity for many men being withdrawn from duty to attend upon them, and increased the pressure on the remainder.

"The routine of duty in particular regiments is thus described by various officers:—

"Lord West, commanding the 21st Regiment, states that:—   21st Regiment.

"Those for the day covering party are roused out of the tents at 4 o'clock in the morning, have about a mile and a-half to march down through snow and mud, and get back to their camp about 7 o-clock in the evening, being thus exposed in open trenches for 15 hours to such inclement weather as now prevails. Most of them will go on the following evening at 5 o'clock, and remain out all night till 6 o'clock the following morning; this routine has been kept up incessantly for the last six weeks."

"Lieutenant-Colonel Maxwell, commanding the 46th Regiment, a corps which was nearly annihilated by sickness in the months of November and December, states that the number of hours his men were in the trenches in every 24, was 12 in the first of these months and 10½ in the second; and it was stated by the Surgeon and verified by the Lieutenant-Colonel, that at one time the men were in the trenches for six successive nights, and had only one night in bed in the course of a week, but that afterwards the duty was better regulated.   46th Regiment.

"The duties in the Light Division are thus described by Deputy Inspector-General Alexander, in a letter dated 10th December, 1854:—

" 'In the 7th Fusiliers, men were in the trenches 24 hours, without relief, up to or about the 17th November: on the 14th two companies were kept on piquet for 36 hours, when, of course, no cooking took place.   Light Division.

" 'In the 19th Regiment, taking the total number of hours for November, viz. 720—304 have been passed by the men either on duty in the trenches or on piquet, which is 10 hours daily for each man, the remaining 14 being passed in bringing water, seeking for fuel, cooking,

190

and other duties, &c. In the 23rd Fusiliers, the average return gives to each man, one night in camp and one on duty; many men, however, had to go on duty with their companies two or three nights running, doing 24 hours' duty to 12 in camp.

" 'In the 33rd Regiment, the men, on an average, were something less than one night in their tents, with water and fuel fatigues when off duty; they are in consequence weak and wasted from the incessant and severe duty.

" 'In the 77th Regiment, the men were either in the trenches or out-lying piquet every second night; on the intervening days, guards, besides water and fuel fatigues, &c.

" 'In the 88th Regiment, no man has ever more than one night in his tent, has 12 hours in the trenches, and 24 hours on piquet, and then has to look after wood for cooking, water, &c., &c.'

Rifle Brigade, 2nd Battalion.

"A Return and letter from Captain Forman, commanding the right wing of the 2nd Battalion of the Rifle Brigade, also shows that in November that wing was on duty 17 times, namely: 9 in the trenches and 8 on piquet, and that the average daily duty performed by each man was about 10½ hours, in addition to two hours spent in going to and from the trenches, besides the fatigue of procuring wood and water, and other regimental duties.

"In December the amount of duty in that corps is described as being rather less, viz., only about 9 hours in the trenches or piquets exclusive of other duties.

"These few individual instances will be sufficient to show how the system worked, and there appears no reason to suppose that (except, perhaps, in the 46th Regiment) they differed from the ordinary routine of duty in other corps during this period."

Comparison.

"It will be found that after dividing, according to the several arms of the service in which it occurred, the aggregate loss from sickness alone, during the winter of 1854—55, in the Crimean army, including what took place at Scutari, and on the passage, the following results are obtained:—

"The average loss of Infantry, as roughly estimated, was 39 per cent. But in the Naval Brigade, which took a very prominent part in the operations during the whole siege,
it was under . . . . 4 per cent.
The loss of Cavalry was. . . . . 15 per cent.
Of Artillery . . . . 18 per cent.
While the loss of Officers, of all arms, was about . . . . 6 per cent.

"But dividing the Infantry into groups, according to the periods of their arrival in the Crimea and the localities they occupied, the following are the results:—

The average loss of four Regiments which arrived
in and about January, and did not for nearly a
month take any part of the duties in the front
was only . . . . 7 per cent.
The average of four other Regiments, which arrived
in December, and were sent immediately to the
front, was . . . . 27 per cent.
In the Highland Brigade, stationed at Balaclava,
the average was . . . . 24 per cent.
While in the Regiments employed in front, on which
the duties of the siege chiefly devolved, the average
was . . . . 45 per cent.
And in eight of these Corps which suffered most, it
was. . . . . 73 per cent.

"This loss, be it observed, occurred within the short period of seven months, and was exclusive of men killed in action, or who died of their wounds. How far it may have been caused by the privations of the troops hereafter referred to—how far attributable to the excessive amount of duty they had to perform, must remain matter of conjecture; but that it could not have been in any important degree the result of climate, must be inferred from the circumstance of this loss having occurred in a country which, by the concurrent testimony of nearly all the Medical Officers, as well as the experience of the following year, appears to have been almost as healthy as Great Britain, except perhaps as regards cholera.

"Out of about 10,000 men who died during these seven months belonging to the Crimean Army, only 1,200 were cut off by that epidemic, the remainder perished by no foeman's hand—no blast of pestilence, but from the slow, though sure, operation of disease, produced by causes, most of which appeared capable at least of mitigation.

"Compared with this, the mortality in our Army on all previous occasions sinks into comparative insignificance; even that of Walcheren, which threw the nation into mourning, and for years convulsed our Senate, did not exceed a fourth part of the average here recorded. Armies have perished by the sword—they have been overwhelmed by the elements, but never, perhaps, since the hand of the Lord smote the Host of the Assyrians, and they perished in a night, has such a loss from disease been recorded as on this occasion."

It will be at once perceived that the above loss is calculated not as we are accustomed to see it upon the per-centage per annum, but upon the per-centage for seven months only. It therefore looks less than it really is. The actual loss, as stated in the text was at the rate of sixty per cent. per annum of the whole Army, from disease alone, during eight months, viz., October 1854 to May 1855.

FURTHER REMARKS ON THE GREATER MORTALITY IN CERTAIN CORPS,
WITH STATISTICS OF THE NUMBER CONSTANTLY SICK.

Details of Mortality in certain Corps.

It has already appeared, in the preceding note, that the mortality in certain Corps was in great excess of the general rate. In the 46th, 95th, 63rd, 33rd, 23rd, 44th, 28th, and 50th Regiments it averaged 73 per cent. during the seven winter months from October 1854 till April 1855, a rate of mortality which would have extinguished the whole of these Regiments in ten months, or, in other words, a mortality of 125 per cent. per annum. The details are present in the following Table.

TABLE A.*

Corps.	Average Strength of Seven Months.	Deaths within that period in the Crimea and Scutari.	Whereof from Wounds & Injuries Received.	Remains Mortality from Disease alone.	Add Ten per Cent. for Deaths not Reported.	Total Mortality in each Corps.
46th Regiment.	378	405	7	398	40	438
95th "	417	354	32	322	32	354
63rd "	448	353	15	338	34	372
33rd "	424	324	32	292	29	321
23rd "	579	359	21	338	34	372
44th "	598	316	11	305	30	335
28th "	522	276	10	266	27	293
50th "	520	327	19	308	31	339
	3,886	2,714	147	2,567	257	2,824

Admissions into Hospitals shown by Regiments.

The next Table, not the least remarkable, explains itself. It shows, Regiment by Regiment, what the Admissions into Hospital were, and what the Deaths, during those fatal seven months. This has been shown before; but it has not been shown before how much of that mortality was due to the frightful state of the Hospitals at Scutari; how much it depended upon the number which each Regiment was unfortunately enabled to send to those pest-houses.

The eight Regiments, above mentioned, which were almost annihilated, and the three Regiments of Guards, have been distinguished by the letter S in the column of "Died at Scutari;" the preponderance of Deaths in that terrible column showing how much Scutari contributed to swell the mortality by which these unfortunate Corps were thus swept away.

* As given by Sir A. Tulloch.

193

TABLE B.
General Abstract, showing the Total Number of Admissions into Hospital and
Deaths, together with the Numbers Invalided, of the Troops serving in the
Crimea, for the whole period of Seven Months, commencing 1st October, 1854,
and terminating 30th April, 1855; and including those under treatment at
Scutari.

Division and Corps.	Average Strength.	Admitted into Hospital.	Total. Died in the Crimea, &c.	Total. Sent to Scutari, &c.	Total. Died at Scutari, &c.	Total. Invalided to England, &c.	Remarks.
2nd Division.							
30th Foot	522	934	108	308	93	99	
55th „	695	1,462	61	265	96	100	
62nd „	430	949	96	135	42	24	
95th „	417	1,250	199	345	155s	114	
41st „	684	1,323	104	320	94	81	
47th „	637	1,223	91	280	71	102	
49th „	655	1,071	66	274	90	89	
3rd Division.							
1st Foot	771	1,048	229	354	118	63	
14th „	‡423	878	8	42	2	6	
38th „	689	1,728	149	319	118	73	
39th „	‡401	623	23	32	16	48	
50th „	520	1,033	231	278	96a	84	
89th „	§433	993	111	129	59	38	
4th „	508	1,044	96	354	95	46	
9th „	309	754	117	217	56	52	
18th „	‡475	636	29	95	18	18	
28th „	522	1,209	175	373	101s	77	
44th	598	1,140	204	394	112s	65	
4th Division.							
17th Foot	§561	846	59	47	23	9	
20th „	532	1,438	132	370	122	116	
21st „	582	1,388	145	294	113	86	
57th „	715	975	66	189	53	65	
46th "	378	1,573	259	431	146s	84	
68th "	503	2,042	73	229	79	53	
68th Detachment	154	371	3	22	-	-	
Rifle Brig., 1st Bat.	601	1,311	124	397	281	176	The Deaths

Each of the four Corps marked ‡ having been in the Crimea for four months only,
the Strength has been reduced in a corresponding proportion. Ditto ditto marked
thus §, ditto ditto for five months only the Strength has been reduced.

Division and Corps.	Average Strength.	Admitted into Hospital.	Total.				Remarks.
			Died in the Crimea, &c.	Sent to Scutari, &c.	Died at Scutari, &c.	Invalided to England, &c.	
Light Division							
7th Foot	562	783	105	347	125	129	at Scutari
23rd "	579	949	219	331	140s	115	include
33rd "	424	1,194	189	345	135s	144	those of
34th "	§504	652	54	86	30	21	both
97th "	646	695	172	224	86	41	Battalions,
19th "	548	837	132	276	112	118	as we have
77th "	736	1,147	124	286	96	84	no means of
88th "	624	1,603	81	319	101	105	separating
90th "	§419	642	95	207	61	25	them.
Rifle Brig. 2nd. Bt. R.W.	449	1,114	43	272	*	-	* Deaths at Scutari included
1st Division							with 1st
42nd Foot	704	775	72	135	51	30	Battalion.
63rd† "	448	602	183	383	170s	96	
71st "	‡330	348	12	43	5	3	
79th "	714	932	156	241	65	39	
93rd "	727	797	87	71	53	62	
Rifle Brig. 2nd Bt. L.W.	192	271	8	43	..	..	Ditto ditto
Grenadier Guards*	487	716	63	271	238s	189	Half the strength only
Coldstream Guards*	478	1,234	115	441	166s	98	included, the Returns being
Scots Fusilier Guards*	553	904	95	353	169s	147	only available for four months.
TOTAL INFANTRY	23,775	45,437	4,963	11,167	4,052	3,214	

* The Guards Brigade was serving in front up to the end of February, but has been included here with the Force at Balaclava, as it was there at the time the Returns were made up.

† The 63rd was also with the 4th Division, in front, till the end of January, but has been included here with the Force at Balaclava, for the same reason.

It may, from the data here presented, be probably inferred that to the excessive mortality (described above) of certain corps, the condition of the Hospitals at Scutari contributed quite as largely as the amount of military labour. In the extracts presented in the last note too large a share in the calamitous result has most likely been assigned to the severe pressure of the soldier's duties.

Number constantly Sick.

A third table, which may here follow, gives a view of the amount of men constantly sick, the number of soldiers at all

Division and Corps.	Average Strength.	Admitted into Hospital.	Total.				Remarks.
			Died in the Crimea, &c.	Sent to Scutari, &c.	Died at Scutari, &c.	Invalided to England, &c.	
Cavalry Division							
1st Dragoons	247	226	7	100	23	18	
2nd „ . .	205	480	15	126	23	16	
4th Dragoon Guards	250	490	11	63	8	18	
6th Dragoons	241	483	20	42	18	23	
5th Dragoon Guards	172	370	9	73	14	39	
4th Dragoons	163	427	12	75	19	29	
8th „ . .	155	301	3	78	16	25	
11th „ . .	143	314]	13	70	21	24	
18th „ . .	185	256	7	67	15	29	
17th „ . .	154	312	6	75	20	25	
TOTAL CAVALRY	1,915	3,659	103	779	177	246	
Royal Artillery							
Right Attack	575	600	70	179			
Left "	587	517	45	..			
A Battery	155	137	12	29			
H "	146	121	6	24			
F "	161	418	16	45			
B and G Batteries	268	385	42	71	258	379	
E Battery	150	169	12	51			
C "	193	447	8	..			
P "	138	239	12	42			
W "	254	331	15	29			
I "	189	317	9	21			
SAPPERS& MINERS. {Right and Left Attack}	433	1,136	28	91	35	42	
TOTAL ARTILLERY AND ENGINEERS	3,249	4,817	275	582	293	421	
Genl. Hospital, Balaclava	..	2,144	190				

times to be deducted, as ineffective by reason of sickness, from the Strength of the Army.

There has been no attempt made in any of the elaborate Reports of Commission, or Committee, which have been placed before the public, to arrive at this fact, to obtain an estimate, for the seven months of disaster in the Crimea, of the number "constantly sick." Yet this must, on all occasions, be one of the most important questions as regards the welfare of an Army.

The fact is, with our imperfect statistics, it is next to impossible to estimate the sickness correctly. The only perfectly correct deduction which can be made with regard to them is that of a well-known statistical authority: "I do not profess to make anything tally which depends on Crimean information."

Statistically, the figures given in Table C are certain to be incorrect, although deduced from Adjutant-General's and Medical Returns. But, for sanitary purposes they give a rough idea of the disabled state of our Army during the seven months in question.

TABLE C.

	Strength.*	Sick.†	Per-Centage of Sick.	Effectives.
October 1854	18,547	4,508	24.2	14,039
November	22,047	6,744	30.5	15,303
December	25,776	8,342	32.3	17,434
January, 1855	26,578	11,070	41.6	15,508
February	27,045	13,428	49.6	13,617
March..	25,003	12,772	51.0	12,231
April	23,047	9,982	43.3	13,065

So that, during this period, the average of "constantly Sick" in our Army was 38.9 per cent.

* The Strength here given does not include the Highland Brigade because these troops were not on duty on the pleateau before Sevastopol. But it includes the Strength at Scutari, which has been generally omitted. It is derived from Medical Returns, the Sick at Scutari being added and the Highland Brigade deducted. It includes the men on command and the Batmen, and those otherwise employed, and is supposed to be the Strength of the Infantry Divisions before Sevastopol.

† The "Sick" are derived from the Adjutant-General's Returns and are the average of those "Remaining in Hospital," both "Present," i.e., in the Crimea, and "Absent," i.e., at Scutari, &c., on four days in each month, according to those Returns. But the "Absent Sick," to all appearance, include a great many who were dead. These would, however, also be included in the Strength, so that the two errors compensate each other, in some degree.

CONCLUDING REMARKS

I have tried, in obedience to command, to give what idea I could of the Sanitary state of the Army. It was necessary, in order to illustrate its Medical or Sanitary organization, to show the results which exist as tests of its efficiency, both in peace and in war.

The tests which exist under the former condition are, the Barrack and the Military Hospital at home and in the colonies, together with the rate of mortality, and that of inefficiency from sickness of the troops. In the state of war, the histories of the Duke of Wellington's campaigns, of Walcheren, and of the late expedition to the East, exist as tests of our sanitary condition.

But, with regard to the last War, it has been here dwelt upon with greater detail, not only because we have much more information on the sanitary history of the Crimean campaign than we have upon any other, but because it is a complete example (history does not afford its equal) of an army, after falling to the lowest ebb of disease and disaster from neglects committed, rising again to the highest state of health and efficiency from remedies applied. It is the whole experiment on a colossal scale. In all other examples the last step has been wanting to complete the solution of the problem.

We had, in the first seven months of the Crimean campaign, a mortality among the troops at the rate of sixty per cent. per annum from disease alone—a rate of mortality which exceeds that of the Great Plague of 1665 to the population of the metropolis, and a higher ratio than the mortality in Cholera bears to the attacks; that is to say, that there died out of the army in the Crimea an annual rate greater than ordinarily dies in time of pestilence out of sick.

We had, during the last six months of the war, a mortality among our sick little more than that among our healthy Guards at home, and a mortality among the troops two-thirds only of what is among the troops at home.

The mortality among troops of the Line at home has been, on an average of ten years,* 18.7 per 1,000 per annum, and among the Guards, 20.4 per 1,000 per annum. Comparing this with the Crimean mortality for the last six months of the war, we find that the deaths to sick were no more than 24 per 1,000 per

---

* 1837–1846

annum, and the mortality among the troops in the Crimea did not exceed 11.5 per 1,000 per annum.*

Is not this the most complete experiment in army hygiene?

But we cannot try this experiment over again for the benefit of inquirers at home, like a chemical example; it must be brought forward as a historical instance.

An experiment, however, equally (perhaps more) important is annually tried at home.

The Recruiting Returns, showing the number of rejections and their causes, are the first step in this important problem. They show the excessive care taken to obtain the best possible men for the Service. The Mortality and Invaliding Returns show the excessive ingenuity displayed in getting rid of them afterwards.

From an examination of these Recruiting Returns may be gathered how perfect is the system for excluding all who are not only likely to yield a high rate of mortality but who are, in any way, physically weak or inefficient; hence the British army consists of only the finest specimens of the finest physical race in the world, with the exception perhaps, of some part of our aristocracy. The ingenuity which, among this selection of first-rate physical frames, made for health and long life, produces scrofula, consumption, and premature mortality, far surpasses any ingenuity with which we are acquainted. Majendie and others have produced scrofula among rabbits and other animals by the same causes; but they did they did their work far less extensively and quickly.

The comparative health of men of the army-ages in England, and of soldiers in barracks on home stations is the proof.

It is, when carefully examined, a more striking experiment in army hygiene than that of the Crimea. But the difference is this—in the Crimea, the remedies applied and the results obtained in health and efficiency formed the last step of the problem which is wanting here.

I have tried to show, therefore, the relative mortality of the army at home and of the English male population, at corresponding ages.

I have tried to show (Preface to Sanitary Section), the same comparison for the whole army at home and abroad.

* In taking this average, the last month, June 1856, which would have reduced it much lower, has been purposely excluded, because troops were embarking. This would have made it unfair. The Deaths to Strength in June were under 2¼ per 1,000 annum. But troops left their sick behind them, which has made us comprise the mortality of sick.

A complete picture is thus given of the changes of life of the soldier compared with those of the civilian at the same ages in time of peace.

I have shown the chief classes of disease by which these awful results are brought about, in order to see how far it is within the powers of preventive science to diminish the risks to which the soldier is exposed, whether at home or in the field.

The comparison between the changes of life of the soldier in the field and those of the civilian at home is thus given; and it will there be found how insignificant, comparatively, to the former are, in his estimated dangers, the results from wounds.

It is, however, now, with the results of our sanitary experiment at home that we have to do.

The relative mortality of the Foot Guards and of the English male population in large towns, at the corresponding ages, is the strongest illustration.

The Guards are, physically, the select lives out of the select. They are chosen by practised Medical Officers out of the strongest and best looking recruits, how well let our Recruiting Returns show. Any weakness or disease is enough to prevent a man being chosen for Service. The young Guardsman is, in every sense, a "picked" life, and would be selected as a first-class life in any Insurance Office.

As soon as the recruit enters the Service, he is placed under the entire control of educated Officers. His diet, cleanliness, personal habits are strictly attended to. He is lodged in Barracks which have cost the country many times the price of the house in which he was born. He never leaves the country in time of peace, but passes from his Town Quarters in London to his Country Quarters at Windsor or at Winchester; and, whenever he suffers from the slightest ailment, his Medical Adviser is instantly beside him; he has Hospital accommodation, medicine, and attendance immediately.

Of all men, a soldier in Her Majesty's Household Troops is the most likely, it would seem, to enjoy perfect health and long life.

The men rejected, when the Guardsman was chosen, have passed back into Civil life. The Civil population has lost a certain proportion of its good life, which has gone into the Army. It has received back those lives which were not good enough for the Army. The Civil population has had all the loss, the Army all the gain.

We have seen how the Guards die off under circumstances, so very favourable to life, apparently, as those we have mentioned.

200

We have seen that the mortality in the Guards, great as it appears, appears less than it really is.

The rate of mortality exhibits all the deaths in the Civil population which take place between the ages of 20 and 40, but does not exhibit all the deaths which take place among the men *selected* for the *Guards*. Every year, between the ages of 20 and 40, men are rendered unfit for service by organic disease, and are discharged to die among the Civil population and to raise its rate of mortality; and these are included in that of the Civil population, and are consequently not shown in that of the Army. These deaths are, in fact, deducted from those of the Guards, and added to those of the Civil population, so that in the comparison the Guards have a double advantage from their not receiving bad lives and from their invaliding bad lives.

The Guards, though the most unhealthy corps in the Service, are not the only corps which suffers a great excess of mortality. All the Line, even on home service, suffers, although at a somewhat lower rate.

It has been shown what is the excess of mortality among the Line on home Stations over the mortality among the general English population, and over the mortality in large towns, subject to the same correction as to invaliding, which has been already mentioned as necessary to be made for the Guards.

The whole Army, like the Guards, consists of carefully "picked" lives, and the lives rejected are thrown back into the general population. But, notwithstanding this process of selection, and the apparently favorable circumstances under which the troops are placed, we have, from some cause or other, the extraordinary results summed up.

To show the full bearing, too, of this process of selection in any comparison between the health of the Army and that of Civilians, it is necessary to state that, of the Civil population at the recruiting age, a certain part is unable, from illness, to present itself to the recruiting officer; that deaths among that part go to raise the Civilian mortality; that of those who do present themselves for recruits, a third part at least, though probably a much larger proportion, is rejected as unfit for service; that of those rejected, at least a fourth part is suffering from diseases which shorten life.

Mortality on the whole Army, at Home and Abroad.

The wide extent of the British Empire, and the great variety of climates which it presents, as well as the topographical peculiarities of our Sovereign's various colonies and possessions scattered over the whole earth, would lead us to expect a higher rate of mortality among soldiers born in the British Islands, when these soldiers are sent on service abroad, than would exist among the home population at the same ages.

Accordingly, in some years, it will be found that the mortality in the Troops is from five to six times greater than it is in Civil life.

The mortality of the whole Army at home and abroad, compared with that among Englishmen of the Army ages, in healthy districts, is given in the Preface to Sanitary Section.

If we can imagine the total sum of life among 10,000 men, between 20 and 40 years of age, entering the Army, and remaining on home-service, and among the same number of Englishmen, taken (1) all over the town and country districts, and (2) in the healthy districts, at home at the same ages—all starting alike, we shall see a very different rate in the progress of death among the various classes. The proportion of death increases and that of life diminishes in a very different ratio and to a very different extent in each.

The mortality is greater and progresses more rapidly among the English male population generally than among that in healthy districts. The general population has lost a third more by the time it arrives at the age of 40 than the healthy population, while the soldiers have lost above a third more of their numbers than the general population, and more than twice as many as the healthy population.

If we can also imagine the total money value of 10,000 men between the ages of 20 and 40, as well as the loss of value from loss of life at each succeeding year between the two ages; and, further, the relative value of the amount of life in the Army, as contrasted with that of two classes of civil population, passing on from 40 years to the succeeding periods of life, we shall see that the Nation loses the money value of the excess of mortality existing in its general population over that of the population in healthy districts—we shall also see that while, among healthy civil populations, about 8,500 lives, out of 10,000, survive the wear and tear of the ages between 20 and 40, and thereafter add their quota to the wealth of the community, only 6,900 of the Army lives are available for the same purpose.

In the case of the Army, the country incurs great expense in educating the soldier for his duties, and it is difficult to overestimate the value of a good soldier, for he can hardly be replaced. In the present state of sanitary knowledge, it may be fairly stated that the whole excess of money-loss between that in healthy districts and that in the Army, might be saved to the tax-payers of the country. The general community incurs a still

Sum of Life among 10,000 Men in Army on Home-service, in general Population and in country Population, at home.

Loss of Life, of Service, and of Money-value entailed on country in case of Army, taken on Home-service only.

further loss of productive labor, because it will be at once seen
that the number of lives at 40 years of age, passed back into the
general population (supposing that the average age of discharge from service is 40 years), is much smaller in the Army
than the proportion which survives in the healthy Civil population; and the productive power of the country is further taxed
for the support, by Poor Rates and otherwise, of a large proportion of men, temporarily or permanently disabled by diseases contracted in the Service.

The loss from invaliding has been already referred to as a
serious cause of inefficiency in the Army in its present state.
The tables in the Preface to Section X have been constructed to
bring under one view the whole great loss sustained. In Table
IV is shown the number of effectives, young soldiers and veterans, (1) who remain in the Army as it is, (2) who would remain,
if the Army were as healthy as the Civil population. The Army
serving at home, in time of peace only, between the ages of 20
and 40, has been taken as the example. Under the present system, 10,000 annual recruits would be required to sustain a
force of 141,764 men; while, under the improved conditions as
to health, 10,000 annual Recruits would sustain an Army of
166,910 men.

The great experiment, then, which is annually going on
under our very eyes, proves what is the loss of life, service, and
money-value entailed on the country by the neglect of sanitary
measures in the Army, taken in time of peace, on home-service
only.

Classes of
Disease from
which this
Mortality
arises, on
Home-service.

It is, in the highest degree, important to know the classes of
disease from which the great losses in the Army in time of
peace arise; for it is in this way alone that we can ascertain
whether, and to what extent, we can mitigate or prevent these
diseases by known sanitary precautions.

The classes of mortality from disease most prevalent in the
Infantry on home stations, as compared with the extent of the
same types of disease in Civil life at the same ages, has been
shewn in Appendix I to Section XI.

Two Classes of
Disease, viz.,
1, Zymotics, 2,
Consumption,
the Scourges of
the Army at
Home.

We are at once struck by the remarkable fact, that more than
seven-ninths of the mortality in the Infantry are due to two
classes of disease alone—viz., to Zymotic Diseases, such as
Fevers, Cholera, Diarrhoea, and to Chest and Tubercular
Diseases, such as Consumption, &c. In fact, the mortality from
Chest and Tubercular Diseases alone, in the Infantry on home
service, exceeds the total mortality from all causes among the

Civil population at the same ages; while the deaths from Zymotic Disease are above double what they are in Civil life. Again, Chest and Tubercular affections are the scourge of the Civil population, and yet the Civil population suffers less than one-half the mortality from these diseases which occurs in the Infantry while the deaths from Zymotic Disease in the Infantry nearly equal the total deaths from Chest affections in the Civil population. It is necessary here also to repeat that, while the mortality of the English male population exhibits all the deaths occurring from each class of diseases, that of the Infantry does not. It takes no account of men discharged on account of Chronic Tubercular and Chest Diseases, whose deaths, taking place after discharge, go to swell the mortality, from these diseases, among the Civil population.

I have now exhibited the frightful mortality, continually and year by year going on, in the British Army at home, and the classes of disease to which this mortality is to be attributed.

The first question which arises is—What can be the cause of all this? By what possible procedure can it be that the first-rate lives selected out of the British working population can be so deteriorated as that such a terrible result should follow? Is there anything in the food, clothing, duties, habits of the men, to which such a loss can be attributed? Are the Army medical men less skilful than those in Civil life? To these last two queries we must reply generally in the negative. There is, on the contrary, everything in the soldier's favor in these particulars, except that perhaps he is not sufficiently worked. His barrack accommodation too has cost the country enough of his money. There has been no expense spared in this either. Can there be anything here to occasion such a fearful annual loss of life?

Causes of this excessive Mortality in the Army at Home.

Let us see what sanitary experience teaches as to the causation of the diseases from which soldiers suffer:—

1. Consumption, and diseases of this class, are the result of breathing fouled air, contaminated by the breath of other persons. It is air polluted in this way which appears to be the special agent which predisposes people to consumptive diseases. How is such a state of the air chiefly produced? Simply by crowding too many people into unventilated rooms, especially to sleep. If barrack-rooms are crowded and unventilated, and if the atmosphere is close or foul during the hours of sleep, when the system is more peculiarly predisposed to its effects, the elements and seeds of Consumption and Tubercular Disease are there. To develop these seeds into activity, all that has to be

1. Causes of Consumption.

204

done is to make the men out of such an atmosphere which they
have been breathing night after night, and to expose them on
guard to wet and cold. The disease will soon show itself. But
exposure to wet and cold alone will not do it. This the Crimean
experience has proved, as it is proved daily and nightly in night
trades and occupations, always excepting the case of the soldier
at home.

To know whether the conditions requisite to produce
Consumption and Tubercular Disease exist in Barracks, it is
only necessary to read the disgusting evidence given before the
Barrack Committee, and to consult the tables given previously,
shewing the amount of cubic space allowed to the men in
Barracks and to the sick in Military Hospitals. It would be difficult to frame conditions more likely to generate such diseases
than those to which soldiers are exposed in barrack-rooms.
They are, in fact, the self-same conditions as those which have
been determined by direct experiment to be necessary for the
production of Tubercular Disease in animals. When a sufficient
case is found, it is not necessary to look for another.

2. Causes of Zymotic Diseases.

2. Zymotic Diseases, Fevers, Diarrhoea, Cholera, Dysentery,
&c., are known in Civil life to be most intense in their activity
where certain local conditions are present.

First in prominence amongst these conditions are again over-
crowding and defective ventilation—the repeated breathing, in
fact, of air already breathed, such air being further contaminated by moisture and exhalations from the skin.

Next in importance are emanations proceeding from animal
excretions or from decaying vegetable matter, together with
moisture. The want of drainage and the foul state of the
latrines and urinals in Barracks as described in various
reports, are sufficient illustrations of this class of causes.

There are others of minor importance which need not be mentioned. Those enumerated are quite sufficient to account of the
excess of zymotic mortality from which the army on home stations suffers. If men, returning from foreign service, happen
occasionally to be more susceptible to the operation of such
causes, they will, of course, suffer more severely. But allowance
is made in the "Statistical Reports on the Sickness and
Mortality of the Troops serving at home," for even this contingency, as they do not exhibit any deaths occurring for the first
six months after men have returned from foreign service.

The next query is one which it is almost superfluous to put. It is, whether there be any known means of preventing this excessive mortality, and whether there be any hope of reducing the disease and mortality among the Troops to the same amount as appears among the Civil population? Can this excessive Mortality be prevented?

The reply, if one were wanted, is, that the soldier's mortality on home service should, to say the least of it, never have been greater than that of the Civil population, and that it might be less.

The mortality and disease among the Civil population are the very evils, towards the reduction of which to smaller dimensions, the whole sanitary procedure under every sanitary Act of Parliament is directed. It was the largeness of those very evils which led to the sanitary agitation which ended in the Legislature giving a sanitary code to England; and, to say the least of it, it is hardly credible that it should be necessary, at the present day, to advocate similar measures for the Army.

There is no reason why, with proper sanitary measures, the general health of the population should not be raised to the standard of the most healthy districts of the country, as indeed it has been in certain marked instances; and why should the health of the Army on home service be any exception, seeing that the personal conditions of the soldier are so much more favourable? If this were done, and if our Home Army consisted of 100,000 Guards, we should save nearly 1,500 good soldiers yearly, who from all experience in other cases, are as certainly killed by the neglects specified as if they were drawn up on Salisbury Plain and shot.

By referring to the Preface to Sanitary Section where is found the Army mortality at home and abroad, as compared with that of an English population at the same ages, we cannot fail to be struck with the immense loss of life entailed on the Army, and the corresponding cost to the country from foreign service. This loss is much less than it was in former times, as will be seen by referring to the Preface to Sanitary Section. It has been diminished by various sanitary means, and there is no reason whatever why, if intelligent enquiry were instituted, and proper sanitary precautions taken, all the Army mortality on that melancholy table might not be very materially lowered. Loss of Life excessive in the whole Army, at Home and Abroad, although less than it was. Pp. vi, vii, Preface to Sanitary Section.

It is to be regretted that, with the materials existing in the Army Medical recesses, from which the valuable returns of Sir A. Tulloch have actually be drawn, a report should not have been published at least twice a year. This, it is hoped, will now

206

be done, by the new Statistical Branch, the formation of which is at present under consideration at the War Department.

From these returns has been gathered what is set forth at pp. viii, ix, of the Preface to the Sanitary Section, X, viz., which Stations have stood still in sanitary progress, which have advanced, which will still want a "Barrack Commission."

There is here to be found—1, satisfactory evidence how much has already been done, by the good sense of Commanding Officers, to reduce, with sanitary means, the mortality of the troops; and—2, convincing proof how much may still be done.

Now, if ever, is the time.

Reasons for seizing on this opportunity to introduce Remedies.

First. We have a Sovereign whose personal regard for Her troops has been exemplified in so many touching instances, who has been to them indeed so truly a royal mother, that the loyalty which, with the English soldier, has always been a duty, is now become an enthusiasm.

Secondly. We have an Army in whose memory is still fresh the greatest example of heroic endurance in modern, or indeed in any times—fresh, not as that which it may have read in history, but that which it has seen, shewn in itself, and accomplished. They have a pride in the power they have proved in themselves to "endure hardness" without complaint—our soldiers—and well they have earned their right to it.

Thirdly. We have Officers, of whom, in the late War, many instances could be cited, known only to God and to their men, of willingness to "endure hardness" with them, and to do whatever could be done, at their own private cost, to alleviate those hardships to their men.

Fourthly. We have, at this moment, a Royal Commission sitting, composed of some of the best men of the country for information in Army matters, and with a President at their head who is, perhaps, the man who has shown most knowledge and feeling as to the wants and constitution, physical and moral, of an Army, in this day. They have already elicited a mass of evidence regarding the Sanitary state of the Army, such as we have never had before—they have brought together a treasure of information and suggestions, which will be a manual for Army sanitary matters in all future times—they will have the privilege of working out practically their own suggestions.

Fifthly. We have a War in India, which will require a large addition to our forces, and which will, without sanitary foresight, prove a most unhealthy and destructive war, destructive solely from disease.

And, lastly, with regard to the men who are gone, who need our words no more, what shall we say? The fittest tribute to them is to be silent—as they were. For their courage and their griefs were too big for our words, although they seemed to them too little for theirs—but, for the sake of the survivors, not for theirs, let the remarkable lines be here quoted of one who best knew the deeds he was writing about:

"The sufferings of the army in the course of the winter, and especially during the months of December and January, must have been intense. It has been only by slow degrees, and after the frequent repetition of similar details, as one witness after another revealed the facts that had come under his own observation, that we have been able to form any adequate conception of the distress and misery undergone by the troops, or fully to appreciate the unparalleled courage and constancy with which they have endured their sufferings. Great Britain has often had reason to be proud of her army, but it is doubtful whether the whole range of military history furnishes an example of an army exhibiting, throughout a long campaign, qualities as high as have distinguished the forces under Lord Raglan's command. The strength of the men gave way under excessive labour, watching, exposure, and privation; but they never murmured, their spirit never failed, and the enemy, though far outnumbering them, never detected in those whom he encountered any signs of weakness. Their numbers were reduced by disease and by casualties to a handful of men, compared with the great extent of the lines which they constructed and defended, yet the army never abated its confidence in itself, and never descended from its acknowledged military pre-eminence.

"Both men and officers, when so reduced that they were hardly fit for the lighter duties of the camp, scorned to be excused the severe and perilous work of the trenches, lest they should throw an undue amount of duty upon their comrades; yet they maintained every foot of ground against all the efforts of the enemy, and with numbers so small that, perhaps, no other troops would even have made the attempt.

"Suffering and privation have frequently led to crime, in armies as in other communities, but offenses of a serious character have been unknown in the British Army in the Crimea. Not one capital offense has been committed, or even alleged to have been committed, by a soldier, and intemperance has been rare.

"Every one who knows anything of the constitution of the Army must feel that, when troops so conduct themselves throughout a long campaign, the officers must have done their duty and set the example. The conduct of the men, therefore, implies the highest encomium that can be passed upon their officers. They have not only shared all the danger and exposure, and most of the privations which the men had to undergo, but we everywhere found indications of their solicitude for the welfare of those who were under their command, and of their constant readiness to employ their private means in promoting the comfort of their men. Doubtless there has been, as there always must be, better management in some regiments than in others, but amongst much that was painful in the evidence that we have heard, it was always gratifying to observe the community of feelings and of interests that appeared everywhere to subsist between the men and their officers, and which the regimental system of the British Army seems almost always to produce."

Among these men there never was heard a murmur—there never was seen one moment's unwillingness to go back to their hardships, until their country's cause was won.

Upon those who watched, week after week and month after month, this enduring courage, this unalterable patience, simplicity, and good sense, this voiceless strength to suffer and "be still," it has made an impression never to be forgotten.

The Anglo-Saxon on the Crimean heights has won for himself a greater name than the Spartan at Thermopylae, as the six months' struggle to endure was a greater proof of what man can do, than the six yours' struggle to fight. The traces of the name and sacrifice of Iphigenia may still be seen in Tauris; but a greater sacrifice has been there accomplished by a "handful" of brave men who defended that fatal position, even to the death. And, if Inkermann now bears a name like that of Thermopylae, so is the story of those terrible trenches, through which these men patiently and deliberately, and week after week, went, till they returned no more, greater than that of Inkermann. Truly were the Sevastopol trenches, to our men, like the gate of the Infernal Regions. "Lasciate ogni speranza, voi ch'entrate." And yet these men would refuse to report themselves sick, lest they should throw more labour on their comrades. They would draw their blankets over their heads and die without a word.

Well may it be said that there is hardly an example in history to compare with this long and silent fortitude.

But surely the blood of such men is calling to us from the ground, not to avenge them, but to have mercy on their survivors!

We can do no more for those who have thus suffered and died in their country's service. They need our help no longer. Their spirits are with God, who gave them. It remains for us to strive that their sufferings may not have been endured in vain for us—to endeavour so to learn from experience as to lessen such sufferings in future by forethought and wise management.

If we really desire to draw into the ranks of our Army the best and strongest men of the working classes, we must hold out positive inducements to them quite other than those negative ones which have been so much in use, viz., drink, want of work, disappointment in love. It must not be forgotten that the intelligence of these working classes has undergone a great advance of late years, and that the details of the Crimean catastrophe as well as the neglects from which it arose are perfectly well known among them. All over the three kingdoms there are those who mourn the loss of friends and kindred, not because they died in battle against their country's enemies, but because they perished from neglect of the conditions absolutely necessary for their health and lives. The events of that war have made an impression, never to be wiped away, on the soldier-classes of the country. And, if we would make them more ready than they at present are to flock to the ranks, it must be by looking to their health and comfort, by reforming their Barracks, by introducing a better system for securing their physical and moral well-being, whether in peace or in war—not forgetting their domestic relations. It must be, in short, by sweeping away those abuses which have hitherto led to such serious losses from sickness and premature mortality in all times, seasons, and countries. It must be by making the Service as attractive to the soldier-spirits of the country as it ought to be made, when dealing with a broad and intelligent people. And no moral and intellectual progress can be, by any means of ours, effected, without Sanitary progress.

For the mere purposes of Recruiting it is imperative to put forth inducements to Enlist, suited to the present state of intelligence of this country.

This is a short summary of our Sanitary condition in time of peace. Unfavourable as it is to the Sanitary System, or rather want of System, in the British Army, it exhibits results which might be considered as, in the highest degree, favourable, when contracted with the mortality from disease among the British Troops in time of war.

Mortality from Disease of Armies in time of War.

It is at such times that the excessively defective state of Sanitary Science and practice in the Army becomes pre-eminently remarkable, and leads to the most disastrous results. It is right, however, to remind ourselves that such defects are not confined to the British Army; all Armies, during war, have suffered from the neglect of very ordinary hygienic precautions, and some Armies have been all but destroyed in consequence. Nearly six-sevenths of the vast Army, with which Napoleon I. invaded Russia, had perished before the setting in of the fierce cold which destroyed the remainder, and to which it was convenient to that gigantic vanity to ascribe the destruction of the

French Invasion of Russia.

210

whole. Of this we have statistical proof; and of this our own great Duke was well aware.

The actual losses in battle form a very small part of the calamities of a war—so small indeed that, if the excess of mortality caused by disease could be cut off, the loss from wounds would be hardly deemed worthy of the familiar phrase, the "Horrors of War." How just that expression is *now*, those only who have seen the Crimean Expedition can well appreciate!

Walcheron.

The facts connected with the disastrous Walcheren Expedition, as well as the ignorance and neglect of the most ordinary precautions which led to so great a loss of life, are matters of history. But, up to the present time, the experience of that expedition seems to have led to no beneficial result, so far at least as can be gathered from the still more disastrous Crimean War.

Comparison of Mortality from Disease in the Crimean Army and in the Civil Population.

At p. 157 are given the comparative results of the mortality among the English male population of the Army ages and among the British Army in the East. For every Englishman of the Army ages who died at home, nearly 23 died in the East. The proportion of deaths from wounds, excluding of those killed on the field, during the War, was 30 times greater among the soldiers than among the Civil population. But, even at that rate, the mortality in Hospital from wounds did not exceed 3 per cent. of the strength, while the deaths from all causes were nearly 23 per cent. of the force in the field.

When we examine the cause of this great mortality, we learn that, for every man of the ages and numbers who died at home from Zymotic Disease, 93 died in the Army in the East! The remaining diseases shewn are not worth notice. If they were all expunged, and the deaths from wounds, taking place in Hospital, with them, the fact would remain that the Army in the Crimea almost perished from Zymotic Disease.

At Manchester.

The awful Mortality in that noble Army is shown still more strikingly when compared with that of the town of Manchester, one of the most unhealthy in England, and one very subject to Zymotic Diseases.

Had the Crimean Army been as healthy as Manchester, it would have lost 1¼ percent. per annum. It did lose, during eight months, 60 per cent. per annum; or 58¾ per cent. more than one of the most unhealthy towns in England.

Vital Statistics of Crimean War.

We have seen how healthy the Army was when it landed in the East; how, immediately on its reaching Varna, sickness and death began to increase, shewing the sudden exposure of the Troops to some very unusual causes of mortality. We have seen that, the whole time the Army was in Bulgaria, it suffered severely—that the mortality declined when it left that pestiferous region for the Crimea—that, from the moment it broke ground before Sevastopol, in a comparatively healthy district of country, the mortality began to rise during October—that it increased with frightful rapidity during November and December, attaining during January 1855, a higher fatality than the maximum mortality of the Great Plague of London in September 1665.

Page 162 gives a representation of that great calamity during the first year of the War. Excepting, perhaps in one or two of the mediaeval epidemics, no pestilence, of which we have any record, would form such a picture for eight consecutive months.

Page 163 gives the mortality of the second year of the War. It was great in the beginning, as compared with the most unhealthy cities in England; but when compared with the first year's mortality it is insignificant. It will be seen that, for the last six months, January to June 1856, inclusive, the mortality retires within the Manchester rate and all but disappears. We have here at a glance the vital statistics of the Crimean War.

The immense preponderance of Zymotic Diseases has already been referred to, and a glance at p. 157 will show that these diseases were the cause of the whole catastrophe. The total mortality from wounds at Alma, Inkermann, and during five months in the trenches, exclusive of the killed in action, is insignificant; so is the total mortality from diseases not Zymotic. While the Zymotic Diseases are shewn to be the pests and scourges of camps and armies now, as they were of cities and towns in the middle ages before the dawn of Sanitary knowledge.

Zymotic Disease the cause of the whole Catastrophe in Crimea.

The analysis of the second year's mortality exhibits an immense reduction in the deaths from all causes, except from wounds, the legitimate result of war, but even to nearly the end the Zymotic mortality retains its preponderance, and disappears only when the Army has arrived at its most healthy condition.

On comparing the total mortality, as shown at p. 162, with the Zymotic mortality, as shewn at p. 157, it will be seen that the very first diseases from which the Army suffered (as shewn by the dates) in Bulgaria, were Zymotic Diseases. They were chiefly Fever and Cholera, brought on by neglect of sanitary precautions, principally in the first bad selection of Camp sites. The first outbreak began to subside in September only and continued to decline until the Army sat down before Sevastopol.

212

Another and far more terrible invasion of Zymotic Disease followed that event.

The men were hard worked. But hard work of itself never induced Zymotic Disease. Other causes must be looked for: and these causes once existing, fatigue would co-operate powerfully with them. The men had no sufficient shelter. They were in want of clothing suitable to the weather. They suffered from wet and damp. They were exposed to the elements at all times and seasons. Their food was not sufficiently nutritive nor varied. They had no proper means of cooking, little or no fuel, and they could not eat their rations. What wonder, then, if scurvy and scorbutic disease appeared at a very early period, if Fever, Cholera, Diarrhoea, Dysentery followed, so as to threaten the total destruction of the Force! Every possible neglect of hygiene had been committed, and these figures show the natural results. During the summer of 1855, Zymotic Diseases still prevailed, though to a comparatively insignificant degree. Sanitary defects in draining, cleansing, ventilation and overcrowding were then the prevailing causes. During the winter of 1855–56, all the previous causes of disease had been removed. The men were well clothed, fed, and sheltered. Their huts were properly drained and ventilated, and nuisances had been removed. The hard work had also ceased. Compare the two periods of September to May 1854–55 and 1855–6, and no more instructive lesson on army hygiene could be given. The men were the same, the conditions only had been altered.

Could an Æschylus or a Sophocles appear again, what a subject would he here find for his delineation of Fatality! How much grander is the Christian fate than that of the Greeks! How much greater a conception for a Tragedy! Do this, says the Greek fate, and a family shall be extinguished or an individual hunted down by the Furies. Do this, says the Christian fate, and 18,000 men shall die; and Providence would not be good, if it were otherwise. Do the other, and 18,000 men shall live. The requirements of Health had been disobeyed in every particular during the first winter in the Crimea; and she has left on those figures an everlasting vindication of her broken commands. During the second winter she had been more perfectly obeyed, and the sign of her displeasure has almost ceased to appear.

Sanitary Treatment of Sick in Hospital, in Crimean War.

In discussing the causes of the terrible mortality of that fearful winter, another important point must not be overlooked, viz.—what chances a sick man had of proper care and treatment.

It is well known that the Medical Staff exerted itself to the very utmost, and incurred a large proportionate mortality among its members in consequence; but the accommodation for the sick in camp was for several months most defective. There were no proper Hospitals and no suitable beds or other appliances. The suffering from exposure among the sick was perhaps greater, considering their diseased state, than even among the Army generally.

The transport ships were, for many months, defective in the highest degree, overcrowded, badly ventilated; and, moreover, many cases were shipped in a state wholly unfit for removal, particularly those of Choleraic Disease. There was a great mortality on board the ships in consequence. During the period of four months and a half from the landing in the Crimea to the end of January 1855, out of 13,093 shipped for Scutari, nearly 75 per 1,000 died on a passage of only 300 miles. Had the embarkation of sick gone on for 12 months and the same high rate of mortality prevailed among them, no less than 3,182 per 1,000 would have died. In other words, the population of the Sick Transports would have perished on the Black Sea upwards of three times. In the month of January, we lost 10 on the passage to every 100 we received alive. The terrible episode of these Transport Ships is given in the Preface to Section II.

On board Sick Transports.

Of these sick who thus arrived in the Bosphorus, there died, in the month of February 1855, 415 per cent. per annum, and in one Hospital, that of Koulali, actually 608 per cent. For when the sick were landed, they were crowded into buildings which had undergone no sufficient sanitary preparation for their reception. The drainage, ventilation, lime-washing, &c., were so defective that the buildings were little better than pest-houses; and the result was an enormous and needless mortality among the sick, which went to swell the losses of the Army, and to raise its proportionate rate of mortality.

In Hospitals of the Bosphorus.

The Scutari mortality was, in fact, a separate problem, and must be considered by itself. It was the case of thousands of sick removed 300 miles from the causes which had occasioned their disease, and exposed to another class of risks in the buildings into which they were received. The buildings were spacious and magnificent in external appearance; far more so, indeed, than any military buildings in Great Britain, and several of them were apparently better suited for Hospitals than any Military Hospitals at home.

The mere external appearance was, however, fatally deceptive. Underneath these great structures were sewers of the worst possible construction, loaded with filthy, mere cesspools, in fact, through which the wind blew sewer air up the pipes of numerous open privies into the corridors and wards where the sick were lying.

The wards had no means of ventilation, the walls required constant lime-washing, and the number of sick placed in the Hospitals during the first winter was disproportionately large, especially when the bad sanitary state of the buildings is taken into consideration. The Hospital population was increased, not only without any sanitary precautions having been taken, but while the sanitary conditions were becoming daily worse, for the sewers were getting more and more dangerous, and the walls more and more saturated with organic matter. Some light improvements were made in the beginning of March, 1855 but it was not till the 17th that effectual means were put into operation for removing the causes of disease in the buildings, viz., by the Sanitary Commissioners. By the month of June the improvements were nearly completed, and the proportion of sick had fallen off.

Page 141 shews the whole history of that frightful Scutari calamity. It exhibits the annual rate of mortality per cent. on the sick population of the Hospitals. It will be seen that, even from the very beginning of the occupation of these buildings in October 1854, and before the sufferings of the winter had begun , the mortality was very high, although the number of sick was small, indicating the unhealthy state of the buildings at the very beginning. Nothing was done to improve them even then—only fresh ship-loads of sick were passed into them. The mortality, of course, continued to rise—still nothing was done. Then came the great Crimean catastrophe, and ship after ship arrived with sick in so susceptible a condition, that the foul air of these Hospitals was almost certain death to them; and, accordingly, they died, in the month of February, at the rate of 415 per cent. per annum. So that in twelve months, at such a rate, the whole sick population of the Hospitals would have perished four times. In the month of February, 1855, we actually lost two out of every five men treated in the Hospitals of the Bosphorus, and one out of every two at Koulali, the worst of all the Hospitals. Well might we learn from our incredible mortality a terrible Sanitary lesson! The reduction in the mortality, after the sanitary works had been begun, is most striking, and it falls eventually, in June, 1855 to less than a sixth part of what it was when the Barrack and General Hospitals were occupied together in October 1854, and to a nineteenth part of what it was in February 1855. Our General Hospitals have been so deplorably mismanaged in all our wars that men have come to ask the question, whether it would not be better to do without them altogether? The experience of Scutari has proved that General Hospitals may become pest-houses from neglect, or may be made as healthy as any other buildings.

The question of Zymotic Diseases is of infinitely greater importance during war than during peace; for no weapons are so destructive of Armies in the field as they are. The slaughter of battles and of sieges is cast into the shade by that of pestilence, which, during long wars, is the real arbiter of the destinies of Nations, for it exhausts their resources more completely than all other losses in the field.

Zymotic Disease the real destroyer of Armies in War.

In a country like ours, with a limited population, an entirely voluntary system of recruitment, and colonies and possessions in all climates and latitudes, the question of military hygiene is rapidly becoming a question of vital importance to the interests of the Empire. The time appears to have arrived, when by the British race alone must the integrity of that Empire be upheld. The conquering race must retain possession. And experience has shown that, without special information and skilful application of the resources of science in preserving health, the drain upon our home population must exhaust our means.

Value of the Soldier.

A competent authority states, that "It is calculated that we shall require something like 25,000 to 40,000 men now in a year to keep up the strength of our army everywhere. There must *all* be for a considerable time in barracks at home, if we can find the requisite number. But, while it is doubtful whether we can find men enough to meet the necessary expenditure of soldiers abroad, we are squandering our means at home, and needlessly expending men in barracks here, who might be preserved to maintain our strength and our dominion elsewhere. What would be thought of a brewer who treated his dray-horses in like manner—or a huntsman who so dealt with his horses or his hounds? A dairyman would be ruined in a twelve-month who suffered his cows to be so fatally crowded. Independently of all moral and political considerations, it is the most wretched mismanagement on the part of the nation. It is doubtful whether our Military Statesmen are yet alive to the truth of sanitary science—they admit it, but they do not feel it—their minds, in some instances, still run in the old rut. While the Board of Health is warning us all to put our houses in order, to attend to our sewerage, ventilation, &c., the dwellings of our soldiers, under the special care and superintendence of the Government, are the most neglected, in these respects, of the habitations of our fellow-subjects. Public attention is now concentrated upon India, and thinks little of what is being done or left undone at home; but men are not in a mood to be trifled with. They are in that sort of savage frame of mind which would delight in tearing somebody to pieces—they would prefer a Brahmin, or a Mussulman, but as they cannot get that, they would take what they could get. If Cholera should break out badly in our Barracks, and should be traced to the neglect of timely and repeated warnings, it would fare ill with the responsible."

That we shall have another epidemic of Cholera soon is, speaking as men speak, certain. The signs are already here. We have put our house in order (in a certain measure, at least,) as far as regards the civil population. Upon them it will bear less hardly than it did in 1849 and 1854. Shall the Queen's troops, and troops which have deserved so well of us, be the only portion of Her subjects which shall not escape, whose chance of life shall not be looked to?

It has been shown that they have suffered more than twice as much in past years, even when the rest of the population was at its worst, from Cholera and other epidemics, as their civil fellow-subjects have done. This fatal preponderance will be seen, as still more glaring, now that the Sanitary state of Civilians has somewhat improved.

The Queen's Household Troops in London have suffered in their Barracks a yet higher proportion of mortality from Cholera, in comparison with the civil population. More than five times the proportion of Royal Horse Guards actually died, in 1849, from Cholera, in Knightsbridge, compared with Civilians, although including all ages, and both sexes, in the same parish*. Shall this proportion be raised yet higher by the mortality of the metropolis falling, while that of the Household Troops does not, and thus be made still more fearfully striking? Such, however, will, in all probability, be the case, unless the Barracks are improved, before the next epidemic comes.

To introduce, therefore, a proper sanitary system into the British Army is, especially at this juncture, of essential importance to the Queen and the Public Service.

The principal defects pointed out and the principal suggestions for their remedy offered, in the preceding notes, will now be subjoined.

---

* Deaths per 1,000, from Cholera, 1849, of Troops and Civilians, in same Parishes.

Per 1,000.

Civilians—St. Pancras 2ˑ2
Troops—2nd Life Guards, Regent's Park 10ˑ4

Civilians—Kensington 3ˑ3
Troops—Royal Horse Guards, Knightsbridge 17ˑ5

Civilians—Marylebone and St. Martin's in the Fields 2ˑ7

Troops—1st Batt. Gren. Guards, Barracks, Portman Street ⎫
       1st Batt. Coldstream Guards, Barracks, Trafalgar Sq. ⎬ 3ˑ2

Civilians—St. John's and St. Margaret's, Westminster 6ˑ8
Troops—2nd and 3rd Batt. Gren. Guards, Wellington Barracks† 2ˑ0

Civilians—East London and Whitechapel 5ˑ4
Troops—2nd Batt. Coldsteams, 2nd Batt. Scots Fus. Guards, Tower . 10ˑ0

Civilians—Marylebone. 1ˑ7
Troops—1st Batt. Scots Fus. Guards, St. John's Wood and
      Portman Barracks 2ˑ0

The Deaths of the Civilians are taken on the whole population, without distinction of age or sex.

---

† The Wellington Barracks are in St. James's Park, the most healthy spot in the district.

NOTES ON HOSPITALS:*

BEING

TWO PAPERS READ BEFORE THE NATIONAL ASSOCIATION FOR THE PROMOTION OF SOCIAL SCIENCE, AT LIVERPOOL, IN OCTOBER 1858

WITH

EVIDENCE GIVEN TO THE ROYAL COMMISSIONERS ON THE STATE OF THE ARMY IN 1857

BY

FLORENCE NIGHTINGALE

LONDON: JOHN W. PARKER AND SON, WEST STRAND. 1859

* Excerpted from "Evidence given to the Royal Commission on the State of the Army in 1857" as reproduced from *Notes on the Hospitals*, First Edition, 1859. This excerpt includes a comment on the problem of clothing for the Scutari patients and a cost analysis of nurse staffing for two different designs for inpatient wards. With this cost analysis, Nightingale was arguing that the proposed Netley Hospital was inefficient and should not be built as planned. It was built anyway. The last table shows the mortality by month for all hospitals during the Crimean war.

Editor's Note: A frotteur is one who rubs or gives massage.

Major Sillery

'I was commandant from the time the army left till within ten or twelve days. When convalescents or invalids leave the hospital, they come under my command. *Many of the sick and wounded men arrived with little or no clothing. From the want of any establishment for the purpose at this depot there is the greatest difficulty in supplying such men with necessaries.* There is a non-commissioned officer of each regiment here in charge of the men of his own regiment. It is the duty of that non-commissioned officer to meet the wants of the men if possible, getting the money for the purpose from the paymaster, who stops the amount from the soldiers' pay. The corporal must get the shirts when he can. In the case of boots, which are a heavy article, there is more difficulty. We cannot get the regimental boots here. For men going up to the Crimea, we look very closely as to boots. Till the last draft we sent up about a fortnight ago, we generally got boots from the commissariat for men going up; but I do not know if we got any for invalids. Every man is examined before he goes to the Crimea or home, but not when he comes out of hospital. We endeavour to complete the outfits as much as we can. This is done partly out of commissariat stores and dead men's effects. In the same way we give the red coatees of dead men.

'We want a quartermaster's establishment,—a large store with necessaries of all kinds. The complication of accounts with so many soldiers of different regiments requires a large staff. In a regiment, a soldier who wants anything is supplied by his captain, who inspects him and draws the articles wanting from the quartermaster's stores. Here we have no officer who discharges the duty of a captain.'

Note E.

Orderlies' Attendance.—With regard to the present 'regulation number of orderlies, viz., 1 to every 10 patients, it is to be observed,—

(1.) *Forty-bed Ward Minimum Size for Regulation Number of* 1 *Attendant to* 10 *Patients.*—A ward of 40 patients might be efficiently served (but it would be hard work) with

1 Head Nurse—Female.
3 Orderlies.

Provided always there were lifts and hot and cold water laid on.

With no number under 40 of patients to a ward, can the Regulation proportion of 1 attendant to 10 patients be adhered to.

(2.) *Twenty-bed Ward requires* 3½ *Attendants.*—A ward of 20 patients cannot be efficiently served (if the orderlies be men) with less than

½ Head Nurse—Female.

3 Orderlies.

And the other ward of this head-nurse ought to be on the same floor.

N.B.—The same number would quite as efficiently serve a ward of 30 patients, provided there be lifts and a supply of hot and cold water all over the building.

(3.) *Ten-bed Ward cannot be served by* 1 *Orderly.*—The Army system of 1 orderly to 10 patients, with a number not exceeding 10 patients to a ward, is upset as immediately by one bad case among the 10, as by 9 to the 10.

For, is the same orderly to be on duty for the 24 hours?

The difficulty is practically got over by the Army, with a permission that any 'bad case' may select any one he likes of his comrades (out of the depot) to be 'told off,' to attend upon him.

This extraordinary regulation is equivalent to (and affords little other practical result, than) granting opportunity for any quantity of spirits, and illicit food, to be smuggled into hospital, and it is clear that it would be totally inadmissible in a general hospital, where the whole system of nursing would be under the most stringent discipline and supervision.

(4.) *Naval Hospitals Regulation number of Attendants* 1 *to* 7 *Patients.*—In all naval hospitals, the regulation number of attendants is 1 to every 7 patients, or 2 attendants for each ward containing more than 7 patients and up to 14.

In civil hospitals the proportion is as great, generally, of attendants to patients, and is mainly determined by the size of the ward:

E.g., in one hospital, where there are quadruple wards of 44 or 48 patients, 11 or 12 in each compartment, the number of attendants is 7.

In exceptional cases extra night-nurses, sometimes extra day-nurses serve particular patients. The labour, both of cleaning and of night-nursing, is much increased by the compartments being four, and separated by a large lobby.

In another of the large London hospitals,* where there are to each ward,

PATIENTS.		ATTENDANTS.
22 }	there are	{ 1 Sister.
24 }		{ 2 Nurses.
30	"	{ 1 Sister.
		{ 2 Nurses.
		{ 1 Scrubber.
34	"	{ 1 Sister.
		{ 3 Nurses.
40	"	{ 1 Sister.
		{ 3 Nurses.
		{ 1 Helper.

In the Lariboisiere Hospital at Paris, where the wards hold 32 beds, 1 sister, 1 nurse, and 2 orderlies on the men's side, 1 sister, 2 nurses, and 1 orderly on the female side, serve the ward efficiently. In this hospital there are no lifts.

(5.) *Same number of Men will not do same amount of Work as an equal number of Women would.*—One woman does the work of more than a man in a hospital, speaking of the duties discharged by under-nurses in civil hospitals; for men are not accustomed to these duties in England, as women are from their childhood.

From this it is by no means inferred that women of the class of under-nurses in civil hospitals should be employed in military hospitals, which unquestionably they should not. But it is to be inferred that the work will not be done efficiently, with a smaller number of men than would be employed of women.

(6.) Practically, it is impossible to serve 4 wards of 9 beds each, with

1 Head Nurse,
4 Orderlies.

---

* It is singular how little, even in civil hospitals, attention has been directed to the comparative cost of nursing in larger and smaller wards. In two civil hospitals, the distribution of sick in which is nearly as in the two instances above, the annual cost of nursing each bed is about one-third *more* in the former than in the latter case. It is true that the average number of constantly occupied beds is about one-third less in the former than in the latter hospital. But the difference of cost seems mainly attributable to the difference of the number of beds in each ward. And the efficiency of the nursing is certainly not less in the latter than in the former hospital.

For, as has been said, one bad case in each ward makes this economy as unmanageable as nine.

1 Female Head Nurse } to { 50 Patients, in (say)
6 Orderlies . . . . }   { 6 Wards,

would be wholly insufficient, though this attendance would be more than sufficient for 50 cases in one ward; but such a ward is considered in a sanitary sense too large. Two wards of 30 beds each on the same floor would be efficiently served by such a staff, however; and there would be no sanitary objection.

(7.) *One Orderly should be the Frotteur.*—One orderly should be trained to be the *frotteur* to each ward. He should also be the porter to fetch and carry everything to and from the ward.

(8.) *Comparison of Cost of Nursing with larger and smaller Wards.*—The plan of Netley, with its wards for 9 sick, is by far the costliest for administration, as the following facts will prove:

I. It is proposed to provide the hospital with orderlies and nurses to conduct the nursing in wards of 9 sick, as mentioned.

II. On sanitary grounds wards may safely be large enough to accommodate 25 to 30 sick.

We may therefore choose the larger wards, being guided only by the cost of the nursing.

III. A ward of 9 sick would require 1 day and 1 night orderly, and a-third of a nurse (that is, a nurse could superintend three such wards).

A ward of 30 sick would require 2 day and 1 night orderlies, and 1 nurse = 4 persons in all.

Or if two such wards were on one floor, 1 nurse could serve both.

IV. We cannot count the cost of orderlies and nurses, including lodging, rations, wages, at less than 50*l*. a year, which when capitalized at 3 per cent. (33 years' purchase), would amount to 1650*l*. for each.

V. A ward of 9 sick would cost in nursing 1650*l*. x 2⅓ = 3850*l*., or 427*l*. 15s. 6*d*. per bed.

VI. A ward of 30 sick would cost for nursing, in perpetuity, 1650*l*. x 4 = 6600*l*. = 220*l*. per bed.

[One nurse to each ward is here allowed.]

VII. The cost of the two plans relatively for a hospital of 1000 sick would stand thus:—

Wards with 9 beds	=	£427,775
Wards with 30 beds	=	220,000

Capitalized difference of cost in favour of large wards £207,775

Suppose the sanitary requirement of 25 sick to a ward be combined with the greatest economy of administration, the cost would stand thus:—

For each ward of 25 sick, 3 orderlies, at 1,650*l*. = £4,950

If two such are built in line close to each other, with the nurse's room between them, one nurse could superintend both wards, or half a nurse to a ward. The cost would be for the ward 825

£5,775

Or cost for each bed $\frac{5775}{25}$ = £231

The comparative cost of wards with 9 beds and 25 beds, would stand thus for 1000 sick:—

Wards with 9 beds..	£427,775
Wards with 25 beds	231,000
Saving	£196,775

The cost of the administration per 1000 beds at Netley and at the proposed hospital at Aldershot would stand as follows:—

Netley £427,775

Aldershot, pavilions, with 3 superimposed wards and 25 sick in each, would require 3 orderlies and 1 nurse* to each ward, and would cost 264*l*. per bed in perpetuity, or per 1000 sick 264,000

Difference of cost in favour of Aldershot £163,775

Some abatement would have to be made, as regards the cost of Netley, as there are a few wards with 16 or 18 sick.

* One nurse might possibly be able to serve the whole pavilion. The highest estimate is here taken.

NOTE F.

The Director-General in 1858 states the Admissions and Deaths in the General Hospitals of the East, 1854 to 1856, thus:—

		SCUTARI.		KOULALI.		VARNA.	
				Feb., 1855—June, 1855.		June, 1854—Jan., 1855.	
		Admissions.	Deaths.	Admissions.	Deaths.	Admissions.	Deaths.
June,	1854	631	6			201	4
July,	"	267	13			824	70
August,	"	359	19			445	99
September,	"	3520	112			874	146
October,	"	1401	235			268	23
November,	"	3864	320			150	26
December,	"	3814	601			57	1
January,	1855	4761	1393	Included under Scutari.		27	5
February,	"	1894	1084	794	302		
March,	"	2385	421	448	134		
April,	"	1629	149	138	52		
May,	"	1623	79	255	16		
June,	"	1519	41	328	5		
July,	"	2473	63	Not distinguished from			
August,	"	2981	58	Scutari.			
September,	"	2195	46				
October,	"	1187	44				
November,	"	1124	163				
December,	"	724	29				
January,	1856	448	20				
February,	"	279	7				
March,	"	595	8				
April,	"	737	8				
May,	"	586	1				
June,	"	329	3				
		41,325	4923	1963	509	2846[c]	374[d]
		Scutari and Koulali		43,288[a]	5432[b]		

[a] 4161 only from wounds. [c] 197 from cholera.
[b] 395 only from wounds. [d] 148 from cholera.

		GENERAL HOSPITAL, BALAKLAVA. Oct., 1854—June, 1856.		CASTLE HOSPITAL, BALAKLAVA. March, 1855—June, 1856.		CAMP GENERAL HOSPITAL, CRIMEA. April, 1855—April, 1856	
		Admissions.	*Deaths.*	*Admissions.*	*Deaths.*	*Admissions.*	*Deaths.*
June,	1854						
July,	"						
August,	"						
September,	"						
October,	"	512	58				
November,	"	514	60				
December,	"	598	66				
January,	1855	752	50				
February,	"	421	34				
March,	"	295	37	218	3		
April,	"	164	9	123	7	4	2
May,	"	324	31	85	5	72	5
June,	"	230	29	505	16	286	37
July,	"	192	13	208	17	34	27
August,	"	194	12	401	13	15	5
September,	"	218	12	470	20	297	85
October,	"	191	5	174	12	151	13
November,	"	152	5	5	1	146	14
December,	"	102	3	20	2	1	11
January,	1856	82	2	2	—	8	3
February,	"	60	2	64	—	28	—
March,	"	105	3	82	—	24	1
April,	"	54	—	13	—	17	1
May,	"	186	4	30	—		
June,	"	341	3	154	—		
		5686[e]	438[f]	2554[g]	96[h]	1083[i]	204[j]

[e] 333 from cholera. [g] 1834 from wounds. [i] 740 from wounds.
[f] 141 from cholera. [h] 83 from wounds. [j] 184 from wounds.

		MONASTERY HOSPITAL, CRIMEA. July, 1855—June, 1856		ABYDOS. Dec., 1854—Sept., 1855		SMYRNA. Feb., 1855—Nov., 1855.	
		Admissions.	*Deaths.*	*Admissions.*	*Deaths.*	*Admissions.*	*Deaths.*
June,	1854						
July,	"						
August,	"						
September,	"						
October,	"						
November,	"						
December,	"			352	3		
January,	1855			9	16		
February,	"			117	14	737	30
March,	"			20	18	256	97
April,	"			226	13	94	9
May,	"			23	13	224	6
June,	"			29	4	38	5
July,	"	182	—	19	—	56	—
August,	"	104	10	18	—	26	1
September,	"	67	7	2	—	17	1
October,	"	115	6			417	—
November,	"	40	2			22	5
December,	"	48	1				
January,	1856	41	1				
February,	"	43	1				
March,	"	49	—				
April,	"	57	—				
May,	"	147	—				
June,	"	18	—				
		911	28	814	82	1887	154

228

		RENKIOI. Oct., 1855—June, 1856. *Admissions.* *Deaths.*	
June,	1854		
July,	"		
August,	"		
September,	"		
October,	"		
November,	"		
December,	"		
January,	1855		
February,	"		
March,	"		
April,	"		
May,	"		
June,	"		
July,	"		
August,	"		
September,	"		
October,	"	232	6
November,	"	234	1
December,	"	263	5
January,	1856	345	12
February,	"	226	16
March,	"	11	9
April,	"	4	1
May,	"	8	—
June,	"	7	—
		1330	50

Epilogue

100 Apples Divided by 15 Red Herrings: A Cautionary Tale from the Mid-19th Century on Comparing Hospital Mortality Rates*

By Lisa I. Iezzoni, MD, MSc

Abstract

In 1863, Florence Nightingale argued that London hospitals were dangerous, especially compared with provincial facilities. She bolstered this contention with statistics published in William Farr's Registrar-General report, which claimed that 24 London hospitals had mortality rates exceeding 90%, whereas rural hospitals had an average mortality rate of 13%. Farr had calculated mortality rates by dividing the total number of patients who died through-out the year by the number of inpatients on a single day. When calculated as the annual number of deaths divided by the total number of inpatients during the year, the mortality rate of London hospitals was 10%. A raucous debate erupted in the London medical press over how best to calculate hospital mortality rates. Critics claimed that Farr had not adjusted for differences in severity of illness between urban and rural hospitals and that his figures would mislead the public. Farr and Nightingale, in turn, criticized the poor quality of hospital data. This story reinforces the need to understand the methodologic derivation of statistics intended to compare provider quality.

Concerns about quality are increasingly surfacing as the U.S. health care system undergoes radical change. Although quality measures remain limited, many health care marketplace competitors, especially for-profit insurance plans, are leading the development of new

*Reprinted with permission from the *Annals of Internal Medicine,* Vol. 124; No. 12, 15 June 1996.

approaches. Quality is central to the marketing of some providers and plans, which claim that improved quality decreases costs.

A worrisome byproduct of this commercial emphasis is the trend toward proprietary quality measures disseminated as "black boxes," with the clinical and empiric logic guarded as a competitive trade secret[1-5]. Organizations claim to assess quality but reveal few details about their methods. Understandable documentation is also frequently unavailable for noncommercial approaches. Specific methodologic choices, however, can skew perceptions of provider performance. Even hospital mortality rates, a seemingly straightforward staple of many provider "report cards," can be modulated by the manner in which they are calculated [6,7].

A provocative example of a methodologic choice that had substantial implications for assessing hospital performance comes from mid-19th century Great Britain. This choice produced a distorted impression of hospitals, especially large urban facilities, as dangerous places that not only "did no good" but "positively did harm"[8]. This misperception lasted more than a century. This historical example underscores the need to open black boxes and look inside.

The Calculation
In 1863, Florence Nightingale (1820–1910) published the third edition of her *Notes on Hospitals*[9], recommending fundamental changes in the configuration, location, and operation of hospitals to reduce the number of deaths caused by unsanitary conditions. Seven years earlier, Nightingale had returned from Crimean war service at British military hospitals, perhaps the first wartime celebrity created by the new media[10]. As crafted by a correspondent from *The Times,* her image as a lone lady nursing sick soldiers by the light of her hand-held lamp earned Nightingale an admiring lifelong audience. This gentle, ministering angel persona, however, belied

Nightingale's tough-minded, laser-focused administrative acumen: In 1855, 6 months after arriving in Scutari, Albania, she cut military hospital mortality rates from 42.7% to 2.2%[10].

Upon returning home, Nightingale continued to target military installations. Needing statistical help, she turned to William Farr (1807–1883), a physician and prominent social reformer who had done analyses for the Registrar-General since 1838. In 1856 they made a pact: Farr would assist Nightingale with army reforms, and Nightingale would aid Farr in his efforts to reduce the number of civilian deaths[11]. In her 1863 *Notes on Hospitals,* Nightingale concentrated on civilian hospitals.

Farr and Nightingale believed that the dangers posed by urban mid-19th century hospitals were obvious, as shown by the number of deaths at the "106 principal hospitals of England" in 1861 (Figure 1). Most startling was the 90.84 "Mortality per cent. on Inmates" at 24 London hospitals. Taken from *Farr's 24th Annual Report of the Registrar-General,* death rates were calculated as follows: total number of deaths at the hospital in 1861/number of patients at the hospital on 8 April 1861. Thus, the numerator reflected figures from an entire year, whereas the denominator encompassed a single day. Farr had calculated death rates per occupied hospital bed, not mortality rates per the total number of hospitalized patients.

This methodologic choice inflated apparent mortality rates. Not surprisingly, hospital mortality rates improved considerably when calculated as the annual number of deaths divided by the total number of inpatients treated during the year. By using this method, mortality rates in 1861 in the "general wards" at 14 London hospitals averaged 9.7%[12].

The Policy Context
British authorities had long collected information about mortality rates, primarily to track epidemic illness.

FIGURE 1
Mortality Percentage In The Principal Hospitals of
England: 1861

	Number of SPECIAL INMATES on the 8th April, 1861	Average Number of INMATES in each HOSPITAL	Number of DEATHS registered in the year 1861	MORTALITY per Cent. On INMATES
IN 106 PRINCIPAL HOSPITALS OF ENGLAND	12709	120	7227	56.87
24 London Hospitals	4214	176	3828	90.84
12 Hospitals in Large Towns	1870	156	1555	83.16
25 County and Important Provincial Hospitals	2248	90	886	39.41
30 Other Hospitals	1136	38	457	40.23
13 Naval and Military Hospitals	3000	231	470	15.67
1 Royal Sea Bathing Infirmary (Margate)	133	133	17	12.78
1 Dane Hill Metropolitan Infirmary (Margate)	108	108	14	12.96

Source: Nightingale F. *Notes on Hospitals,* third edition. London: Longman, Green, Longman, Roberts, and Green, 1863.

Overwhelmed by plague-related deaths, Henry VII began gathering weekly "Bills of Mortality" in 1532[13]. starting late in the 18th century, the massive social upheavals of the industrial revolution heightened this interest. As populations shifted from the countryside, amassing within congested industrial centers, statistics clearly showed egregious public health consequences. By the 1830s statistical societies had arisen throughout England, founded by civic and business leaders intent on quantifying the effects of these social changes. The archetypal member was "a liberal Whig, Unitarian, reform-minded"[11]. these early Victorian statisticians viewed "facts" as the scientific means to prompt political change. Farr himself published the first Registrar-General reports on deaths in 1839, claiming that "these facts will [promote] . . . practical medicine" by identifying areas rife with disease[14].

British hospitals had accumulated statistics on their patients since the 1600s. In Victorian England, hospital statistics served several purposes. Because hospitals were primarily charitable institutions serving the poor, statistics quantified for wealthy benefactors the results of their charity and encouraged new subscribers. As can be seen today, those paying for hospitals wanted to ensure that they were getting their money's worth. In addition, as noted in an 1863 report for the Medical Officer of the Privy Council[15], "the public as a rule still look to the death-rates of hospitals as the best indication of their relative healthiness."

Not all Victorians shared a passion for numbers. Social critic Charles Dickens parodied statistical fixations in his dark 1854 novel *Hard Times* in the character of Thomas Gradgrind, eminent citizen of sooty Coketown, who intoned, "In this life, we want nothing but Facts, Sir; nothing but Facts!" Dickens believed that individual persons were lost among statistics. Nonetheless, Nightingale's experiences during the Crimean War had taught her that facts were the best way to prod recalcitrant military authorities into action[16, 17]. She and Farr thus used statistics to wage their civilian reform campaign.

The Methodologic Context
Today, observers might view Farr and Nightingale as erring in their calculations or intentionally skewing statistics to bolster political arguments. In the 1860s, however, little consensus surrounded statistical techniques,

let alone the manner in which hospital mortality rates should be calculated. Victorian statisticians emphasized subject content rather than methods, accepting "men of little mathematical ability" into their field[11]. Although Quetelet (much admired by Nightingale) investigated the "law of error" in the early 1800s, the 20th century's standard statistical techniques and ways of thinking about error and uncertainty were decades away. For example, W.S. Gross proposed the t-test (under the pseudonym "Student") in 1908[18], Fisher's refinement appeared in 1925[19], and Pearson introduced chi-square goodness-of-fit tests in 1900[20].

Hospitals calculated mortality rates in different ways to suit their particular goals[8, 15]. The most effective way to skew statistics involved specifying the numerators of mortality rates. As the 1863 Privy Council report[15] noted,

In the majority of hospitals, it is . . . the custom to reckon among their deaths those who have been brought dead to the institution; but there are many hospitals where such cases are not reckoned, and there are some indeed where even those who die within 24 hours are, on the ground that they were moribund at the time of admission, excluded from computation.

Another factor skewed comparisons of mortality rates between urban and provincial hospitals. Many provincial hospitals explicitly refused patients with phthisis (tuberculosis) or fevers and the "dead or dying," whereas urban facilities took everyone[15]. Urban facilities objected to being compared with outlying hospitals that excluded such patients. As the 1846 Glasgow Royal Infirmary report[8] stated, "the reception of moribund cases greatly swells the number of deaths recorded in the Hospital, and very materially increases the proportionate mortality thereby producing misconceptions in the public mind. . . ."

As described below, Farr and Nightingale were criticized primarily because of their denominator.

Nonetheless, in the mid-19th century, some viewed the number of deaths per bed as an indication of the hospital's productivity—another measure to show charitable donors. A further rationale for calculating per-bed mortality rates was the notion that having low occupancy rates (low average daily census) was healthy, giving patients more space and lessening the fear of contagion. In his 1877 report on English hospital mortality, Lawson Tait, a fellow of the statistical society, emphasized this point by explicitly calculating rates by bed and by patients[21].

In 1865, surgeon Fleetwood Buckle raised concerns about biases from calculating per-bed mortality rates, especially when comparing rates across hospitals[22]. Buckle was troubled about attributing deaths to unoccupied beds. In this pamphlet on the mortality rates for English hospitals in 1863, Buckle stated, "no 'bed-rate' has been given, as it is obvious that in many country hospitals, where perhaps only half the number of beds are occupied at a time, the rate would be much lower than it should be, while in others, where the beds are constantly full, it would be correspondingly high"[22]. At least Farr had used occupied beds.

Nightingale herself wrote few original reports on statistical methods[23], focusing instead on graphic ways of presenting information. Nightingale nevertheless emphasized concerns about underlying data quality, generally viewing hospital-reported data with suspicion. With an eerily modern ring, she wrote,

. . . Accurate hospital statistics are much more rare than is generally imagined, and at the best they only give the mortality which has taken place *in* the hospitals, and take no cognizance of those cases which are discarded in a hopeless condition, to die immediately afterwards, a practice which is followed to a much greater extent by some hospitals than others.

We have known incurable cases discharged from one hospital to which the deaths ought to have been

accounted and received into another hospital, to die
there in a day or two after admission, thereby low-
ering the mortality rate of the first at the expense
of the second[9].

The Response

Today, hospital mortality rates exceeding 90% would
prompt a swift and vigorous outcry from the popular
press. Review of indexes to *The Times* from 1861 through
1865, however, found few articles about hospitals and
none about controversies over Nightingale's publication
and hospital mortality statistics. That debate occurred
in the London *Medical Times and Gazette* and *The
Lancet,* and the major critics were men practicing at
urban hospitals[11].

An anonymous reviewer of *Notes on Hospitals* began,
"It is sad to see a work of so much value—full of such
useful information—disfigured by a few serious and ele-
mentary mistakes. Much as all Medical men must
appreciate the philanthropic labour of its authoress, it is
a false kindness to pass erroneous views without
protest"[24]. The reviewer observed that because the mortality rate table came from the Registrar-General, "perhaps Miss Nightingale can hardly be held responsible for
it." He nonetheless excoriated the methods, noting.

The inmates of a single day are balanced with the
deaths of a whole year, and no wonder the results
are "striking enough." It is to be hoped there are
valid reasons for giving to the world what seems to
us a simple piece of arithmetical legerdemain.
Surely it is the very essence of percentages and of
averages (both, we believe, fruitful sources of error),
that the figures dealt with should stand on one and
the same bottom, and that deaths for one year
should be compared with admissions or discharges
for that period, and no other. There is something
audacious in the last column of this table, were
twenty-four London Hospitals are accredited with a

"mortality per cent on inmates" of 90.84. No doubt it will be said this is the quotient of the figures employed; but we entirely deny their validity and the accuracy of the impression thus conveyed. The problem as here put is exactly that so often asked of forward schoolboys—What is the quotient of a hundred apples divided by fifteen red herrings[24].

Farr's arithmetic choices were slyly caricatured by John Bristowe, a prominent London physician, who showed that hospital "recovery" rates calculated using Farr's methods would range from 899.5% to 953%[25]. Timothy Holmes, a London surgeon, indicated that by Farr's method, one hospital had a mortality rate of 130%, clearly a "misleading" figure[26].

Another anonymous critic objected to the absence or risk adjustment, viewing comparisons between inner-city and rural hospitals as hopelessly flawed: "Any comparison which ignores the difference between the apple-checked farm-laborers who seek relief at Stoke Pogis (probably for rheumatism and sore legs), and the wizzened [sic], red-herring-like mechanics of Soho or Southwark, who comes from a London Hospital, if fallacious"[27], Bristowe[25] concurred:

has Dr. Farr . . . really overlooked the differences in relative severity of cases admitted into this different classes of Hospitals, the different relative length of stay of their inmates, the different numbers of patients treated in them in relation to the numbers of constantly-occupied beds? Has he no suspicion that his death-rate is determined almost wholly by these causes?

Bristowe also questioned how the public would interpret Farr's mortality rates: "That Dr. Farr understands the mathematical meaning of his figures no one will doubt; but that the majority of his readers understand them neither in this sense nor in any other, and are utterly mislead by them, is certain"[25]. Bristowe directly challenged the motivations of Farr and Nightingale, stating that when they "try to mislead others into the belief that the unhealthiness of Hospitals is in proportion to Dr. Farr's death-rates of Hospitals, we are bound to protest against the whole matter as an unfounded and mischievous delusion"[25].

The Defense

In her book, Nightingale clearly argued that "in all hospitals, even in those which are best conducted, there is a great and unnecessary waste of life . . ."[9]. In the Crimean War, statistics had helped her overcome the resistance of military officials. Perhaps anticipating similar hurdles in her civilian crusade, Nightingale chose the statistics that best supported her case.

Medical leaders did sometimes minimize concerns about hospital mortality rates. In the 1860s, eminent physician Sir John Simpson railed against "hospitalism"—the "hygiene evils" of hospitals. Finding much higher mortality rates from amputation at hospitals than in "country practices," Simpson asked, "Do not these terrible figures plead eloquently and clamantly for revision and reform of our existing hospital system?"[28]. His colleagues apparently remained unconvinced:

. . . I have conversed on many occasions with many medical men upon this subject. I have found, however, that to most professional minds it seemed to be altogether a kind of medical heresy to doubt that our numerous and splendid hospitals for the sick poor could by any possibility be aught than institutions as beneficial in their practical results as they were benevolent in their practical objects[29].

Although Nightingale was a celebrity, as a non-physician, she may have felt even less able to motivate change[8, 17].

Two weeks after the review of *Notes on Hospitals,* the *Medical Times and Gazette* published Farr's response. He took exception to an anonymous reviewer "who could treat a lady roughly"[30], although he later accurately acknowledged that Nightingale was "well able to defend herself"[31]. Farr argued that if hospitals would provide accurate figures on the number of patients who were treated and died, few disputes would arise. He did not refute specific attacks on his calculation, instead emphasizing a fundamental reservation about most mortality rate calculations:

This [Farr's approach] is one method; there is another which is less correct, but more common. The deaths are divided by the mean number of cases admitted and discharged . . . The defect of this method lies in this: it does not take the element of time into account, which is important, as it so happens that cases are scarcely ever admitted as in-patients of Hospitals at their origin, and that many cases are discharged from Hospital before they have terminated[30].

Thus, Farr wanted to hold constant the window of observation, saying, for example, that it was unfair to compare death rates at St. Thomas's in London (average inpatient stay, 39 days) with rates at two Dublin hospitals (average stay, 27 days)[30]. At least, Farr argued, his calculation was clear in exactly what it was observing.

One year later, when the Statistical Society, with Farr as treasurer, published hospital mortality rates for 1863, the rates were calculated according to the following formula: annual number of deaths/annual number of admissions + (number of patients at the beginning of the year – number of patients at the end of the year)[12]. The publication noted that lengths of hospital "residence" were very long, averaging 30 days for 14 London hospitals. Despite this methodologic shift, Farr continued using statistics to urge reform, writing to Nightingale in 1864, "What are figures worth if they do no good to men's bodies or souls?"[17].

Discussion
The statistical arguments between Farr and Nightingale and their critics arose against the backdrop

240

of a more fundamental debate between the "contagionists" and "noncontagionists" that had begun in the 1830s over causes of hospital deaths[11], Nightingale clung tenaciously to the central role of sanitation and miasmas (noxious vapors spreading disease), fiercely resisting the increasingly popular "germ theory." She advocated architectural changes to allow more air circulation and shifting hospital sites to fresher outlying environments as the way to reduce the number of deaths, and she downplayed the benefits of antiseptic techniques. Farr was torn between his allegiance to Nightingale and his growing acceptance of the germ theory. In the end, statistical evidence tipped Farr into the contagionist camp and distanced him from Nightingale; his final conversion was confirmed by observing the 1866 cholera epidemic[11].

Ironically, however, in the ensuing decades, Nightingale's voice sometimes rose over that of her methodologic critics. The statistical debate in the *Medical Times and Gazette* and *The Lancet* receded, whereas *Notes on Hospitals* remained much read. Nightingale's proposals for changing ward configuration and hospital location were widely adopted and reduced the number of hospital deaths. Nightingale's view that urban hospitals were dangerous was shared by other for more than a century[8].

Victorian statisticians such as Farr and Nightingale were almost religiously zealous, aiming to introduce the certainty of scientific rigor into political discourse. These statisticians viewed any aspersions on their integrity as outrageous; Holmes wrote that conducting statistical analyses "really intended to bolster up a private scheme" was a "piece of personal dishonesty"[32]. Today's public no longer views statisticians as seekers of truth. Especially in today's political arguments, statistics are available to prove any point. Farr took his figures from public documents, and he was open about his methods—his calculations were not a black box. To interpret his figures, however, one had to understand how they were calculated and the consequent methodologic implications. Today, many users of statistics immediately seek "bottom lines" that advance their views; organizations generating statistics frequently withhold their methods from public scrutiny.

Nonetheless, points raised in the debate following Nightingale's publication precisely parallel themes cited frequently about today's efforts at measuring provider performance, including the requirement for severity or risk adjustment[1-4]; the need to hold windows of observation constant (such as examining mortality 30 days after admission rather than in-hospitals deaths [33]); suspicions about data quality[34]; concerns about providers avoiding high-risk patients because of fears of public exposure[35]; and reservations about the public's ability to understand reports on provider performance[36]. At various times since the mid-1980s, each concern has been raised about highly publicized provider performance reports in the United States, such as the Health Care Financing Administration's publications of individual hospital mortality rates for Medicare[37] and reports in New York[36, 38] and Pennsylvania[1, 7, 39] on hospital- and physician-specific mortality rates for coronary artery bypass graft surgery.

The statistical methods used in these high-profile performance reports for comparing hospital mortality rates have frequently generated esoteric debates among methodologists, but even such basic issues as specifying numerators and denominators remain controversial. For example, in comparisons of rates of death from coronary artery bypass, one particularly problematic issue is how to handle patients transferred from other acute-care facilities. According to the June 1995 Pennsylvania coronary artery bypass hospital mortality report,[39] 12 of 227 patients at a prominent academic center died, compared with the predicted 2 to 11 deaths. Hospital representatives argued that his higher than expected mortality rate was due to transfers: Fifty-two percent of their patients having bypass surgery were transferred from other institutions, some from facilities with open-heart surgery capabilities.

Another example involved a Massachusetts hospital report card produced by the *Boston Globe* using data annually produced by hospitals and submitted to the state. Because of a specific attribute of their severity adjustment methods, The *Boston Globe* excluded from their mortality rate calculation all persons dying within 2 days of hospital admission. The reporters further rationalized that patients who died within 2 days would probably have died anyway, regardless of the quality of hospital care. Their strategy had obvious implications for comparing mortality rates across hospitals[40].

Fortunately, most government-sponsored reports have technical appendices that describe their methodologic black boxes. Even the *Boston Globe* revealed, in fine print, their exclusion of early deaths. Concerns arise, however, with the increasing number of proprietary quality measures that do not detail their methods[1-7]. In addition, calculating hospital mortality rates is easier than producing provider performance reports for populations (for example, beneficiaries of specific insurance plans). For populations, specifying numerators and denominators for calculating rates is often challenging. Nevertheless, knowing the manner in which rates are calculated is essential to understanding comparisons across populations (see example in Table 1). Otherwise, grossly misleading impressions about provider performance could arise.

In fairness to Nightingale's substantial contributions, one postscript is essential. Although Nightingale drew heavily on mortality rates to further her arguments, she recognized that counting the number of deaths neglected the main goal of hospitals. As she noted,

If the function of a hospital were to kill the sick, statistical comparisons of this nature would be admissible. As, however, its proper function is to restore the sick to health as speedily as possible, the ele-

TABLE 1
Example of Calculating Screening Mammography Rates for Two Health Plans

	Health Plan A	Health Plan B
Older women enrolled, n	10 000	10 000
Older women who saw their primary care physicians during the year, n	5000	5000
Older women receiving screening mammograms, n	4000	4000
Calculation approach chosen by each plan	4000 ÷ 10 000	4000 ÷ 5000
Screening mammography rates calculated by each plan, %	40	80

ments which really give information as to whether this is done or not, are those which show the proportion of sick restored to health, and the average time which has been required for this object . . .[9].

Today, most would agree. Nevertheless, 130 years after Nightingale's observations, information on patients' "health" after medical encounters is rarely available.

Acknowledgments

In a brief overview of Nightingale's contribution to examining outcomes of care, I fell into the trap of seizing her "bottom line" on hospital mortality rates, without investigating her methodology. Duncan Neuhauser, Ph.D., alerted me of my failing and kindly pointed me to selected sources that revealed the full story. I thank Dr. Neuhauser for his gentle rebuke and for giving me a rich opportunity to investigate and learn the lessons of history.

I am also grateful to Christen Miller who scoured the Countway Medical Library Rare Books Room and the Harvard University libraries, capably assisting me in this research.

244

References

1. Localio AR, Hamory BH. A report card for report cards. *Ann Intern Med.* 1995; 123: 802–803.
2. Epstein A. Performance reports on quality—prototypes, problems, and prospects. *N Engl J Med.* 1995; 333:57–61.
3. Wu AW. The measure and mismeasure of hospital quality: appropriate risk-adjustment methods in comparing hospitals. *Ann Intern Med.* 1995; 122: 149–50.
4. Kassirer JP. The use and abuse of practice profiles. *N Engl J Med.* 1994;330:634–636.
5. Iezzoni LI. 'Black box' medical information systems: a technology needing assessment. *JAMA.* 1991;265:3006–3007.
6. Iezzoni LI, Shwartz M, Ash AS, Hughes JS, Daley J, Mackiernan YD. Severity measurement methods and predicting pneumonia deaths. *Med Care.* 1996;34: 1128.
7. Iezzoni LI, Ash AS, Shwartz M, Daley J, Hughes JS, Mackiernan YD. Judging hospitals by severity-adjusted mortality rates: assessments may depend on how severity is measured. *Am J Pub Health.* (In press.)
8. Woodward JH. *To do the sick no harm. A study of the British voluntary hospital system to 1875.* London: Routledge & Kegan Paul, 1974.
9. Nightingale F. *Notes on Hospitals,* third edition. London: Longman, Green, Longman, Roberts, and Green, 1863.
10. Cohen IB. Florence Nightingale. *Scientific American.* 1984;250:128–137.
11. Eyler JM. Victorian *Social Medicine. The Ideas and Methods of William Farr.* Baltimore: The Johns Hopkins University Press, 1979.
12. Statistical Society. Statistics of metropolitan and provincial general hospitals for 1863. *Journal of the Statistical Society of London.* 1865; 28 (December): 527–535.
13. Walker HM. Studies in the History of Statistical Method. Baltimore: The Williams & Wilkins Company, 1929.
14. Farr W. The first annual report of births, deaths, and marriages. *The Lancet.* July 13, 1839:572–575.
15. Bristowe JS, Holmes T. Report on the Hospitals of the United Kingdom. *Sixth Report of the Medical Officer of the Privy Council.* 1863. London: George E. Eyre and William Spottiswoode for her Majesty's Stationery Office, 1864.
16. Keith JM. Florence Nightingale: statistician and consultant epidemiologist. *Int Nurs Rev.* 1988;35:147–150.
17. Diamond M, Stone M. Nightingale on Quetelet. Part 1. The passionate statistician. *J R Statis Soc.* 1981; 144:66–79.

References *continued*

18. "Student." The probable error of a mean. *Biometrika.* 1908;6:1–25.

19. Fisher RA. Applications of "student's" distribution. *Metron.* 1925;5:90–104.

20. Pearson K. On the criterion that a given system of deviations from the probable in the case of a correlated system of variables is such that it can reasonably be supposed to have arisen from random sampling. *Philosophical Magazine.**1900;50: 157–175.

21. Tait L. *An Essay on Hospital Mortality Based Upon the Statistics of the Hospitals of Great Britain for Fifteen Years.* London: J. & A. Churchill, New Burlington Street, 1877.

22. Buckle F. *Vital and Economical Statistics of the Hospitals, Infirmaries, &c., of England and Wales for the Year 1863.* London: John Churchill & Sons, New Burlington Street, 1865.

23. Nightingale F. *Notes on Hospitals.* London: John W. Parker and Son, West Strand, 1859.

24. Review. *Notes on Hospitals.* By Florence Nightingale. *Medical Times and Gazette.* January 30, 1864: 129–130.

25. Bristowe JS. Hospital Mortality. *Medical Times and Gazette.* April 30, 1864: 491–492.

26. Holmes T. Mortality in hospitals. *The Lancet.* March 26, 1864:365–366.

27. Response to letter by William Farr. *Medical Times and Gazette.* February 13, 1864: 187–188.

28. Simpson JY. *Hospitalism: Its Effects on the Results of Surgical Operations.* Edinburgh: Oliver and Boyd, 1869.

29. Simpson JY. *Hospitalism: Its Effects on the Results of Surgical Operations. Part 1.* Country Amputation Statistics. Edinburgh: Oliver and Boyd, 1869.

30. Farr W. Miss Nightingale's "Notes on Hospitals." *Medical Times and Gazette.* February 13, 1864: 186–187.

31. Farr W. Mortality in hospitals. *The Lancet.* April 9, 1864:420–422.

32. Holmes T. Mortality in hospitals. *The Lancet.* April 16, 1864:451–452.

33. Jencks SF, Williams DK, Kay TL. Assessing hospital-associated deaths from discharge data: the role of length of stay and comorbidities. *JAMA.*1988;260:2240–2246.

34. Green J, Wintfeld N. Report cards on cardiac surgeons. Assessing New York state's approach. *N Engl J Med* 1995;332:1229–32.

35. Omoigui NA, Miller DP, Brown KJ, Annan K, Cosgrove D, Lytle B, Loop F, Topol EJ. Outmigration for coronary bypass surgery in an era of public dissemination of clinical outcomes. *Circulation.* 1996;93:27–33.

246

References *continued*

36. Chassin MR, Hannan EL, DeBuono BA. Benefits and hazards of reporting medical outcomes publicly. *N Engl J Med.* 1996;334:394–398.

37. Sullivan LW, Wilensky GR. *Medicare HospitalMortality Information.* 1987, 1988, 1989. Washington, D.C.: U.S. Department of Health and Human Services, Health Care Financing Administration, 1991.

38. Hannan EL, Kilburn H, O'Donnel JF, Lukachik G, Shields EP. Adult open heart surgery in New York State. An analysis of risk factors and hospitalmortality rates. *JAMA* 1 990;264:2768–2774.

39. Pennsylvania Health Care Cost Containment Council. *A Consumer Guide to Coronary Artery Bypass Graft Surgery.* Volume IV. 1993 data. Harrisburg, PA: Pennsylvania Health Care Cost Containment Council, 1995.

40. Kong D. High hospital death rates. *Boston Globe.* October 3, 1994:1, 6, 7.